Enterprise

ENTERPRISE
Creation, development and growth

Tom Cannon
Director, Manchester Business School

BUTTERWORTH
HEINEMANN

Butterworth–Heinemann Ltd
Halley Court, Jordan Hill, Oxford OX2 8EJ

PART OF REED INTERNATIONAL BOOKS

OXFORD   LONDON   GUILDFORD   BOSTON
MUNICH   NEW DELHI   SINGAPORE   SYDNEY
TOKYO   TORONTO   WELLINGTON

First published 1991

British Library Cataloguing in Publication Data
Cannon, Tom
    Enterprise: creation development and growth
    1. Entrepreneurship
    I. Title
    338.04

ISBN 0 7506 0014 4

Typeset by BP Integraphics Ltd, Bath, Avon
Printed and bound in Great Britain

Contents

Preface

Each of us has a notion of enterprise. It might be the colleague who quits her job to start a business. Perhaps, the venture is based on the idea you rejected. It can be a neighbour who forms a help group for parents with children affected by Down's Syndrome. You can see it in teachers who provide a new way of looking at problems and students reaching a new insight. It is hard to imagine anything which is more central to modern life than the concept of enterprise. Personal endeavour lies at the core of every attempt to create, shape or develop oneself or one's community. Individual and group initiatives supply the dynamics which drive society forward.

This book is about how enterprise can be understood, applied and developed in its many guises and in various capacities. Throughout, the relevance of enterprise to a host of situations is emphasised. This extends beyond the conventional view that enterprise is about building businesses and creating wealth. Anita Roddick, Richard Branson, Bill Gates, Guilliana Benetton, Liliane Bettancourt and Reinhard Mohn show the same type of enterprise as every creator of a new business. Similar determination and endeavour is shown by Ralph Nader, Olwen Jones, Simon Rattle, Gertrude Elion and others.

Their achievements are built on an ability to reshape situations they face. But, enterprise is about building not destroying. This turns on the ability to accept Edison's dictum that the one per cent of inspiration needs to be wedded to ninety-nine per cent perspiration. The effort that is involved can be managed effectively or wastefully. This book reflects my firm belief that good management of personal and group skills and competencies is central to releasing the potential for enterprise that exists in everyone.

Throughout the book this link between insight and action is sustained. Each chapter draws out an aspect of enterprise. The early chapters emphasise the nature of enterprise and the conditions which shape its emergence and role in a community. The connection between the images we hold and the ways enterprise is supported are drawn out in the opening three chapters. The middle chapters concentrate on the organisational context for enterprise. This can be the small venture or the large organisation. The recurrent theme of these chapters is the ubiquitous nature of enterprise. The group of mothers who created MADD (Mothers Against Drunk Drivers) faced the barriers to change and relied on their own initiative to get action. The same determination, responsiveness and practical skills are needed by: the graduate starting a business; the social worker introducing a client database; the drama group raising funds for permanent premises; and the manager launching a new product. The personal and group skills which turn ideas to actions and interests to successful ventures are drawn out in the closing chapters.

The link between ideas and action is seen within each chapter. Ideas are introduced. Typically, they are linked to action. Most chapters close with an 'aid to action'. These range from case studies to questionnaires. Each has been designed to give the reader and user a means of applying the material in the chapter.

Much of this material is linked to the Enterprise in Higher Education initiative of the Department of Employment. This initiative provides the opportunity for all students, regardless of discipline, to gain some insight into enterprise. I am, however, convinced that material and theme have a much wider relevance. In developing and communicating this I have been lucky in winning help from a host of friends and colleagues. Some, like Professors Allan Gibb, Mike Scott, John Dawson and Brian Moores are a constant source of ideas and advice. Others like Bob Hale and Francis Chittenden supply a distinctive personal insight. Much of my understanding of the phenomenon derives from research presented at the annual Small Firms Policy and Research Conference. My students at Stirling University and Manchester Business School are perhaps the greatest influence. They range from entrepreneurs on short courses to graduates on the MBA. Their talent, insight and energy supply a constant reminder of the potential that resides in people.

This book would not have been possible without the support and encouragement of my publishers. As always my family have shown a remarkable willingness to put up with stress and dislocation. A full catalogue of the contributors is impossible but the debt is gratefully acknowledged.

Tom Cannon

Chapter 1

Images of enterprise

The meaning of the enterprise concept

Any meaningful definition of enterprise must contain several different elements. One is the ability to look beyond the obvious:

> The frog in the well say, 'The sky is no bigger than the mouth of the well'.
>
> Mao Tse Tung

There is implicit in most notions of enterprise the principle of risk but typically for a purpose:

> Nothing venture, nothing win.
>
> *Iolanthe*, Sir William Gilbert

Self reliance allied to the talent to make the best of a situation are often linked in definitions of enterprise:

> You only have a problem if you think it is a problem.
>
> Mueller's Law (*1001 Logical Laws*; compiled by J. Peers)

The enterprising individual is often viewed as achievement rather than process or procedure orientated. Tom Lehrer summed this up with his comment:

> It is sobering to consider that when Mozart was my age he had been dead for a year.

Balzac's conclusion (*1001 Logical Laws*; compiled by J. Peers) that:

> there is only one giant machine operated by pygmies, and that is bureaucracy

is the corollary. There is a sense of individuality in most assumptions about enterprise but this can be reflected in group behaviour and in the actions of a single person. In this it is closely linked to creativity and innovation as well as the energy and drive to see projects through to their conclusion.

> While most large metal and engineering producers rolled heavily in the doldrums of

the 1870s and 1880s Vickers' reaction to the 'Great Depression' was to innovate a way
through it, exploiting rather than mislaying their technical strengths ... little wonder
that Tom Vickers could agree with a somewhat bemused Royal Commission on the
Depression of Trade that his firm had turned about to face the ill-winds, and, to beat
through them, had simply 'created a new business'.

> Trebilcock, *The Vickers Brothers* (1977)

A basic assumption about enterprise is the acceptance that novel solutions and
risk may be necessary if challenges are to be faced and solutions found. The motives
which prompt this desire to find solutions and accept risks are complex. They are
seldom centred solely on acquisition.

> While the exploratory drive may be adulterated by ambition and vanity, the quest in
> its purest form is its own reward.
>
> Koestler, A., *Bricks to Babel* (1980)

From these and the *Oxford English Dictionary* definition,

> Disposition to engage in undertakings of difficulty, risk or daring.

A full definition looks like this:

> Enterprise is the characteristic of people, groups and organizations which produces a
> disposition to self realisation through achievement. It encompasses the self reliance to
> innovate, accept risk and act independently, if these are needed to complete tasks effec-
> tively. People and organizations showing enterprise have the drive, energy, creativity and
> leadership to see tasks through to completion by individual effort or successful team-work.

Enterprise can be shown in a wide variety of ways. The classic, commercial form
is the entrepreneur who identifies a business opportunity and builds a company.
The 'heroic' form of enterprise is epitomized by those Elizabethan adventurers who
set out to challenge empires.[1] In describing Drake, Raleigh commented:

> A single purpose animates all his exploits and the chart of his movements is like cord
> laced and knotted round the throat of the Spanish monarch.

In science, enterprise has characterized most of the breakthroughs in knowledge.
Here, painstaking attention to detail allied to insight seems to distinguish outstanding
contributors.

> Newton had a grasp of mathematics many times more exact and more powerful than
> his contemporaries, so that he was able to turn his sensible speculations about gravity
> into precise formulations that observation could verify ... The work of Isaac Newton
> is technically so powerful that we easily miss the lucid originality of outlook which
> underlies it.
>
> Bronowski, J. & Mazlish, B., *The Western Intellectual Tradition*

In the humanities, these features of enterprise are often combined with an ability to innovate and challenge the accepted order while re-creating it.

> Our way of life changes, under pressure of material changes in our environment; and unless we have those few men who combine an exceptional sensibility with an exceptional power over words, our own ability, not merely to express, but even to feel any but the crudest emotions will degenerate.
>
> T.S. Eliot, *The Social Function of Poetry*

In all its forms, enterprise retains this sense of the individual, the group or the organization taking responsibility for its own fate and seeking to produce a successful and appropriate outcome.

Different types of enterprise

The diversity of form which can be encompassed by this concept of enterprise has already been touched on. The entrepreneurial form is perhaps the simplest to identify. The individual when acting as entrepreneur literally 'undertakes' a venture to achieve a desired outcome. Typically, he or she has identified an opportunity or need which is not satisfied in the present environment. Existing large organizations are unwilling or unable to act or simply ignorant of the opening. The founders of Friends of the Earth did not act in a vacuum. There were existing bureaucracies which had shown themselves unwilling to respond to the grassroots concerns about the environment that were emerging. Large corporations have consistently shown themselves unable to respond as effectively as newly formed businesses to innovative technologies and their applications (see Table 1.1).

The entrepreneur performs a crucial economic role by accepting risks which the established firm shuns. This can be the gap in the market described by Schumpeter.[2] Bearing the risks associated with innovation and development is probably more important today. Rapid change is closely linked with high rates of failure. The costs can be met socially as in the case of large firms or public institutions. These organizations tend to avoid these risks by resisting change. The costs are enormous especially when borne by enterprises with high overheads and historic investments. The entrepreneur takes on the risk personally but keeps overheads low and historic investments are minimized.

The social entrepreneur makes a similar contribution. Significant changes in the ways in which groups or organizations operate usually requires people who are willing to step outside convention. These people can act singly or together. Dr Barnardo's, Oxfam, Shelter and Greenpeace are just some the organizations which have emerged to fill gaps left by established systems of provision. Often the link with the innovator(s) is self evident; as with Dr Barnardo's, elsewhere the creators have acted together to meet a need, such as Oxfam. Comic Relief illustrates the ability to devise novel approaches to a problem. Large, established institutions may respond when the need and the approach has been validated by the pioneers.

The same combination of individuality and vision abounds in the Arts: Beethoven's

Table 1.1 Sixty-three important innovations* by US small firms in the twentieth century

Acoustic suspension speakers	Link trainer
Aerosol can	Nuclear magnetic resonance scanner
Air conditioning	Nuclear magnetic resonance spectrometer
Airplane	Optical scanner
Articulated tractor chassis	Oral contraceptives
Artificial skin	Outboard engine
Assembly line	Overnight national delivery
Automatic fabric cutting	Pace-maker
Automatic transfer equipment	Personal computer
Bakelite	Photo typesetting devices
Catalytic petroleum cracking	Polaroid camera
Computerised blood pressure controller	Precast concrete
Continuous casting	Prefabricated housing
Cotton picker	Pressure sensitive cellophane
Tape defibrillator	Programmable computer
Double knit fabric	Quick frozen food
Dry chemical fire extinguisher	Reading machine
Electrical wire nuts	Rotary oil drilling bit
Fibre optic examination equipment	Safety razor
Fluid flow meter	Six axis robot arm
Foam fire extinguisher	Soft contact lenses
Front end loader	Sonar fish monitoring
Gas chromatograph	Spectrographic grid
Geodesic dome	Stereoscopic map scanner
Gyrocompass	Strain gauge
Hand held fluoroscope	Strobe lights
Heart valve	Vacuum tube
Heat sensor	Variable output transformer
Helicopter	Winchester disc drive
Heterodyne radio	Xerography
Hydraulic brake	Zipper
Large capacity computer	

* *Note:* An innovation is the first sale using a discovery.
Source: State of Small Business; A Report of The President (1983) US Government Printing Office, p. 127.

combination of energy, drama and statements of human ideals; Picasso's redefinition of shape and Joyce's 'impressionistic' use of language reflect the willingness to create something new, if necessary, in defiance of convention. Frequently they show an ability to return to fundamentals shorn of the accretions which may blind large organizations or establishments to their true purpose and value.

Different forms

The variety of situations in which enterprise can emerge is reflected in the different ways in which it can be manifested. The dedicated, 'driven' individual is a common stereotype. On occasion, this combination of dedication and sacrifice may be necessary for progress and change to occur. Kuhn[3] argues that scientific progress has largely been shaped by the conflict between 'a strenuous and devoted attempt to force nature into the conceptual boxes supplied by professional education'[4] and the attempts to challenge this consensus based on new insights: 'Scientists ... often speak of the *scales falling from the eyes* or of the *lightning flash* that *inundates* a previously obscure puzzle, enabling its components to be seen in a new way' (Kuhn, 1962).

Individual enterprise has a crucial role in most models of human progress and development. Effective personal endeavour is usually associated with a relentless dedication to particular outcomes. This uncritical approach creates problems as well as opportunities. Most research into failure highlights the lack of review and appraisal by the champions of the project.

Single-minded endeavour can lead to intolerance of others who lack this commitment. Artists, scientists and entrepreneurs may find it hard to understand others who fall short of their dedication. This can produce a reluctance to build teams or larger organizations. Many small business people deliberately restrict growth to avoid employing more workers. There is a growing body of evidence that much of the stress observed in research teams derives from the clash between the uncompromising demands of leaders and the desire of colleagues to follow a 'more normal' lifestyle.

This type of conflict is not inevitable. Individual enterprise is consistent with effective team work. The vision of the individualist can stimulate loyalty which can be as self-sacrificing as that shown by the originator. Enterprise can be channelled through more conventional attempts to build teams and organizations. It requires a recognition of the need to work with and through others to achieve goals. It seems that this is not consistent with conventional organizational hierarchies as shown in Figure 1.1.

This type of structure presupposes clearly defined levels and lines of authority. It is hard to break out of the confines of the hierarchy because of the implicit challenge to more senior staff and functions. Enterprise-orientated teams are characterized by more open, flatter and organic configurations. Hub-based configurations (Figure 1.2) seem to be more successful at combining individual enterprise and successful teams. In this form of organization, all team members have access to the key decision makers on basis of need rather than a role or right basis. Information and authority flows are on the same footing. Effort in team building and bonding ensures that the group works successfully together while individual enterprise is channelled effectively. Control is vested in the individual. Direction is achieved through a clearly worked out and clearly communicated strategy which is internalized by members of the team or organization. Those who need to act are *empowered* to act.

Most management literature places the onus on managers to create the type of environment in which enterprise can flourish. Peters & Waterman[5] discuss the ways in which this can be created as well as supplying examples at a personal and corporate

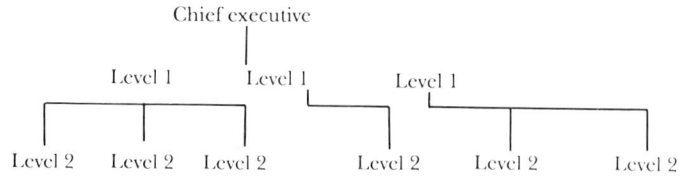

Figure 1.1   Conventional hierarchy

level. Kantor[6] develops a similar theme. Even Pinchot (1985) slips into the same top-down, employee mentality. The first action required of the Chief Executive is to 'Clearly state your vision of the company's future'. In the enterprising organization, every member accepts responsibility for the nature and direction of the concern.

An obligation to create the appropriate climate, developing and achieving strategic goals is shared. It is not only the Chief Executive's job to 'Look at every level for

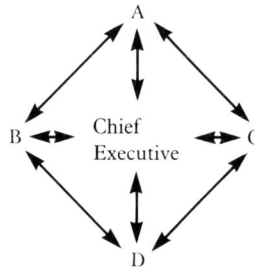

Figure 1.2   Hub-based organizations

intrapreneurs with ideas',[7] there is an identical duty on the members of the organization. They should develop their own enterprise; play their part in shaping and implementing strategy, besides championing their own development ideas in an open and constructive way. Success depends on creating teams in which individuality is combined with a sense of group responsibility. The leader may get the followers he or she deserves but the followers get the leader they deserve.

Visions

Research into enterprise might be described as consisting of many strands but little pattern: the attempt to understand why some individuals and groups show the self reliance, drive, energy, creativity and leadership to innovate, accept risk and act independently is at least as old as the social sciences themselves. McGregor[8] alludes to this in the preface to his book, *The Human Side of Enterprise* when he quotes Alfred P. Sloan asking 'whether successful managers are born or made'.

The view of enterprise as a something 'you are born with' remains an important part of the general view of this phenomenon. Many early researchers placed considerable emphasis on the personal or psychological origins of enterprise.

> For Babson, the required intelligence, drive to achieve, energy and necessary qualities of leadership were products of ancestry and, to a considerable extent, were outside our control.
>
> Ronstadt, R.C., *Entrepreneurship*, Lord Publications (1984)

It is a view which recurs in much of the lay literature which describes the origins of famous entrepreneurs.

> Tales of Henry Ford's infant mechanical prowess, his devising of gadgets and tinkering with tools, have clustered around the accounts of his youth.
>
> Lacey, R., *Ford*, Pan (1986)

> Somewhere in his thick Scotch Presbyterian bones, the eight-year-old Jack Simplot was an irrepressible entrepreneur.
>
> Gilder, G., *The Spirit of Enterprise*, Viking (1985)

Researchers have sought to explore the forces which shape the values, attitudes and approaches to life which lead certain people to take on the challenges of initiating, organizing or developing which are generally associated with enterprise. The 'born not made' theory requires this type of framework if it is not to be reduced to a simple random event model.

Most of the research which has been undertaken from this perspective has sought to explain the relationships between the internal, individual factors and the external, social components. Chell[9] explored the questions which are raised by various researchers in this area. She identifies three broad strands of work which are classified as:

- The Traits Model – often associated with McClelland[10]
- The Psychodynamic Model – generally linked with Kets de Vries[11]
- The Social Development Model of Gibb and Ritchie[12]

The 'traits' model of behaviour argues that there exists a single trait or group of traits in the personality of the enterprising individual which differentiate him or her from others. A 'trait' is a persisting dimension(s) or characteristic of the personality. McClelland saw the enterprising individual as one who was willing to accept risk, had a high achievement need and sought self realization to action. McClelland explicitly rejected the 'born not made' model. He argued that these behaviour 'traits' could be developed through appropriate training and specific social circumstances.

Other writers have put forward additional personality traits to explain enterprising or entrepreneurial behaviour. These included 'anxiety or neuroticism'[13] and 'leadership aspirations'.[14] The notion that there are these kinds of features in the personality make-up of the enterprising individual goes some way to explain the persistence of enterprising action over time in some people. It does not fully explain why individuals can be enterprising in some aspects of their behaviour and in certain spheres of activity but cautious elsewhere. Nor does it account for change over time. In the UK, for example, it is suggested that many entrepreneurs have a low 'comfort factor', i.e. once their business is established at a particular, acceptable level they avoid risk and resist growth.

Many of the same problems face the psychodynamic approach. This proposition is based on the notion that enterprise; especially in its entrepreneurial form is a form of deviant behaviour. It emerges in people whose attitudes have been shaped by a harsh, hostile or deprived background. They compensate by reducing their dependence on others and the wider community or society. This individualism will express itself in several forms which will reflect the lessons learned during the period of deprivation. An emphasis on personal achievement is in part a measure of increased control over destiny and an outward display of success in the face of adversity.

Together, these characteristics tend to produce an aggressive, self-orientated approach to social intercourse. Boissevain[15] saw this desire for control and self realisation as especially important for 'small entrepreneurs [who] perceive [the] disadvantages as secondary to the feeling of independence; of freedom; of being able to build; of being able to implement one's own ideas'. There is ample evidence to support the notion that a desire for freedom of action and a 'world view' which sees the individual as a focus for liberating behaviour are closely linked with personal enterprise. There is, however, far less evidence that harsh, prior experiences are consistently linked with individual endeavour.

Gibb and Ritchie[12] have examined in some depth the 'antecedent influences' which are associated with personal enterprise. They place considerable emphasis on the domestic, social, educational and work experiences which affect the probability of a person or group acting in an enterprising way. This type of social development model highlights the impact of peers especially within the family, the value of positive reinforcement through reward, role models and feedback as well as the contribution of particular types of work, life and educational experiences.

It is hard to separate these social and economic pressures on the individual from wider cultural influences. There do, however, seem to be wide variations between communities in the way people respond to those pressures. Simultaneously, people faced with the same pressures will respond differently. This is especially notable in the type of semi-controlled environment found in the large organization. People working, being educated or operating in this context will exploit, ignore or respond in a wide range of ways to opportunities to demonstrate their enterprise.

Expectations

Views of enterprise in an organizational context are closely linked with visions of how people work together. Organizations are not fixed and rigid entities. They are made up of people who come together to achieve different things. Their motives differ and the way they interact depends as much on their expectations of each other as on any formal roles they perform and offices they hold. These expectations are shaped by communication and reward systems.

Communication is a complex process based on a mixture of tangible and intangible elements. Success depends on the ways in which the desired message is accepted and interpreted by the recipient. A positive approach to enterprise in an organization requires more than the transmission of this message.

> I don't want any yes-men around me. I want everybody to tell me the truth even if it costs them their jobs.
>
> Samuel Goldwyn

People interpret signals in a variety of ways which may differ significantly from the objective of the individual sending the message. This will depend on the way it is sent, background 'noise' and the perspective of the recipients. The impact of the signals can be seen at a social, organizational and individual level. A society which undervalues or denies access to enterprise is not likely to see many examples among its citizens. A firm which fails to recognize or reward enterprise may find enterprising individuals leave or seek recognition elsewhere. The individual who sees enterprise as 'not for me' or is ignorant of the scope for personal enterprise will not realize the opportunities offered by personal endeavour.

There is ample evidence that once certain preconditions are met very large numbers of people are willing and able to express their enterprise. These preconditions include a sympathetic culture in the society or the firm, awareness of the range and diversity of situations in which enterprise can be expressed, recognition of its relevance and accessibility and desire to act.

Learning

Learning is a crucial aspect of the transition from awareness and interest to desire and action. There is increasing evidence that education, training and development can play a part in stimulating enterprise in individuals, groups and organizations. This has been especially notable over the last decade in projects designed to increase new business formation rates. In the UK, programmes such as Graduate Enterprise and institutions such as Enterprise Trusts seem to have tapped new reservoirs of individual enterprise (Figure 1.3). In other European countries co-operatives such as the Mondragon group of co-operatives in Spain are associated with a surge of enterprising behaviour. In the USA, the Small Business Development Centres are linked with increases in entrepreneurship from Atlanta to Washington DC.

Much of the initial success of the Enterprise Agencies in Britain grew from their success in making enterprise accessible. Large numbers became aware that it was possible to express their desire for independence through self-employment. The Trusts are easily accessible. They are often located on the High Street of major cities. Their organizers deliberately seek to reduce the barriers between the potential entrepreneur and the helper. The same features are found in Graduate Enterprise. For the first

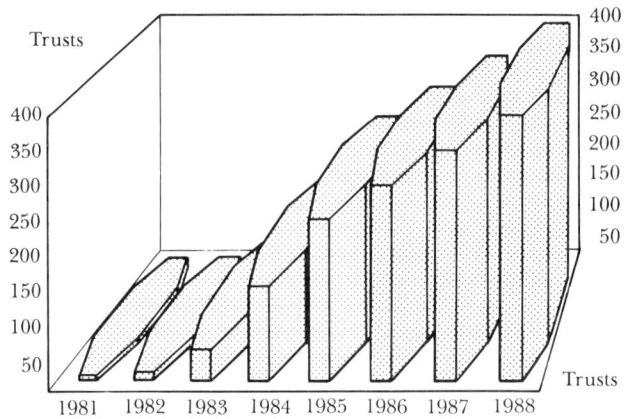

Figure 1.3   The number of Enterprise Trusts in the UK

time students were made fully aware that self realization through personal enterprise was open to them. The latent interest was vividly illustrated by the high initial rates of involvement and the rapid growth in numbers of those participating (Figure 1.4).

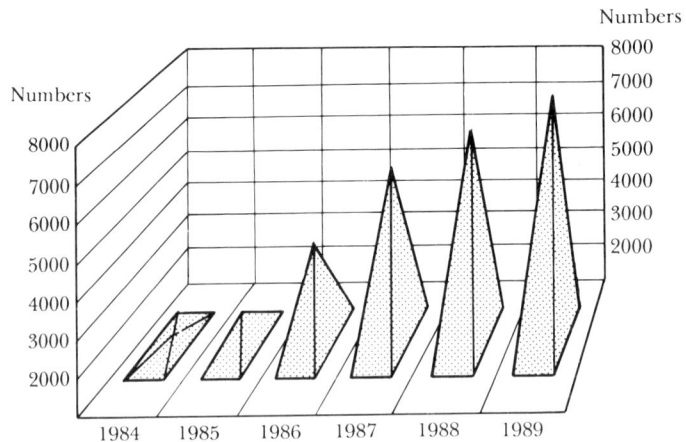

Figure 1.4   The growth of Graduate Enterprise

These are the more recent illustrations of the interest in enterprise which emerges once people are aware of the opportunity to express themselves in this way. In other fields of endeavour examples abound. The success of the 'fringe' at the Edinburgh Festival derives, in part, from the enterprise of people who find the institutional constraints of the Edinburgh Festival unacceptable.

The interest in enterprise depends on a combination of environmental and personal features. The appeal of enterprise is shaped by broad environmental forces such as the culture, technology, politics and economy of the society. These are interpreted by intermediaries such as the media, education, political parties and bankers. The pattern of these relationships is described in Figure 1.5.

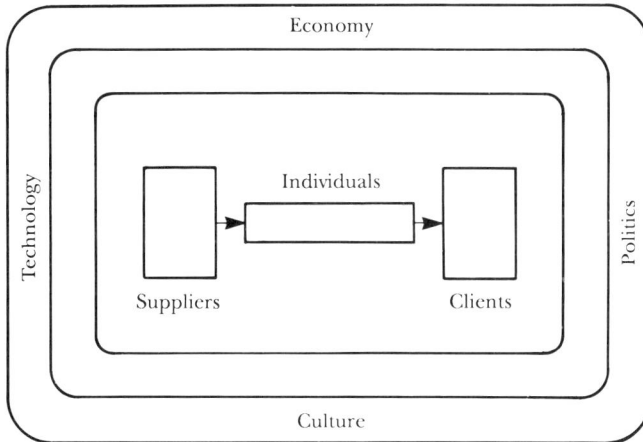

Figure 1.5   The environment for enterprise

The forms of enterprise reflect the ways in which people respond to these external pressures and the opportunities opened by suppliers and clients. The former can provide ideas as well as goods and services. Customers determine the extent to which projects, concepts, products or services can be sustained.

Perhaps the greatest barrier to any personal endeavour is the view that 'it is not for me'. This seems to be closely linked with the attitudes communicated by family and peers. Research into entrepreneurial behaviour by women indicates that parental and other family pressures often discourage business formation. Educational experiences have a major effect on the extent to which opportunities are recognized, their nature and the willingness to exploit them.

Translating interest into desire calls for a learning experience which helps individuals to appreciate the benefits while preferring these to other opportunities. Peer group behaviour is an especially important aspect of this. It can reassure as well as reinforce positive aspects of the experience especially during the initial stages. Group-based, self-directed, experiential and action learning approaches to learning are effective means of building up support systems. At the same time they can provide participants with the means to manage their long-term learning more effectively.

Group-based work has not played a large part in education in the UK. Recent interest in this approach reflects a recognition that the majority of people spend the bulk of their life working in groups. The group learning experience resembles the most, situations faced after university or college. There is a need to learn how to cope with these situations during more formal education. Project-based learning is an effective way of developing this knowledge. It does, however, pose new challenges to the student and the educator especially in terms of project definition, team construction, role and task definition, project management, and integration of contributions beside production and evaluation of results.

Self-directed learning is not new to education in the UK. Current interest reflects a burgeoning awareness that its effectiveness depends on the creation of the right kind of environment and initial training of participants in the opportunities and problems it creates. The best environment for self-directed learning is one in which access to materials and sources is good, peer support is available and feedback is quick and relevant. It creates the opportunity for the 'teacher's' role to become more that of a mentor. It leads to the student gaining a greater sense of ownership of learning which continues after the specific exercise is completed.

Experiential- and action-based learning complements self-directed learning. It is based on the notion that 'learning through doing' can lead the student into new areas of experience beside reinforcing more conventional teaching. The approach is closely linked with the work of Reg Revans.[16] He indicated the benefits gained when managers could identify problems or issues of concern and link the knowledge sought to these tasks. He argued that the projects undertaken should be outside the manager's direct area of work. Others have applied the same approach to projects which fall within the direct competence of those involved.[17] Attention has been paid recently to the relative advantages of 'close' and 'open' projects. The former are externally determined and usually focus on specific areas, e.g. exports. 'Open' projects are identified by participants and may be very wide ranging.

These approaches present an opportunity to shift ownership of the learning experience to the student. They seem to be effective at breaking down the barriers between subjects. In the longer term they seem to support a move from interest in the issue or subject towards a desire to pursue and use knowledge.

Conclusion

A recurrent question in the recent discussion of enterprise is, to what extent can enterprise be taught or developed in others? Some answers to this complex issue are possible. Enterprise can certainly be released. Awareness of the opportunities prompts some who may show no initial signs of enterprise to realize their potential. People show enterprise in many situations. The passive worker may be the driving force behind the local dramatic society or sports club. The energetic and venturesome entrepreneur may be conservative in his approach to finance or technology.

Circumstances will affect this. The founder of a business may be ambitious for growth and development up to a point. Once a comfort level is reached progress might stop. The open, flexible scientific researcher can be a narrow and nervous manager. Some societies seem able to encourage high levels of individual and group enterprise. Elsewhere, artistic creativity, new business formation and other forms of enterprise are far less evident.

Case study

Physician know thyself

Self knowledge is the key to self realization. Complete the following appraisal and check your responses against the candid views of someone you trust.

- *Performance*: Does your performance match up to your promise or do you fall down for avoidable reasons?
- *Handicaps*: Do any aspects of your behaviour stop you achieving your full potential?
- *Your actions*: They speak louder than your words but do they say the same thing?
- *Intelligence*: This separates those working smarter from those working dumber. Do you think before you act?
- *Cool views*: Avoid errors – do you act in haste and repent at leisure, and what does it cost?
- *Inferiority complexes*: These limit horizons – do you have the ambition to realize your potential?
- *Analysis of opportunities and resources*: This is the first step towards mobilizing yourself to capitalize on opportunities. Do you know your strengths, weaknesses, opportunities and challenges?
- *Now*: This is the time to act to make the best of yourself. Do you have a plan of action?

References

1. Black, J. B. (1959) *The Reign of Elizabeth*, Oxford, Oxford University Press.
2. Schumpeter, J. (1936) The Instability of Capitalism, *Economic Journal*, pp. 361–86.
3. Kuhn, T. (1962) *The Structure of Scientific Revolutions*, University of Chicago Press.
4. Kuhn, T. (1972) Reflections on my Critics, in *Criticism and the Growth of Knowledge* (Laktos, I. and Musgrave, A., eds.), Cambridge, Cambridge University Press.
5. Peters, T. J. and Waterman, R. H. (1982) *In Search of Excellence*, New York, Harper and Row.
6. Kantor, R. M. (1983) *The Change Masters*, London, Allen and Unwin.
7. Pinchot, G. (1985) *Intrapreneuring*, New York, Harper and Row, p. xii.
8. McGregor, D. (1987) *The Human Side of Enterprise*, London, Penguin.
9. Chell, E. (1985) The Entrepreneurial Personality: A few ghosts laid to rest, *International Small Business Journal*, vol. 3, no. 3, spring, pp. 43–54.

10. McClelland, D. C. (1961) *The Achieving Society*, New Jersey, Van Nostrand Reinholt.
11. Kets de Vries, M. F. R. (1977) The Entrepreneurial Personality Person at the Crossroads, *Journal of Management Studies*, February, pp. 34–57.
12. Gibb, A. A. and Ritchie, J. (1981) Influences of Entrepreneurship: A study over time, in *Bolton Ten Years On*, Proceedings of the UK Small Business Research Conference, November.
13. Lynn, R. (1969) The Personality Characteristics of a Group of Entrepreneurs, *Occupational Psychology*, vol. 43, pp. 151–2.
14. Hornaday, J. A. and Bunker, C. A. (1970) The Nature of the Entrepreneur, *Personnel Psychology*, vol. 23, pp. 47–54.
15. Boissevain, J. (1981) *Small Entrepreneurs in Changing Europe*, Maastricht: European Centre for Work and Society.
16. Revans, R. (1971) *Developing Effective Managers*, London, Longman.
17. Cannon, T. and Willis, M. (1983) The Role and Application of Action Learning to Management Development in the Small Firm, *Management Education and Development*, vol. 14, part 2, summer, pp. 91–102.

Chapter 2

The entrepreneurial economy

The term 'the entrepreneurial economy' has achieved a great deal of popularity over the last twenty years. Its prominence reflects a widespread view that the individual can play a more important role in shaping economic processes than was assumed for most of the post-war period. A number of specific issues provoked this shift in thinking. First, there was the growing concern among academics about the failure of conventional economic theory to account for the distinctive contribution of the individual. Baumol[1] highlighted this omission. The notion that 'impersonal market forces' explained all economic outcomes did not fit well with personal experience and observation of the crucial role that key individuals had played in the competitive success of individual firms or economies. Increased domestic and international competition led to greater attention to the factors which gave certain firms or communities a competitive edge. The entrepreneur and the successful manager seemed able to make a real and substantial contribution to increased competitiveness.

Growing anxieties about national economic performance among policy makers were more important than the recognition of an intellectual gap in stimulating interest. These concerns centred on the growing belief that the failure to support individual enterprise could lead to negative economic consequences. In Britain, the Bolton Report[2] highlighted the low start-up rates and small numbers of self-employed in key industry sectors. It was subsequently suggested that a link existed between these features of the economy and the UK's poor, overall performance in the post-war period. The stronger, advanced economies of West Germany and Japan appeared to have higher rates of start-up and a higher proportion of their workforce in small- and medium-sized firms.

The economic downturn of the late 1970s and rapid increases in unemployment provided an immediate spur to interest in the entrepreneurial economy. Research[3] was published which seemed to indicate that smaller firms employed more people and were more stable local employers than larger enterprises. This struck a chord with policymakers grappling with unemployment which seemed to grow inexorably while showing massive regional variations.

Initial interest in small firms was linked with unemployment growth. There was, however, an even more powerful inducement for policymakers to develop an interest in entrepreneurship. The rapid rate of technological change created an environment in which those firms able to initiate and exploit new technologies were especially important to industrial economies. Several features of smaller firms make them especially important in the process of innovation. The more open, organizational structure of the smaller enterprise means that barriers to change are reduced. At the same time, information and decision flows occur on a *need to know* basis rather than rooted in bureaucratic procedures. This type of organic structure is closely associated with successful development of novel solutions to problems.

The entrepreneur performs several roles which are linked with effective invention, innovation and development. The 'product champion' helps new ideas, products or services to overcome internal and external opposition. The combination of champion and proprietor is especially powerful. The small firm can combine an open and organic structure with clear and rapid decision making through the entrepreneur. This is especially true in the early years when 'hub'-based organizational structures are faster and simpler than more formal bureaucracies. The hub-based firm described in Figure 1.2 allows entrepreneurs to make decisions, sign-post and direct flows and establish links on a needs basis. There are few barriers between the key players. Innovation is easier and operates at a lower cost.

The bureaucratic structure emphasizes professionalism based on established systems and procedures. These protect the organization from risk but act as a barrier to change. It is hard to bring diverse, interdisciplinary groups together. The formal, highly-structured nature of the enterprise provides considerable scope for blocking novel ideas and developments. This can frustrate those innovators and change agents who will determine the firm's long-term success in a changing environment.

Does the enterprise economy have a meaning?

There are two ways in which the notion of the entrepreneurial economy might have a meaning. There is the specific sense in which economic theory addresses the issue of the role of individual enterprise and the entrepreneur. More broadly, there is the pragmatic perception of an economy – local, national or international – driven by entrepreneurial activity.

It is fashionable to view the current interest in the entrepreneur and the contribution of individual enterprise to economic activity as a novel phenomenon. This is true in a limited sense. Marshall's writings contain 'no clear distinction between entrepreneurial and non-entrepreneurial activity: on the contrary, entrepreneurship is so pervasive that the label is simply never used'.[4]

There is, however, another tradition in economic analysis. Among the first writers to provide a distinct role for the entrepreneur in economic life was Joseph Schumpeter.[5] His interest centred on change in industrial and economic processes. He challenged the conventional preoccupation of economists with equilibrium, and the neglect of theories of change. He saw movement, not equilibrium, as the dominant force in industrial behaviour and asserted that 'it is . . . the producer as a rule who initiates economic change, and consumers are educated by him as necessary; they are, as it were, taught to want new things'. The notion of the entrepreneur as the creator of change has particular relevance when innovation and transformation are seen as the dominant features of economic development.

Recently, Casson[6] has placed entrepreneurial behaviour at the centre of his explanation of economic success or failure. He explains this largely in terms of the choices made about resource allocation. The entrepreneur's contribution centres on three broad roles: intermediary or deal maker, risk taker and co-ordinator of resources. He or she manipulates expertise and information to create markets and obtain a better return in each of these areas to their rivals. The numbers and skills of the entrepreneurs will determine local, corporate and national success.

There is the famous definition of the academic as 'someone who sees something working in practice and wonders whether it will work in theory'. Policymakers and the media have accused those who seek to find a theoretical role for individual enterprise and entrepreneurship in economic success of falling into the trap implied by the joke. The economic contributions of individuals as diverse as Otis, Ford, Singer, Leverhulme, Morris, Krupp, Morita and Aggelli are sufficient evidence for some that the entrepreneurial economy has a real and specific meaning. It is, however, important to develop our understanding of these concepts so that relevant theories of economic behaviour can emerge which will guide policy.

The 'enterprise' economy seems to have several dominant characteristics. These centre on the willingness of individuals to exploit or create change and build successful enterprises out of the opportunities which emerge. Recognition of an opening is only one factor. Individuals must seek out and exploit the opportunities which exist. Society has a crucial part in preparing the ground for this type of development to occur. There are wide variations between communities in the willingness of their members to follow this route. New business start-up rates are very different in North America, Japan, West Germany and the UK. Evidence suggests a much greater acceptance in North America that enterprise creation is a vehicle for self realization. Table 2.1 shows the variations within the UK.

It is wrong to see starting a venture as the sole measure of individual enterprise applied to economic activities. It can occur within existing organizations. Innovation and new product development are crucial to the well being of advanced economies. Managers act as technology gatekeepers, introducing novel ideas, or as product champions advancing the project. In these roles, the acceptance of risk and the determination to progress a project are characteristics of the enterprising individual. The entrepreneurial economy depends on wider social support for these characteristics and their implications.

Creativity, insight, risk and determination are important components in the type of enterprise which produces economic returns. The discussion of Schumpeter above illustrates the emphasis that he placed on the creative spur to innovation. The impact of new products, new ideas and new services on everyday life can be seen in every High Street and store. It is estimated that 60% of all products sold in a large supermarket have been introduced within the last five years. Modern industrial societies

Table 2.1 Occupational grouping by head of household (1983)

Region	Percentage of heads in self-employment
North	5.3
Yorkshire and Humberside	6.7
East Midlands	8.0
East Anglia	9.4
South East	8.8
South West	10.6
West Midlands	7.1
North West	7.2
Scotland	6.2
England	8.1
Wales	8.0
Northern Ireland	11.7
UK	8.1

Source: Regional Trends, 1985.

depend for their long-term prosperity on the ingenuity and innovativeness of their people. Their repression of enterprise in Eastern Europe for fifty years means that the greatest challenge facing their economics lies in reasserting the value of individual responsibility for improvements.

An understanding of creativity is central to its stimulus and support. Two forms of insight underpin most creative acts. First is the ability to bi-sociate. This means bringing two separate phenomena together in a new unity. This skill is associated with creativity in the Arts, Humanities, Science and Business. Second, is the 'logic-leap' or ability to move beyond the existing consensus. Each of these sources of creativity depends on a combination of open-mindedness and confidence. A society which seeks to constrain thinking or undermines the self belief of individuals or groups is likely to discourage creativity.

Creativity alone is not enough. The process of invention, innovation and development is made up of several distinct and complex elements. Invention is the process of creation and discovery associated with novel phenomena. It generally involves a specific addition to the sum of human knowledge. Although new, it is not necessarily useful or desired by any potential market.

Innovation is the technical, industrial and commercial steps which leads to the marketing of new manufactured products or commercial services or to the use of new technical processes, products or services. Development involves the introduction of adaptations, changes or modifications into existing products, brands or services. These are generally designed to extend their viable life, adapt to new circumstances or introduce new customers.

Successful innovation and development lies at the heart of the prosperous, entrepreneurial economy. The innovation matrix described in Figure 2.1 describes the options

open to the individual or firm seeking progress through innovation. The radical innovation is based on the combination of a new product and a novel production process.
The computer game is a good example of the combination of a newness in offering
and technology. The technoshift is based on a new technology but limited change
in the nature or function of the product. The introduction of the Spinning Jenny
was just such a development. The pioneering product takes existing systems of production and uses them to manufacture a new product. Alcohol-free wines and beers
have used established technologies to create new markets. The most common form
of innovation – adaptation – links minor changes in both technology and product.

		Product	
		New	Improved/current
Process	New	Radical	Technoshift
	Improved/current	Pioneer	Adaptation

Figure 2.1   The innovation matrix

Change involves risk. The enterprise economy keeps the cost of entry to, and exit
from, innovative activity to the minimum necessary for sound stewardship and responsible management. There is some evidence that the willingness to start a new venture
is highest in those countries and regions in which re-start opportunities are the greatest.
This can include re-entry into the job market as well as starting another new activity.
Acceptance of risk taking by the wider community is linked with individual enterprise
outside the commercial sector. The progress of scientific knowledge from the seven-
teenth century is closely linked with the willingness of individuals to take risks in
the advocacy of their ideas and acceptance of this behaviour within their community.
The same pattern of behaviour can be seen in the Arts and Humanities.

   The entrepreneurial economy cannot be separated easily from attitudes to individual
and group enterprise in the wider society. Successful response to the rapid rate of
change seen today in science, commerce and society calls for creativity, innovation
and risk taking. This behaviour is linked with individual enterprise.

How permanent is this phenomenon?

The economic and industrial turbulence of the last twenty years has re-shaped the
environment. New business formation, innovation, new organizational forms and more
general shifts in attitudes and behaviour have placed a premium on personal initiative.
Society's long-term response is shaped by the permanence and extent of change.

These transformations may be part of a general evolution in industrial behaviour or represent a second or third Industrial Revolution.

It is impossible for any contemporary to classify with confidence the era of change they experience as evolutionary or revolutionary. There are, however, good reasons for viewing present circumstances in these terms. The best response to current challenges is likely to be that which minimizes the costs of absorbing the most extreme scenario while effectively exploiting any incremental adjustments to circumstances.

The technological, social and economic developments of recent years combine in ways which bear all the hallmarks of a major industrial change or revolution. The pace of change is now so fast that the line between quantitative and qualitative change is hard to draw. This is not only in high-profile areas such as Information Technology. Here, processing power increases and price cutting have a combined impact on industry, which bears comparison with the shift from water to steam power. A similar rate of change in the power output of the internal combustion engine would mean that the typical car engine would be the size of a match-box, cost less than a bottle of whisky, do 100 miles to the litre and produce enough power to drive the *QE2*. Similar technological changes can be seen in materials, energy and other key sectors of industry. The emergence of new biotechnologies adds further support to the impression that a qualitative change in the technological base of modern industrial society is occurring.

These changes have parallels in the restructuring of the world economic order over the last decade. New economic powers such as Korea and other Pacific Basin nations are joining Japan in a challenge to US and European dominance of the industrial world. The re-shaping of the European Economic Community in the early 1990s could mean that the USA will slip from first to third place among the world's economic powers. The dominant position that took fifty years to create could disappear within a decade. The transformation of Eastern Europe has been driven by popular awareness of economic deprivation and recognition by politicians that radical action is needed to stop economic decline. The UK's decline may be slowing. Despite that the coveted place in the top ten economic powers is lost without any sign of being restored.

These changes reflect shifts in systems of production and industrial relationships that neither the USA nor the UK seem able to adopt comfortably. The first is the erosion of traditional forms of industrial structure. The bureaucratic hierarchy is an institutional response to the organizational needs of large-scale manufacturing and processing. These production systems were based on bringing a large number of people together to achieve the maximum economies of scale. Single site operations were especially effective. It was, however, the need to mobilize the efforts of these large numbers of people that produced managerial hierarchies and bureaucracies. Military and bureaucratic systems of management dominated not least because the only prior experience of such large-scale mobilization of labour was in war or large-scale public projects.

Limits on the span of control of managers required subordinates who could manage communication and control systems. The narrowness of job description for operatives was the best route to volume production. Simultaneously, it reflected the limited skill base of the workers. The simplest formulae for calculating span of control illustrate the difficulty in dealing with many subordinates. The number of relationships which exist including those between subordinates and need to be understood can be determined by the following formula devised by Graicunas,[7] where n is the number of subordinates:

$$r = n(2^{n-1} + n - 1).$$

This takes into account the relationship between the superior and the subordinate, the subordinates with each other and the subordinates within subgroups. Hence, a manager (M) with both subordinates (A and B) will have two direct relationships; MA, MB, two group relationships; MAB, MBA. Beside these, the manager will need to recognize the two cross-relationships AB and BA.

The dominant, new technologies of today do not require these patterns of industrial organization. Information technologies can be organized just as easily around small numbers structured as networks as in single, large hierarchically based 'factories'.

There are strong similarities between the network-based structure (Figure 2.2) and the hub-based systems employed in many entrepreneurial concerns. Once the productivity of both systems is comparable, other costs can be taken into account. The capital and social costs of bringing large numbers of workers together is higher than a distributed workforce.

The factory system is a relatively new form of industrial organization. Its dominance dates from the middle of the last century. It is not hard to see this form of organization replaced by smaller units, linked through networks and distributed widely. The ultimate irony would lie in the elimination of 'these dark Satanic mills' and the building of 'Jerusalem in England's green and pleasant land' *by a computer*.

Some forms of heavy and repetitive manufacture seem certain to remain. These are central to the economy of an industrial nation. Many of these will be based on robot production.

> 'One day,' said Wilcox, 'there will be lightless factories full of machines like that.'
> 'Why lightless?'
> 'Machines don't need light. Machines are blind. Once you've built a fully computerized factory, you can take out the lights, shut the door and leave it to make engines or vacuum cleaners or whatever, all on its own in the dark. Twenty-four hours a day.'
> 'What a creepy idea.'
> 'They already have them in the States, Scandinavia.'
> 'And the Managing Director? Will he be a computer too, sitting in a dark office?'
> Wilcox considered the question seriously. 'No, computers can't think. There'll always have to be a man in charge, at least one man, deciding what should be done and how. But these jobs' – he jerked his head round the row of benches – 'will no longer exist. This machine is doing the work that was done last year by twelve men.'
> 'O brave new world,' said Robyn, 'where only the managing directors have jobs.'
>   David Lodge, *Nice Work*, Secker & Warburg, 1988

The shift in the technological imperatives will have knock-on effects across the production system. The most immediate will be that there is no need for a *man*

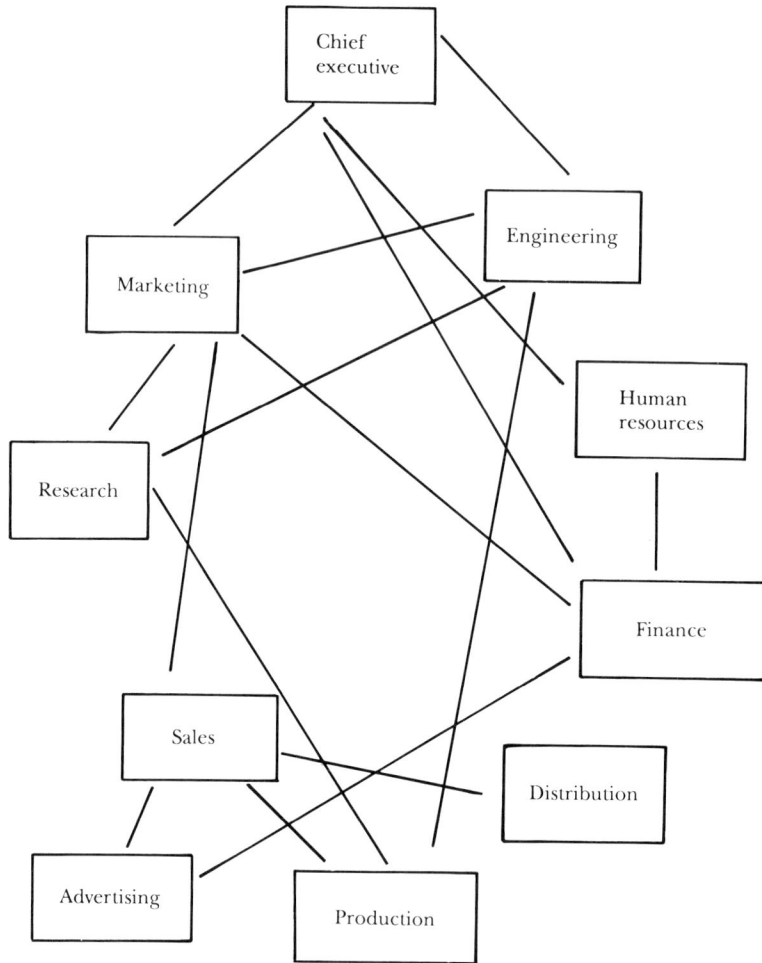

Figure 2.2   Network-based management systems: an illustration of some of the links

to be in charge. The new industries, the service sector and the forms of industrial organization outlined above create far fewer barriers to female employment than the old order.

The effective use of knowledge and expertise will determine success at an individual, company and society level. The pace of development places a premium on those people and groups with skills in accessing and exploiting these resources. Many will be graduates. During earlier periods of economic transformation the age of the typical entrepreneur dropped rapidly. A similar pattern can be seen today. When no-one has any experience, experience is no advantage.

The combination of these phenomena with the rapid rates of change in markets means that the ability to tap individual enterprise and creativity will determine the success of firms and communities. Power- and authority-based systems of control are poor at mobilizing these abilities. Consensus and voluntary approaches to managing people get the best response. These, in turn, depend on the willingness of society to invest in the knowledge and expertise which generates the confidence to act and the skill to manage. Those who demonstrate entrepreneurship within large organizations are often described as intrapreneurs.

Intrapreneurs

The large organizations that have grown to dominate life in the late twentieth century are unlikely to disappear and 'accept their fate' in a new age. The challenge to their leaders lies in combining their advantages of scale with the gains from creativity and enterprise. Part of this response is likely to take the form of new forms of organization. It might provoke 'the creative disintegration of the large corporation'. The large centrally organized firm working through large aggregations of workers will be replaced by a distributed workforce. This can already be seen in engineering, many forms of manufacture and the service sector. Peters and Waterman[8] highlighted one aspect of this when they noted the smallness of the head office functions of many of their successful firms.

Two problems will face these 'disintegrated' businesses. The most well-publicized is the shortage of people with the range of enterprise skills required to manage these activities. The parallel gap lies in finding senior executives with the ability to manage the type of highly delegated system expected by entrepreneurs. The UK Government's 'Enterprise and Higher Education' initiative attempts to address the first of these deficiencies by increasing awareness and use of relevant skills among graduates.

The accomplishments of the entrepreneur are not merely different to those of the conventional manager – they challenge their basis. The giant institutions of today have grown through increased managerial specialization. The salesman was joined by the advertising manager. Soon the promotions executive arrived. Later came the marketing manager who discovered an urgent need for a market research and public relations officer. The same pattern can be seen in production, distribution, finance and all other arms of the public company. This process is mirrored in the Arts, Science and across the public sector. Press agents for actors proliferate at the same rate as finance officers in university science departments.

In contrast, the small enterprise is led by the generalist. He or she expects to move easily from marketing to finance to production. More importantly, the primary task is to mobilize and integrate each set of skills for the benefit of the whole rather than the self aggrandisement of the parts. This priority reflects the second challenge to corporatism. The separation of ownership and management is rejected on a personal, if not a financial, level.

Chandler[9] charts the shift from kinship-based authority and responsibility systems to professional, managerial structures. The former, unambiguously linked ownership and responsibility. The success of the latter required clear separation. Enterprise based approaches bridge the two. The individual accepts responsibility because there is a strong sense of ownership. This might be formal and legal as in the case of the graduate entrepreneur setting up in business. Equally it can be a strong sense of identity or responsibility for outcomes. He or she is a committed 'champion', advocating, developing and seeking a specific outcome. The management challenge to organizations is to identify, support and guide these intrapreneurs.

The potential for enterprise and individual creativity is widely distributed. In commerce, this is vividly illustrated by the evidence of rapid increase in new business start-ups in most open economies. The recognition and legitimacy conferred on entrepreneurship has sparked rapid increases in new formations in countries as diverse as Italy, the UK, USA, Korea, China, Malaysia and Hungary. Similar developments can be seen in the Arts, Science and the public sector. The policy of Channel 4 TV in the UK to commission many of its programmes from independent producers stimulated a wave of new talent to emerge. The changing pattern of university, government and finance produced an environment where innovation driven by individual effort has proliferated. In the public sector, the same pattern can be seen. In Eastern Europe there is a declared wish to tap the enterprise which has only been shown on the black market recently for the new co-operatives and private ventures.

Different contexts for enterprise

The robustness of the enterprise economy depends on its value in different contexts and its substantive contribution to effectiveness in various circumstances. The first of these is important because narrow identification with a particular situation undermines the case for permeating the society with enterprise awareness. The second matters because the claim that more positive approaches to individual enterprise improves effectiveness is crucial to the argument for its centrality. In this context, efficiency and effectiveness can be distinguished.

Measures of efficiency generally concentrate on the internal, process aspects of the ways in which a task is performed. The output is secondary to performance (see Table 2.1). The engine of a car might run efficiently but unless it is attached to the drive shaft it merely 'wastes' energy. Introducing notions of individuality, creativity or enterprise are mere sops to fashion if the quality or output is not improved. It is worth introducing mechanisms to help foster enterprise in hospital management if patient care is improved.

It has no value as a substitute for other forms of investment unless it generates a better return. There is, however, powerful evidence that lack of enterprise can be disastrous regardless of other advantages.

Although there had been several minor fights in 1806, 1811 and 1814, the first employment of British troops against the Ashanti warriors came in 1823 when Sir Charles Macarthy, the British governor at Cape Coast Castle, launched a punitive expedition against them. When the two armies came close, Sir Charles ordered the band to play 'God Save the

Table 2.1 Effectiveness versus efficiency

Do the right things	*rather than*	Do things right
Avoid recurrences of difficulties	*rather than*	Solving specific problems
Optimise use	*rather than*	Safeguard resources
Obtain results	*rather than*	Follow duties
Increase returns	*rather than*	Lower costs

Adapted from: W. J. Reddin, *Managerial Effectiveness*, McGraw-Hill, London, 1970.

King' while he stood to attention in the jungle, confidently expecting the Ashantis to join him. Instead they attacked, and Sir Charles's West Indian regiment and Fanti allies were soundly defeated. Sir Charles was killed and his skull taken to Kumasi where in future it was displayed annually at the Yam festival.

Byron Farwell, *Queen Victoria's Little Wars*, Allen Lane, London, 1973

Private enterprise

The phrase *private enterprise* is such a cliché that the link between business and initiative can easily be lost. This is especially true given the dominance of systems thinking in management theory during much of this century. The notion that the operations of the firm and the activities of its workers could be reduced to a series of formulae and general theories is very attractive. This is especially true when economies of scale, conglomeration and routine seemed to offer external growth and internal stability. The rise of the technocrat in firms like General Motors, Imperial Group, Fiat and Volkswagen seemed to offer institutional bureaucracies painless growth without the challenges posed by individualism and enterprise.

Even innovation could be bureaucratized and converted into a series of sub-routines. Firms created new product development departments. Their task was to manage this process to schedule. Firms planned their launch schedule years in advance. This was necessary to fit into long-range promotional and production schedules. Years in advance it would be decided that a new product or brand would be launched onto the market. This was necessary to 'exploit the product life cycle' or 'maintain positioning' or achieve some other corporate goal. The notion of 'built in obsolescence' discredited a generation of managers. The outcome was a proliferation of trivial and incremental changes – but they did not work. Failure rates of over 80% were common where *no-one ever went broke from underestimating the intelligence of managers who underestimated the intelligence of the American (or British) consumer*. Companies like Volkswagen, who proudly boasted that they had product improvements to the Beetle planned for years ahead, faced major crises. Customers turned to firms who delivered the best product when available but did not eke it out like some miser trying to save the job of a new product manager.

The basic disciplines for the effective management of innovation have a value when wedded to creativity and enterprise. The process is described in Figure 2.3. The success of each stage and the dynamics of moving between stages turns on the enterprise of the people responsible. Managers who oversee the process require the vision to accept challenges to the status quo and support risk takers. Those responsible for the activity must champion and assess projects as if they owned the business. This will mean accepting that the marginal, compromise offering will always easier but may not be right.

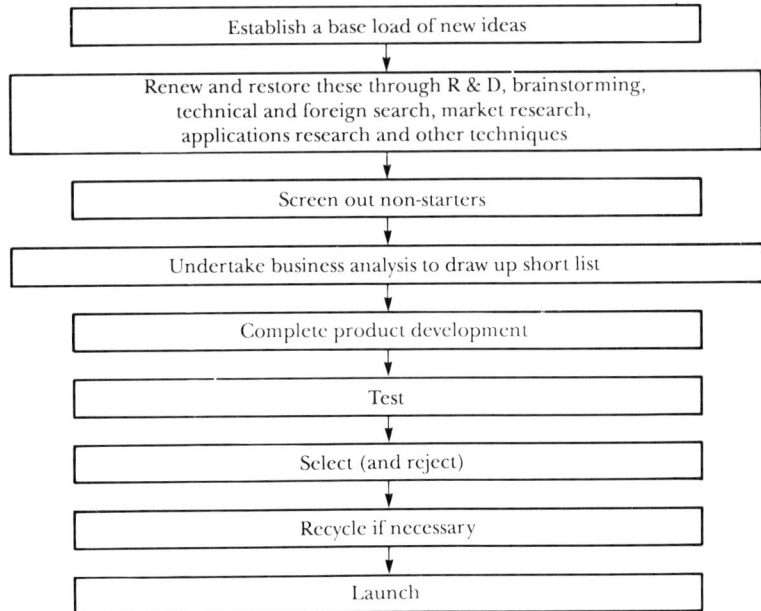

```
┌──────────────────────────────────────────────┐
│       Establish a base load of new ideas       │
└──────────────────────────────────────────────┘
                        │
┌──────────────────────────────────────────────────┐
│  Renew and restore these through R & D, brainstorming, │
│      technical and foreign search, market research,    │
│      applications research and other techniques        │
└──────────────────────────────────────────────────┘
                        │
┌──────────────────────────────────────────────┐
│           Screen out non-starters              │
└──────────────────────────────────────────────┘
                        │
┌──────────────────────────────────────────────────┐
│  Undertake business analysis to draw up short list │
└──────────────────────────────────────────────────┘
                        │
┌──────────────────────────────────────────────┐
│          Complete product development          │
└──────────────────────────────────────────────┘
                        │
┌──────────────────────────────────────────────┐
│                     Test                       │
└──────────────────────────────────────────────┘
                        │
┌──────────────────────────────────────────────┐
│               Select (and reject)              │
└──────────────────────────────────────────────┘
                        │
┌──────────────────────────────────────────────┐
│              Recycle if necessary              │
└──────────────────────────────────────────────┘
                        │
┌──────────────────────────────────────────────┐
│                    Launch                      │
└──────────────────────────────────────────────┘
```

Figure 2.3   The management of innovation

Enterprise in business is closely linked with the role of the entrepreneur. Often, frustration with existing, large corporations propels them into creating enterprises which challenge the hegemony of their former employers. Hewlett-Packard, Wang, and Tandon computers are part of a tradition which goes back to Chrysler and Richenbaker in the USA and Fodens (ERF) and Mars in the UK.

The entrepreneur has shown a persistent skill in identifying new markets and opportunities: Bell with the telephone; Edison with the incandescent lamp; Pilkington with the Float Glass Process and Jobs with the personal computer. The President's Report to Congress on the State of Small Business in 1986[11] noted that beside accounting for the majority of significant innovations, small firm productivity in product development is significantly greater than larger companies.

Two important caveats should be introduced into this analysis. The first is the much greater investment in R&D by larger corporations. Without this, entrepreneurs would not be able to exploit the opportunities created. The second is the acceptance of risk by entrepreneurs. Much of the cost of failure falls on the individual who, in this way, saves society from meeting these expenses.

Public enterprise

Some accounts of enterprise imply a conflict between public service and personal initiative or effectiveness. This approach gives little credit to the needs of management in the public sector or the potential for improved services through the application of enterprise. This view is challenged in the opening and closing sentences of a classic of management literature – McGregor's *The Human Side of Enterprise*:

> Every professional is concerned with the use of knowledge in the achievement of objectives: the engineer as he designs equipment, the medical practitioner as he diagnoses and prescribes for the ills of his patients, the lawyer or the architect as he serves his clients ... And, if we can learn how to realise the potential for collaboration in the human resources of industry, we will provide a model for governments and nations which mankind sorely needs.
>
> McGregor, D., *The Human Side of Enterprise*, New York, McGraw-Hill, 1960

In the same vein, Drucker asserts that

> No better text for the *History of Entrepreneurship* could be found than the creation and development of the modern university.
>
> Drucker, P., *Innovation and Entrepreneurship*, p.21[12]

The separation between policy and practice in the public sector poses a particular challenge. It is generally accepted that policy decisions are in the hands of the elected representatives. The duty of the 'civil servant' is to implement the will of the people as outlined by politicians.

> 'They were going to give me three more red boxes for tonight, by the way. When I jibbed at this a bit, Sir Humphrey explained that there are a lot of decisions to take and announcements to approve. He then tried something on, by saying: "But we could, in fact, minimise the work so that you need only take the major policy decisions."
>
> 'I saw through that ploy at once. *I* insisted that *I* would take *all* the decisions and read *all* the relevant documents.
>
> 'They've given me five boxes for tonight.'
>
> Lynn, J. and Jay, A., *The Complete 'Yes Minister'*, London, BBC, 1985, p.18

In reality, the gap between policy and implementation is neither clear enough or wide enough to permit this distinction. There is, however, a tendency to concentrate on doing things the right way instead of the right things. This reflects the tradition of public stewardship which emphasized established procedures for dealing with issues and primacy of public scrutiny. A combination of technological and social change is bringing into question key aspects of this tradition.

National and local government is affected by a range of new technologies. They have enormous potential for improved efficiency and better services. The introduction of computers into housing departments, child-care units and social services means that databases can be up-dated rapidly and response times improved. The flexibility of microcomputers places better information into the hands of many more professionals.

There are dangers. The adage that computers merely exaggerate faults and highlight failures has been proved many times – 'Anyone can make a mistake, but it takes a computer to really foul things up', sums up this view. More insidious is the gap that new technology can create between the official and client. This sense of powerlessness in the face of technology can extend to the politicians who are responsible for policy. Education can address some of these problems. More immediately, systems are being designed which maximize the inherent potential in new information technologies for greater access and ease of use.

The task of managing change symbolizes wider shifts in the management of public sector activity. Ideas of Marketing, Strategic Planning and Financial Control have been wedded to traditional administrative systems. In many cases, their value was identified initially in new or peripheral aspects of government work. The expansion of leisure services by local authorities encouraged many to use marketing to promote their use. The economic downturn of the late 1970s and early 1980s prompted others to widen their information and employment support services. The earlier lessons were exploited in this new situation. The recent debate on the role of national and local government has led to widespread interest in strategic planning as a means of shaping the direction of services.

Across the public sector, examples proliferate of the scope for integrating the best of modern management and administrative thinking. Ambulance services use advertising campaigns to persuade those who can, to use taxis to get to hospital. This frees the service for emergency use. The police use logistics and routing techniques to win maximum cover of localities. Local education authorities now combine to get the best purchasing deals from suppliers.

The emergence of secondary income activities in several areas of the public sector shows how the combination of management technique and enterprise can produce immediate gains. Secondary income describes all those sources of revenue which can be obtained from commercial activities. Universities have moved into this field over the last decade. Many found that their Halls of Residence were badly underutilized out of term. They discovered a ready market among tourists, conference organizers and other visitors. The combination of extensive facilities and low prices easily compensated for the rudimentary accommodation. In some universities, over 10% of total income derives from this source. This has prompted several to explore the market for upgraded facilities. Recently Stirling and Warwick Universities have followed several US universities in building hotel quality accommodation on their campus.

Hospitals have developed variations on this theme. The vision of a large hospital as a small town has encouraged several to capitalize on the opportunities this creates. A hospital of 2000 patients probably supports a 24-hour population of 20 000 people. This includes staff and visitors beside patients. A cursory examination of the facilities for eating, shopping and personal services vividly illustrates the paucity of provision and the potential for development. Better use of space can produce improved services and substantial increases in revenues.

In each case the challenge to enterprise is the same. New opportunities for the application of skills can be identified. They should not distract from the core activities. Successfully implemented, they make the work of officials more satisfying, reduce pressure on scarce resources and deliver improved client benefits.

Group enterprise

Public and private institutions, such as universities, hospitals and private limited companies, represent only some of the mechanisms used by people to work together to achieve goals. Formal organizations are deliberately set up to achieve certain objectives. There is usually some attempt at organizational design. Some form of rule system defines the tasks to be performed and the status and authority structure. Managers and entrepreneurs need an identifiable portfolio of skills to play their part in the success of the enterprise. In parallel to this formal system, there exist informal or social organizations. These shape the ways in which people behave towards each other. They reflect wider social norms and values. They may coincide with the formal organization or transcend it.

A group of workmates together who regularly support the same soccer team might constitute such an informal group. The relations between the formal and informal group has a profound influence on the workings of each. The relationships between the footballer supporters could be changed if one is promoted to a position of authority over the others. This impact might be increased if the newly promoted manager needed his friends to work overtime instead of going to a game. The social organization helps shape the formal institution. The alleged, anti-enterprise culture in UK education may reflect the traditional source of recruits for UK academics. Few have any industrial experience. Most have developed their attitudes to commerce through interactions with others with a similar lack of experience. Effectiveness often depends on the skills with which both the formal and the informal groups are managed.

Personal enterprise

The evolution of management thinking for most of the period following the Industrial Revolution placed an increasing emphasis on the institution and the organization. The individual's role was to serve their needs. The low point of this type of thinking was the notion of corporate men (or women). Their lives were driven by conformist disciplines and management sciences. Processing power was believed to be far more important than insight when faced with private or public sector decisions. Quantification was emphasized at the expense of qualitative judgements. The personal qualities of leadership, enterprise and self management were neglected.

The dangers of this corporate perspective were vividly illustrated during the early

1980s. Industrial and economic change produced pressures on firms and public institutions that called for novel and creative responses. The contribution of the individual to organizational success was vividly illustrated in those concerns which survived and prospered. John Harvey-Jones of ICI, Gavin Laird in the ETU, John Ashworth at Salford University and Geoffrey Chandler of the Royal Society of Arts are just four examples of individuals who stamped their personality on different institutions. In doing so, they helped them prosper when faced with new challenges. One of the great personal challenges of today lies in realizing individual potential in this way.

Some people appear to realize their potential spontaneously. The 'natural' entrepreneur or leader seems to emerge without any obvious support, even encouragement. But, these are a tiny majority. Most have to work to realize their latent capabilities. The first step in this is a recognition that the potential to achieve exists in all people. Self awareness lies at the core of individual effectiveness.

In group situations, self awareness needs to act along two dimensions: the effects on 'self' and on others. The compulsive worker might achieve personal fulfilment which encourages others to try harder. He or she might equally suffer from stress, be ineffective and alienate colleagues. The process of self assessment depends on regular attempts to appreciate personal strengths and weaknesses. In group situations this turns on the successful contribution to group goals. Reddin[13] outlined this when he presented his 3D Theory on Managerial Effectiveness. He noted difference between the Task and the Relationship sides to group activity. The Task emphasizes the output which the organization strives to achieve. In a manufacturing concern, it is the product. In a public agency it might be welfare purpose. The Relationship highlights the way the individual works through and with others.

The interaction of the Task and Relationship dimensions is shown in Figure 2.4. The 'related' style emphasizes relationships at the expense of task. The 'dedicated' style, in contrast, gives overwhelming priority to the task. The 'integrated' approach gives equal priority to both. The 'separated' style underplays each. Reddin's approach stresses the scope to be effective within each basic style. A bureaucrat can perform an important role in an organization without a strong task or relationship orientation. A compromiser might invest so much effort in balancing high task and high relationship

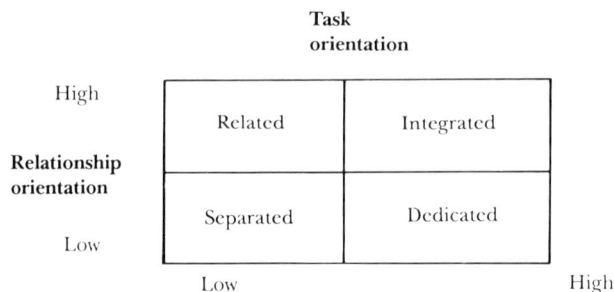

Figure 2.4   Styles of behaviour

orientations that the outcome is failure. The skill to build style flex, i.e. adjusting approach to context, can be crucial to success.

Personal effectiveness in doing tasks is an integral aspect of building credibility among colleagues. The management of self as a resource is often based on simple rules of time and resource management. The basic rules of time management are as easy to describe as they are to neglect. Some of these are:

- Take time to identify the tasks to be done
- Draw up lists
- Plan tasks realistically
- Break work up into manageable chunks
- Allocate and plan time to be spent
- Split tasks into urgent and important (they are not the same)
- Minimize interruptions
- Do hard jobs *first*
- Allocate work you cannot do to others
- If you cannot do it . . . say so
- Establish and keep to completion dates

The word 'No' is perhaps the single most potent aid to personal effectiveness. It is remarkable how seldom it is used as a practical tool.

Time released by more effective time management provides an opportunity to achieve greater control over tasks, work and relationships. The most common cause of stress, frustration and job dissatisfaction is lack of control and a poor sense of direction. The work drives the individual, not the other way round. The common symptoms – lack of direction, fragmentation of effort, poor preparation and low quality output – can only be addressed individually by better planning and time management. In group situations, planning needs to be linked with communication and delegation.

Most tasks will not be executed by their originator. They depend on others for implementation. Their effectiveness turns on how well the work is understood. Generally, this requires some understanding of the desired outcomes as well as the job description. Peters and Waterman[8] highlight the role of 'tight–loose' management. This means that those responsible for implementation are fully briefed on goals and strategies. These objectives are 'tightly' defined. The 'looseness' means giving a great deal of discretion on how the work is performed to those responsible for action; managers and workers. This substitutes pre-planning for crisis management. The traditional UK alternative; 'mushroom management' – *keep everyone in the dark and cover them with manure* – is avoided.

Conclusion

The nature of work has changed rapidly over the last century. The pace of change seems to be increasing. This can seem like a threat to the individual, their colleagues and the community. This threat can be translated into an opportunity for those groups and individuals who are willing to *innovate a way through*, *exploit strengths* and learn to adapt and manage their opportunities. Many established and institutional supports to control and executive are eroding. They are replaced by an increased diversity of opportunities. Quality of labour and effort is replacing quantity as the determinant of success. Colleagues, subordinates and superiors will accept more open, developmental and enterprising work. 'Enpowerment', that is, transferring authority to act to those who need to act is increasingly seen as the key to better results and more satisfied workers. These are the building blocks of the successful organization of the future in the public and private sector, large or small. All place a special emphasis on individual achievement built on improved competence developed through education and training.

Case study

Knoxbridge: A suitable case for treatment?

Introduction

The closure by British Rail of the Knoxbridge Engineering Works brought the problems of this once prosperous town in the Central Belt of Scotland to national attention. The loss of 500 jobs was a severe blow to a community which had seen its major industries and leading firms steadily decline for a number of years but with increasing speed during the recent recession.

Knoxbridge has an industrial history dating back as far as that of Scotland itself. Although links with the railways have always been strong, the industrial base was much wider. Coal and fireclay were mined for much of the last century. The last pit closed as recently as 1962. Although there was a steady rundown in the mining industry, jobs emerged in new industries such as papermaking, refactory brick making, iron castings, general engineering and more recently plastics processing and some chemicals. As recently as the late 1960s Knoxbridge was sufficiently prosperous to offer most of the youngsters leaving its schools a good chance of an apprenticeship or a job.

Besides its manufacturing base, Knoxbridge has been an important commercial centre for the nearby rural community. The shopping centre is large and contains a number of retail outlets, such as Marks & Spencer and House of Fraser. However, business has been lost to nearby Silvertown. The new indoor shopping centre in that town has drawn trade from Knoxbridge.

Although Knoxbridge is within 30 miles of both Edinburgh and Glasgow, access to the motorway network could be improved. Rail links are good but the closure of the engineering works has raised some questions about this.

Recent decline

There are now about 46 000 people living in the Knoxbridge area. The conurbation is bounded by the motorway to the west; with the exception of some more recent housing development, the town is skirted by good 'A' roads to the east and south. The newer developments mentioned were primarily developed to accommodate over-spill from Glasgow. Almost 90% of these houses are local authority owned. An industrial and commercial estate was developed near this. Unfortunately, this has been especially hard hit by the recession. Unemployment in this area is very high.

The rest of the township is less well defined and concentrated. Home ownership is low, with 77% of all houses Council owned. There are a number of relatively isolated communities in outlying areas such as the old mining community of Kintry. Here there are major social problems, especially with the ageing population.

These particular problems have to be seen in the context of the area's progressive decline. Unemployment has grown rapidly. At the same time there is low demand for existing skills. The College of Technology has recently opened an Information Technology Centre. The College of Commerce has a well established programme of work. There has been a dramatic increase in youth unemployment. These have to be seen in the national context of long-term decline in industrial output and rising unemployment of surviving firms and a number of major closures such as that experienced in Knoxbridge recently.

Figures from the Knoxbridge Employment Office show that it is proportionately one of the worst affected areas in Scotland. It is now estimated that the workforce has contracted to just over 7500 in 1982 from just under 14 000 in 1971.

The general picture is dismal with:

• a number of recent closures
• negligible growth in existing firms
• low rate of new company formation
• poor prospects of inward investment.

Between 1974 and 1980 there was a 35% decline in total employment in the area. At least 34 companies have closed and job losses of at least 1400 people have occurred between the beginning of 1978 and March 1983: 25 of these were in manufacturing and construction, accounting for over 1000 of the jobs lost.

Overall employment changes

Knoxbridge Employment Office statistics show the following employment changes:

Sector	1983	%	1988	%	Change
Primary	386	2.7	222	2.0	−164
Manufacturing	7 226	51.5	5 424	54.0	−1802
Construction	1 484	10.6	1 404	14.0	−80
Services	4 946	35.2	3 084	30.0	−1842
Total	14 042	100.0	10 134	100.0	−3908

Although the last few years have seen some new developments, especially a new hypermarket and a major DIY superstore, these have done little to arrest the overall decline.

Community action

The announcement of the closure of the Knoxbridge Railway Engineering Works prompted a number of people from different parts of the community to come together to explore ways of tackling their problems. The Regional and District Councils, along with the Chamber of Commerce and a number of employers, met with the Scottish Development Agency. The latter strongly advised them to *set up* an Enterprise Trust. This has now been done with the Region, the District providing pump priming financial support and ABL Distilleries providing a secondee as director.

The challenge: *Where do you go from here and how do you get there?*

Develop an action plan for the town. This should highlight the main challenges facing the community. Ways to tackle the social and economic problems should be outlined. A clear indication of priorities and the mechanisms for gaining and allocating resources is necessary.

References

1. Baumol, W. J. (1987) Entrepreneurship in Economic Theory, *American Economic Review* (Papers and Proceedings), 58, pp. 64–71.
2. Bolton, J. Chr. (1971) *Small Firms*, Cmnd. 4811 London: HMSO.
3. Birch, B. (1979) *The Job Generation Process*, Cambridge Mass., MIT.
4. Loasby, B. (1988) *Economic Theories of Entrepreneurship*, Stirling, Scottish Enterprise Foundation.
5. Schumpeter, J. (1939) *Business Cycles: A theoretical, historical and statistical analysis of the capitalist process*, New York, McGraw-Hill.
6. Casson, M. (1982) *The Entrepreneur: An economic theory*, Oxford, Martin Robinson.
7. Graicunas, V. A. (1933) Relationship in Organization, *Bulletin of the International Management Institute*, vol. 7. p. 39.
8. Peters, T. J. and Waterman, R. H. (1982) *In Search of Excellence*, New York, Harper and Row.
9. Chandler, A. (1962) *Strategy and Structure: chapters in history of the industrial enterprise*, Cambridge, MIT.
10. Cannon, T. (1990) *Basic Marketing*, London, Cassell.

11. US Government Office (1983) *State of Small Business: A report of the President*, US Government Printing Office.
12. Drucker, P. (1985) *Innovation and Entrepreneurship*, London, Heinemann.
13. Reddin, W. J. (1970) *Managerial Effectiveness*, New York, McGraw-Hill.

Chapter 3
The enterprise support system

A common observation in the mid-1980s was that 'the fastest growing business in the UK was the enterprise support system'. Government, the private sector, voluntary organizations and public agencies vied to introduce distinctive offerings for new and developing small- and medium-sized enterprises. In part, this reflected the weakness of the infrastructure prior to this period. In contrast to much of Europe, the Chambers of Commerce in the UK were generally weak and poorly funded. Few alternatives had developed to fill the gap in local private sector or voluntary provision.

The role of support systems

Support systems perform several roles. They might make it easier for an idea to be adopted. The Enterprise and Higher Education Initiative of the Training Agency of the UK[1] sets out to ensure that:

- every person seeking a higher education qualification should be able to develop competencies and aptitudes relevant to enterprise
- these competencies and aptitudes should be acquired at least in part through project-based work, designed to be undertaken in a real economic setting and they should be jointly assessed by employers and the higher education institutions

More specifically this means:

- securing curriculum development and change so as to enhance personal effectiveness and achievement at work
- extending and strengthening partnerships with both private and public sector employers, including small- and medium-sized enterprises
- offering students the opportunity to develop and apply skills including those of communication, team work, leadership, decision making, problem solving, task management and risk taking
- developing students' initiative
- developing economic and business awareness.

This fits neatly with thinking about the ways in which innovations are introduced.

People are initially made *aware* of the opportunity. The Enterprise and Higher Education Initiative achieves this through the 'cascade' method. A small number of institutions were involved in the first instance. Their efforts were concentrated on staff. These staff encouraged others and transferred ideas to large numbers of students. The institutions themselves became role models for others to copy. The pioneers were used to provide resources which can be used to raise awareness of ideas and programmes. Most development programmes seek to move beyond *awareness* to *interest, desire* and *action.*

Interest exists at a much higher level of consciousness. The idea, scheme or project has provoked a mental response. The literature on the Enterprise and Higher Education Initiative is read rather than consigned to the waste bin. This provides an opportunity to stimulate a desire to know more. Typically, this is associated with the attempt to generate positive attitudes or desire. Ultimately this may lead to action.

Support systems come about to ease access to each stage, assist during these phases and help the transition between levels. Exposure and availability are often the most powerful aids to access.

The Enterprise Agencies in the UK made a powerful contribution to the enterprise movement through their high profile and large number of access points. The existence of an Enterprise Agency office on a High Street or in an industrial park made large numbers of potential entrepreneurs aware of the opportunity for self realization through self-employment. The Oxfam shop provides a similar function for this charity.

During each phase, information and reassurance have a special value. Each plays a part in providing opportunities to learn more and reducing the risk of regression. The National Trust has found that regular contact with members is essential if they are to retain their support.

The shift from one stage to another is perhaps the most difficult. Far more people: desire their own business, wish to do an MBA, or intend to give blood or aim to assist a Charity than ever act. Transition is best achieved through some mixture of push and pull. Unemployment *pushed* many into self-employment during the 1880s, 1930s and 1980s. Generous scholarships can *pull* individuals into choosing to follow an MBA programme. Pressure from family and friends can *push* a young person to give blood but the trigger to act might be a factory visit by the Blood Transfusion Unit. The media cover for Comic Relief might persuade an individual to look for ways to help but the final push might be a company sponsorship. In each of these situations the role of the support agency is to reduce the costs of entry while increasing the benefits of participation.

Sink or swim

The creation of an extensive system of support for enterprise is not easy. Its existence challenges some of the more simplistic notions of enterprise. This view is that people should be left to sink or swim. The history of the development of enterprise on either an individual or organizational base confounds this perspective. Great concerns during their most 'entrepreneurial' periods required extensive systems of support. Ford, General Motors and Mitsui epitomise those companies which survived their early years because of the backing they received from those outside the business. It might be individual financial backers as in Ford. Du Pont gave General Motors support at a crucial phase in its early development. The Japanese government played a similar role for Mitsui.

Advanced industrial societies cannot rely on chance for the survival of personal or corporate enterprise. Their continued prosperity calls for a system of support which enables the most promising to develop while making the costs of failure as small as possible. The system of support which exists in the UK supplies most of the forms of backing seen elsewhere. There are differences in institutions and the way they behave. Some commentators[2] have suggested that the ways in which the financial institutions operate in the UK discourages small firm growth. The creation of the Unlisted Securities Market was a direct response to the criticisms that small firms found the cost of a full quotation too high. It drew heavily on US experience of similar systems. Most systems of support are built around a mixture of private, public and voluntary aid.

Private support

A mature industrial society depends on comprehensive systems of support for commercial activity. The mature state of the UK economy means that this system is comprehensive and well established. In the newly liberalized economies of Eastern Europe, support is rudimentary or non-existent. The lack of a commercial banking system make start-up capital hard to obtain. The 'privatization' of state enterprises cannot be achieved without a stock market.

Most aspects of enterprise are influenced by the private sector support systems which surround them. There are some features which reflect long established, global patterns. Clearing banks and accounting firms exist in virtually all mature, capitalist economies. Others have grown up to meet distinct, local needs.

The Enterprise Boards were developed in Britain during the early 1980s to provide local venture capital from public funds. The pattern of support is not fixed. Change is the norm. Venture finance companies have grown rapidly during the latter part of the last decade. The scope of public sector finance has been restricted. The nature of provision has changed. The thrust of factory construction has moved from large-scale out-of-town development to small-scale, high-amenity projects. Keeping abreast of these shifts is a continuing task for the manager of any enterprise.

Finance

Most pursuits conducted in a modern economy require access to finance. The entrepreneur creating a new firm is no different to the student theatre group planning a new performance. Each requires money to buy or hire premises, purchase equipment, employ people, promote the activity, cover running costs and provide a base on which to build future activity. The primary task of the financial institutions is to meet these needs by deploying the funds made available to them by savers and investors.

Banks

The public face of the banks is most evident through the work of the clearing banks: Lloyds, NatWest, Barclays, Midland, Co-op, TSB, Bank of Scotland, Clydesdale, Royal Bank of Scotland, Allied Irish, Bank of Ireland and Ulster Bank. Each offers a broadly similar portfolio of services.

Banks provide access to two vital services – money and advisory support. Most of the finance provided through the clearing banks takes the form of loans. Sometimes equity is supplied. Generally the banks prefer to arrange this through specialist arms, e.g. Midland Venture or through related subsidiaries. British Linen Bank is the merchant banking arm of the Bank of Scotland. Some years ago the clearing banks came together to create 3I's (*I*nvestors *I*n *I*ndustry). The deregulation of the financial services sector over the last decade has led to the proliferation of new financial services and businesses to provide them. The venture financiers are perhaps the most well known.

The type of finance provided by any of these companies depends on the time horizon, the risk, the likely return and the nature of ownership. Overdrafts can provide short-term finance for projects, firms or individuals. The school parents' association might run up an overdraft to buy stock for the autumn bazaar. Overdrafts are generally seen as the easiest form of loan to arrange and the most flexible. Banks are often willing to take anticipated earnings into account when fixing up overdrafts. The advantages of flexibility and ease works both ways. The bank can withdraw it as quickly as it arranged it.

Long-term loans backed by some form of security provide an alternative. These are especially useful when a fixed repayment schedule can be arranged or a specific payment date exists. The introduction of the Loan Guarantee Scheme has encouraged some firms to exploit new opportunities which require significant funding. The Department of Employment guarantees 70% of loans up to £75 000 and lasting for two to seven years. The cost can be high. It is typically 2.5% higher than the rate set by the bank. This contrasts with the similar US scheme which subsidizes the loan. Traditionally, private individuals supplied significant amounts of loan or investment income.

> He told me that I was still dangerously short of money. I accepted his advice and began to looks around for some more. My family had an acquaintance with a pleasant young man called Peter Burton ... He came in for £1,000 and a job. I also met a man named Roy Marsh ... He put in a couple of hundred pounds and brought in a friend of his, Harry Roberts as another investor. It was still not enough so I went back to Tom Gardner

... 'Look, Tom,' I said brazenly, 'why don't you take a share as well?' ... He made up the balance of necessary capital and I was left with sixty per cent of the business.

Lord Forte, Forte, p. 35

The creation of the Business Expansion Scheme (BES) is an attempt by the Government to encourage larger numbers to provide this type of backing. The conditions for participation are strict. These reflect the generosity of the tax relief allowed for participants. The tax benefits mean that the real price of a share of equity sold this way can be higher than it would be without such benefit.

The growth of venture finance has led to a number of different forms of provision. Most require a significant share of equity before they will supply funds. Often they have a strong local or sectoral bias. Prior research, a clear understanding of needs and a well-designed plan are crucial to success in this area. Venture capitalists expect to realize their investments when the firm expands. Growth may lead to some form of public offer of shares or equity. The creation of the Unlisted Securities Market (USM) was an attempt to reduce the cost of 'going public' to smaller companies. Almost 400 enterprises have now followed this route to bringing in outside investors and unlocking the company's capital base. Some of these firms have since proceeded to get a full Stock Exchange listing.

In the long term, the advice and support services of the banks and other financiers may be more valuable than the money provided. A good bank manager or venture capitalist will make a mark on all aspects of the start-up, development and growth of the enterprise. The basic commodity – money – can be purchased anywhere. The added value comes from the support services. This puts a premium on the ability of the enterprising individual to search out and select a total service. The creation by Midland, Lloyds and other banks of specialist sections, e.g. Small Firm Advisers, reflects their recognition of these needs.

Accountants, solicitors and other professional advisers

The same discipline is involved with the choice of all advisers. The choice of supplier calls for an understanding of needs and alternatives, a willingness to pay and a determination to work at getting the best service. The audit of needs should be split into the 'need to have' and the 'nice to have'. Needs might include 'ease of access' for the community group working to help local disabled. There may be a need for extensive support with book-keeping for the community co-operative. A growing company might need detailed and sophisticated advice on sources of financial help. Accountants exist who can perform each of these and an array of other functions.

The monetary cost will invariably be a function of time spent and labour costs. A large firm of accountants will carry a wide portfolio of specialist services. These might include consultants, project managers and trainers. These can be invaluable to certain clients but merely an expensive overhead to others. The charges are likely to be too high unless these services are needed or some special arrangement is made. It is common for the larger firms to accept significant social responsibilities. Staff might be seconded to a needy organization or charges waived. Individuals or smaller firms will not carry these overheads. This may mean that there are gaps in their knowledge or networks. A banker might be more inclined to support a project if a major accountancy firm is associated.

The same situation faces those choosing solicitors, consultants and other advisers and outside experts. Legal advice is useful on the form of the enterprise. This should be optimized for financial, contractual and stewardship purposes. The private enterprise can be a sole trader, partnership or limited company. Other non-commercial forms can include charities or voluntary association. All forms of association have legal implications. It is advisable to ensure that the right structure is established early to minimize problems. This is particularly relevant if contractual relationships are undertaken. These can include contracts to sell, buy, hire or lease products or services from outsiders. Similar obligations exist where employees or agents are involved. The law is always with us, even if we try to ignore it. This is especially true of the responsibilities of directors. They are answerable to their shareholders and the law for their stewardship of the assets under their control.

Marketing

The long-term viability of any organization depends on the effectiveness with which assets are managed to produce benefits to ownership groups while meeting the needs of customers. Marketing has evolved into those activities which manage the relationship between the concern and its external stakeholders. The latter includes current and potential buyers and users, besides shareholders, funding agencies and all those with a stake in the enterprise. An organization will survive for as long as it can retain their support, at a price which maintains its prosperity, if necessary at the expense of other potential beneficiaries.

Conventionally, marketing is linked with the commercial activities of larger companies. They learnt early, the value of concentrating attention on customer needs rather than the products and services produced. A company preoccupied with its existing offering would find itself soon becoming obsolete. Its position in the market would be taken by more responsive rivals. Individuals such as Charles Revson of Revlon summarized this view when he commented, 'in the factory we make cosmetics, in the market we sell dreams'. The essential features of this approach are:

● emphasis on the totality of the offering
● recognition of the diversity of needs.

The total offering will include the basic product or service, the price charged, its image, the way it is presented, quality and availability. This marketing mix of Product, Price, Promotion and Place defines the true offering in the customer's eyes. Successful integration of these elements means that the user/buyer leaves the transaction feeling he or she has profited from the exchange and wishes to repeat it.

The value of marketing has been recognized by smaller enterprises, public and voluntary agencies. Often, the more successful had an intuitive understanding of marketing. Anita Roddick challenged a host of conventions but showed that she was in touch with new market needs. The defenders of the Glasgow Veterinary School against closure understood and tapped powerful, national sentiments. The success of Ironbridge Industrial Museum confounded sceptics and indicated how a museum could be developed in novel and popular ways. Long-term effectiveness in markets requires a combination of intuition – to create the new, unitary offering – and discipline – to keep up to date and manage change.

The launch of the Enterprise Initiative by the UK's Department of Trade and Industry vividly illustrated this increased marketing awareness. The initiative was backed by large-scale promotional expenditure. Its advertising acknowledged that the owners of small- and medium-sized firms often saw government help as distracting and lacking in relevance. At the same time, the provision of marketing help was placed at the centre of the schemes offered through the programme. Most of the schemes were linked to a greater or lesser extent with the Marketing Initiative. This was made easier by the active involvement of intermediary organizations such as the Institute of Marketing.

Marketing research

Research involves two distinct but interrelated processes. First, there is the process of gathering information. Second, there is the conversion of these findings into meaningful results. Science plays an essential role in the process of gathering and interpreting marketing research.

> Marketing research is the systematic and objective search for and analysis of information relevant to the identification and solution of any problem in the field of marketing
> Green, P. E. and Tull, D. S., *Research for Marketing Decisions*,
> Prentice Hall, N.J., 1986

Initially, this means understanding the nature of the questions or issues being addressed and can take several forms. The most basic is identification of the hypothesis being tested. The marketing researcher faces the same challenge as the physicist. The task is to determine whether the issue is worth researching and can be researched. Some topics are too trivial to justify systematic investigation. Other measuring tools may exist which can be used. It is usually easy to filter out these topics. Establishing researchability is harder. A topic might be fascinating but far beyond the capabilities of the researcher or the available resources. Doctoral students are prone to researching 'the effectiveness of advertising' or other such perennial and hard to complete topics.

The research brief has the dual role of defining the area to be examined and guiding analysis. It includes the following elements:

- A brief summary of the problem(s): This is an overview from the perspective of those initiating the project.
- The key aspects of current knowledge: There is no point in asking researchers

to find information already held. It might be necessary to check or update material but mere repetition has little value.

- The objectives of the study: These should be spelled out as fully as possible. Ideally, they are prioritized and split between the need to know and the nice to know.
- Constraints on the project: There may be absolute limits, e.g. no discussion with certain groups or relative restrictions such as budget.
- Decisions sought: It is useful to indicate the decisions which may be made on the basis of the findings, e.g. enter or exit a market.
- Decision criteria: Often there are specific criteria against which judgements will be made. A firm might not launch a new product if it takes significant sales from its existing products.
- Timing: Many projects are time dependent. Research into an election loses its value if it reports after the vote has been taken.

In management and administration attention is usually focused on the six basic type of decisions:

- What are the problems?
- What immediate solutions are available?
- What can be done in the long term?
- How can we implement the solution(s)?
- Does monitoring implementation lead to revisions?
- Can we establish overall policy for reference?

The sources of information can be classified broadly as primary, secondary, internal and external. Figure 3.1 shows their relationship.

	Internal	External
Secondary	In-house gathered for other purpose	Official statistics and other public or commercial data
Primary	In-house but gathered for this purpose	Market research or other original work

Figure 3.1   The information matrix

Secondary data exist in many forms. A company wanting to know why returns are increasing and market share declining might have letters from customers and suppliers. A university or college department examining student demand for its courses will have applications data. These internal sources might be supplemented with other published data. The firm might subscribe to A. C. Neilsen's retail audit or turn to trade statistics. The university or college department will have access to UCCA data on demand or research done by some other university.

Once these sources are fully exploited there may still be questions unanswered. It is possible to turn to people within the organization. Sales and technical staff can shed light on issues customers are raising with them. Faculty and students can be asked for their views on aspects of the subject's demand. Exhausting this process can leave some issues in doubt. It might even raise other more complex matters. External investigation targeted on these matters might be the only means of gaining insight into these issues. A range of techniques are available to tackle these matters. They include experiments, observation, questionnaire-based and qualitative approaches such as in-depth individual or group discussions.

Communication and promotion

Research is hard to separate from communication. The effective implementation of research findings requires that they are disseminated and understood. This can be a personal process. Newton and Darwin were pressed by their friends to publish their findings so that others could gain access and due credit won for their pioneering efforts. Satisfactory communication builds on a willingness to investigate the needs, expectations and capabilities of those to whom the message is directed. The same principles operate for personal and impersonal media.

The key lies in recognizing that communication starts with the receiver of the message not the transmitter. Lecturers in the classroom probably understand the topic. But, they are fooling themselves if they believe they have communicated a lesson by saying it or projecting it. This is the same problem faced by an advertiser. In Figure 3.2 the communication process is described visually.

Communication starts with the decisions on the message to be sent and the means employed. A clear understanding of the topic and the audience are the foundations on which competent interchange is built. The message should lie within the competence of the person transmitting to deliver and the audience(s) to receive.

Preparing a message for communication means going beyond the substance of the topic. It includes an analysis of the ways in which it will be delivered. Experts can fail to convey their knowledge because the presentation of the issues is badly thought through. The costs of media time have forced advertisers to refine this process. Their success underlines the importance of determining the *specific purpose* or *theme statement* which will hold the presentation together. In advertising this might mean encapsulating the image of the product in 30 seconds. In a press release it might require summing up a major project in 500 words. A research presentation to a Board of Directors can call for a major, long-term investment with less than an hour to put forward a case.

The medium used can have different effects. Marshall McLuhan[3] describes radio as a hot medium and TV as cold. He views radio as hot because listeners can become involved, use their imaginations and play a more active role than in TV. Personal presentation and the telephone allow immediate feedback while TV and cinema cannot achieve this. Newspapers, magazines, periodicals and books have a degree of perma-

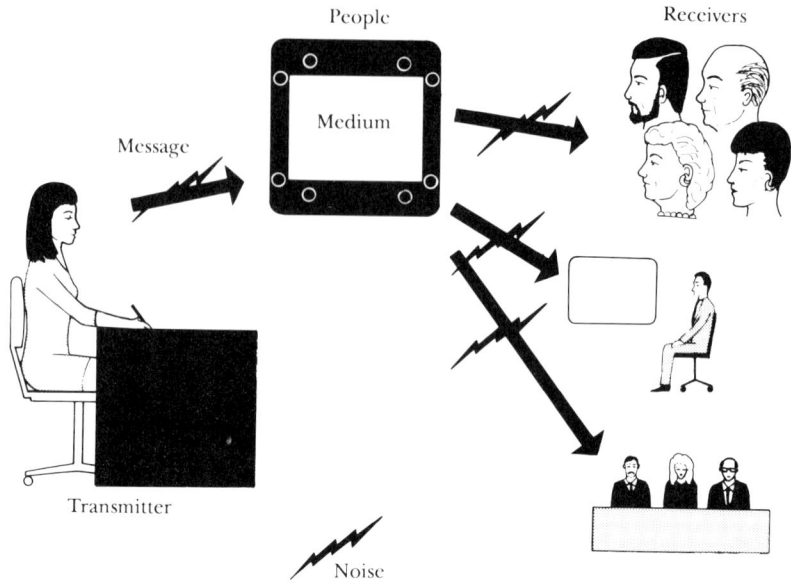

People   Receivers

Medium

Message

Transmitter

Noise

Figure 3.2   *Communication process*

nence while lacking the movement and sound of TV and cinema. The nature of
the message and the ways it is interpreted are directly affected by the medium. A
lecture given as part of a three-year degree course can build on earlier lessons. It
should lead into new areas and contribute to an extensive learning process. An after-
dinner speech will need to encapsulate stimulating ideas in a brief and lively, stand-
alone event. Occasionally, blurring the issues will produce creative results.

> Alexander Graham Bell, while trying to remove defects from the telegraph, discovered
> the telephone.
>
> Marshall McLuhan, *Culture Is Our Business*, 1972, p.28

More often, confusing issues merely confuses.

Different groups will require topics delivered in ways which meet their needs.
Advertisers segment their audiences to ensure that the media and the message fits.
Media are chosen for their access to certain populations. Cinema is especially good
at reaching those in the 14–26-year-old age range. The messages appeal to their tastes
and interests. The more homogeneous the audience the easier it is to be confident
that the issue will be understood. The greater the heterogeneity, the harder it is
to ensure successful communication. The increased affluence of markets in the developed world has led to more fragmentation of markets. The resources exist for groups
to express their individuality in the products and services purchased. This marketing
imperative is having a direct effect on the technical and production systems of society.

Technical and production

The interaction between technology, production and markets has shaped the ways in which industrial society develops. Phyllis Dean[4] underlines the control that technology gives mankind over production and distribution. She sees this mastery of technology as the single most important factor which differentiates pre- and post-industrial society. Machines meant that products could be produced to relatively consistent standards in large quantities. Other machines allowed suppliers to deliver these quickly, reliably and cheaply. This process change transformed communities. The population of Birmingham grew from 6000 people in 1660 to 300000 in 1860 and almost 1000000 by 1960. The character of the populace altered.

> Birmingham had developed two distinctive features during its growth from medieval village to bustling industrial Midlands town. The first was its obsession with manufacturing as a way of life and the second was the independent spirit of so many of its inhabitants, which turned them from working as journeymen for masters to setting up as independent 'little masters' producing goods of all kinds in their own homes.
>
> Nockolds H., *Lucas*, David & Charles, 1976, p. 1718

The UK's initial success in harnessing technology to support manufacturing and distribution created the Industrial Revolution while establishing the basis for current prosperity. The success of other nations: West Germany, the USA, Japan, France and Italy – has secured their affluence and eliminated the UK's early advantage. Figure 3.3 illustrates the extent of the UK's decline.

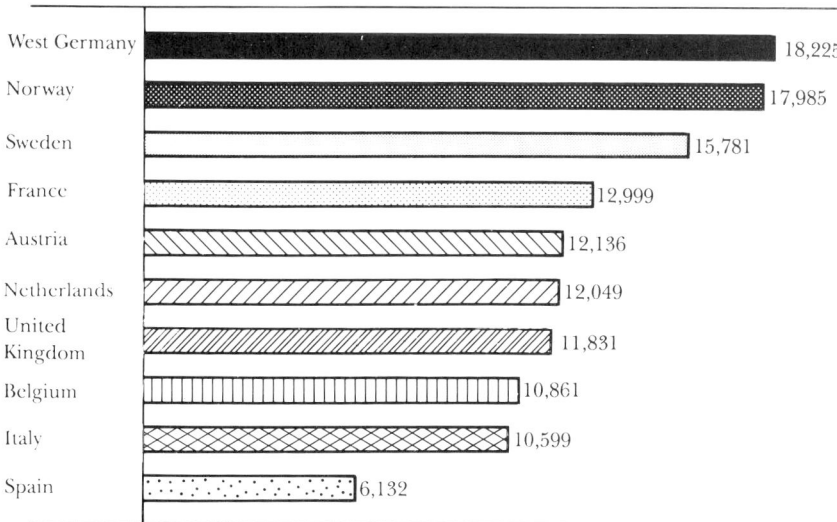

Nation	GNP per capita
West Germany	18,225
Norway	17,985
Sweden	15,781
France	12,999
Austria	12,136
Netherlands	12,049
United Kingdom	11,831
Belgium	10,861
Italy	10,599
Spain	6,132

Figure 3.3 GNP per capita 1989 among European nations (in $US)

The failure to compete effectively has hit the UK.

> One central feature of Britain's economic development is easily found: it is a low rate of growth, compared with similar economies. We have seen that relatively slow growth characterises Britain's performance for at least the past century, and is especially notice-able over the whole of the post Second World War period, a period in which Britain has declined from relative prosperity and economic health to relative poverty and economic debility.
>
> Smith K., *The British Economic Crisis*, Penguin, 1984, p. 98.

More recently, the USA has experienced a similar decline in manufacturing with the same results.

> Our lack of competitiveness has stemmed from our inability to improve productivity and deliver higher-quality products for a lower price than competitors in other high-wage economies.
>
> Magaziner I. C. and Reich R. B., *Minding America's Business*, Random House, New York, 1982, p. 2

Magaziner and Reich[5] describe this decline as the major reversible cause of the USA's economic difficulty. The successful management of technology and product provide the key corporate and national prosperity. For the UK, the key to reversing decline lies in a similar effort to improve productivity through technology and enterprise. This has seen the UK's Gross Domestic per Capita drop from third to twelfth among major economies in the half century since the end of the War.

The requirements for a strong manufacturing base for a firm, mirror those needed in an economy. Research, development, design, supplies, logistics systems, standards and operations are engineered to produce a total manufacturing or production system. The precise character and pattern of integration depend on the nature of the technology involved. The dominant forms are:[6]

- *Jobbing*: Each item is produced to a specific customer's needs. A craftsman might make a table and chairs for a specific buyer; a boatyard will produce to particular specifications.
- *Batch*: A finite quantity is made on a non-continuous basis. A pottery will manufac-ture a series of commemorative plates to celebrate an event.
- *Mass*: The repetitive manufacture of an array of relatively standardized items. The 'run' might continue for years as with a successful new car model. It might be changed occasionally as when new models in a range are introduced.
- *Process*: The flow of output is continuous and homogeneous. Oil, chemicals and certain types of food items, e.g. flour, illustrate this type of production.

Research

Research underpins all types of manufacturing. The output and the form of production are shaped by the investigation which creates the item and determines the optimum form of organization. The research agenda in an enterprise is driven by a combination of internal development and external search. The growth of research investment by organizations reflects the high cost of this activity and the importance of innovation for competitive advantage.

These costs are encouraging collaborative development of work. Normally, this takes two forms – vertical and horizontal. Vertical collaboration extends to suppliers and customers. Horizontal combinations concentrate on links with others at broadly the same point in the development chain. Small firms are especially dependent on links with suppliers to provide access to new materials and technologies. A firm like Clearex Plastics in the north-east of England uses the polymer science of ICI to develop special forms of self-skinned plastic foam for British Rail. Hakansson[7] found marked disparities between the strategies for collaboration adopted in different European countries. The best results seemed to occur in those situations in which prospective customers were involved early and extensively in the research process.

Interest in horizontal collaboration has grown rapidly in recent years. Universities, polytechnics and other institutions of higher education are wedding their research to companies seeking access to ideas, science and technology. International programmes such as Alvey, Commett and Esprite in Europe complement local initiatives. These projects have fostered the creation of more institutional mechanisms for partnership. These range from industrial liaison offices to science and technology parks. Elsewhere, companies are linking their expertise. The European Airbus project brought together a number of corporations who determined that collaboration was the only means of creating the resource base to tackle the project. A similar pattern can be seen in the association between national government programmes and the dissemination and application of research. The most famous of these, the NASA dissemination programme, was an attempt to achieve early commercialization of the research output from the NASA space programme.

Development

Company expenditure is associated more usually with development rather than research. Development falls into two categories – adaptation of existing products or services or the preparation of a novel offering for the market. The evolution of the VW Beetle provided one of the classic cases of continual updating and improvement of a product. Volkswagen systematically planned the introduction of new features. A similar process can occur where a university introduces new electives or features on a degree programme. The 'core' is constant but it is adapted over time. This can be a very cost-effective mechanism for extending the life of a product.

There are also dangers. The organization might fail to recognize the point at which a more profound change is needed. The success of the Beetle blinded Volkswagen to the need for a radical change of direction. Business historians have identified the hyperactivity of established firms as a feature of change. It was seen in the military supplies industry in the second half of the nineteenth century. Foundries introduced large numbers of adaptations to their cannon in a doomed attempt to compete with engineering companies with rifled guns. The proliferation of new features can accelerate decline as costs increase and returns decline. The advertising industry witnessed this in the late 1970s. A host of new services – marketing, planning, merchandising, support, etc. – were added to the facilities offered to clients. Overheads grew while the 'core' business was neglected.

The pre-introduction, development period of a new offering is crucial to its long-term success. Faults can be identified, ways of handling difficulties resolved and improvements introduced in private. The famous, market failure of the Edsel occurred, in part, because technical problems were not resolved before it went onto the market.

> Within a few weeks after the Edsel was introduced, its pratfalls were the talk of the land. Edsels were delivered with oil leaks, sticking hoods, trunks that wouldn't open, and push buttons that, far from yielding to a toothpick couldn't be budged with a hammer.
>
> Brooks J., *Business Adventures*, p. 66

The failure of Stelvatite, perhaps the first technically successful plastic-coated steel was linked with the failure to issue handling instructions to customers. Buyers used conventional handling techniques. These damaged the coating irreparably. The bulk of the first product run was returned before explanatory leaflets were issued. These had been prepared prior to the launch of the product. The rush to get the first batch of product onto the market had led to delays in preparing the support literature. The concept of 'poisoned apple marketing' – let someone else take the first bite – has evolved to exploit the opportunities created by these errors.

Design

Design is now recognized as a central element in the technology and manufacturing process. Organizations which build design into rather than adding design onto the product or service gain many benefits. Products are more reliable. Quality standards are easier to maintain. The fit between functions and appearance is natural rather than artificial. The prerequisites for this integration are:

- early involvement of the design group
- extensive participation in the programme
- recognition of the process nature of design.

The creation of the Design Council in 1976 reflected widespread concern about attitudes towards design in industry and among the general public. These were reflected in the objects set for the Council: 'the advancement of British Industry by the improvement of design in the products thereof'. The tasks that were set reflected the concern to 'display ... well designed products', provide 'information', hold or participate in 'exhibitions', encourage 'education' in the area as well as 'increasing knowledge and educating opinion'. Many of the current discussions about the future of design in the UK reflect the progress that has been achieved in all these areas of the last decade. Simultaneously, there have been major changes in the economic and industrial environment as well as the pattern of government support.

The major challenges facing those working in design lie in developing and delivering those offerings which reflect the needs of industry. At one level it means helping firms to manage change especially those innovations associated with new creative or technical processes. Here, the ability to supply a process view of design is crucial. Research by the Design Council suggests that this area is more important than the traditional – design as a transaction – approach. This shift indicates growing maturity and the changing profile of the design professions.

Supplies

The goods and services bought by an enterprise often account for the largest single area of expenditure. The supplies, purchasing or buying function is responsible for all the activities which control this. The main aspects of the work are information gathering, supplier selection, assessment of goods or services inward, evaluation and control of performance. The role varies widely between organizations. In the public sector, it is normal to separate the user from the choice of supplier. Competitive tendering is employed extensively. Private companies are more likely to emphasize the working partnership between the user and the source. This link is especially important in projects which involve adaptation and modification for customer needs.

The work of the buying function varies considerably within organizations. Large, capital items affect the entire establishment. The Chief Executive or Board of Directors will expect to make the final decision on this type of item. In the public sector, the relevant minister or head of the institution will play a similar role. Purchase of items which are used in the manufacturing process may be left in the hands of the production or engineering staff. Sales and marketing will expect to participate in supplier decisions which might affect their work.

The sales link is especially important where there is an element of reciprocity in the transaction. Some customers will only buy if there is a clear understanding that, say, the supplier is placing some of its orders with affiliate companies. Ford might only buy plastic components from companies whose salespeople drive Fords. In the construction industry it is common to see preferred suppliers identified. This means that the contractor must subcontract part of the project to these organizations. The importance of purchasing power is being recognized in economic development. A government department will restrict its orders to companies using a minimum percentage of domestic product. The defence industry is characterized by this type of project.

> Sources at the meeting have confirmed that the M1 Abrams tank dominated discussions, and the company made much of the opportunities for British firms to get in the act by supplying material from gears to electronics. Manufacturers were told that British parts would be shipped to America and then returned for final assembly.
>
> *The Observer*, 10 December, 1989

Despite these developments, the dominant roles of the supplies officer or buyer remain: to gather information and manage suppliers to ensure that the company has access to supplies, at the right time, in the right place, of sufficient quality and at the best price consistent with a strong trading relationship. Price invariably plays a central role in all purchase decisions. It is the simplest, but not necessarily the best, test of a buyer's skills.

The high cost of holding stocks has highlighted the importance of supply schedules and inventory. 'Just in time' stocking brings out the benefits which can be gained if users can schedule goods-inwards close to use. It depends heavily on sound order management and good, quality suppliers. Cost and waste is minimized if it is effectively implemented.

These initiatives reinforce the importance of the supply management function in three ways. First, it confirms the value of attention to detail in processing. Rigorous and clear purchase ordering and documentation underpin this work. This is inseparable from well-defined terms and conditions of trade. Second, the strategic role of supplies is highlighted. Third, the development contribution of supply management is emphasized.

Logistics systems

The primary task of the logistics system is to ensure that the organisation's output is available, in required amounts, at the desired quality, when needed and priced to satisfy the needs of the target population(s). It is made up from several inter-dependent operations. Goods and services 'inward' creates the capability to produce. Labour of the type and in the numbers required has to be mobilized. Capital is required for wages and purchases. Equipment converts raw materials, components, etc. into output. Delivery systems take goods and services to distributors and end users. Fuel and energy make them work. Spares, repair services and other post-purchase back-up ensures long-term client satisfaction.

These components are drawn together in the logistics system. Network planning, flow charts and critical path analysis are among the techniques employed to provide a planning framework in which parts can be drawn together. These techniques help managers, but they only work if they can cope with the different features of the components. Most activities can be broken up into their constituent elements. Some activities cannot be undertaken until another is completed. Certain processes can be proceeded with at the same time as others. The simple chart illustrated in Fig. 3.4 shows how these features are drawn together. The task is to prepare for a new drama production. Activity B is preparation of flats and stage props. It takes 3 days to prepare drawings and send them to a studio for production. Completion will require a further 12 days. Deliver and construction takes 6 days. While this is taking place, activity C, revision of text, casting and rehearsals is taking place. Casting takes 2 days, readings and revisions 4 days and 8 days are needed for rehearsals. Final preparations and the dress rehearsal takes 4 days and 1 day. While these are going on activity A, design, preparation and adaptation of the costumes is completed. The last 4 days between a/2 and a/3 allow the company to complete final dress rehearsals.

The logistics function integrates prior preparation, planning and activity manage-

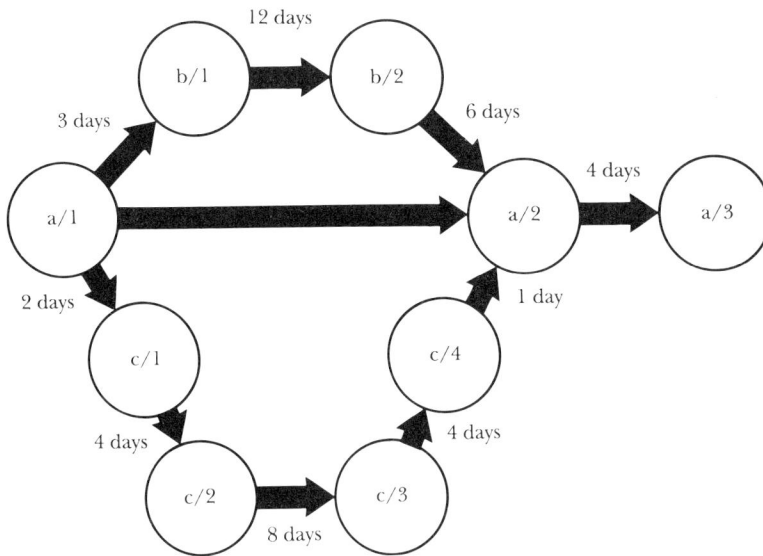

Figure 3.4

ment. PERT (Programme Evaluation and Review Technique) is used extensively with large and complex projects such as the development of a new product or brand. It allows tasks to be identified and resources allocated while giving planners an understanding of the likely time for completion.

Standards

Engineered products should satisfy technical or other standards. The British Standards Institute is the responsible agency in the UK for establishing, regulating and issuing standards. The process of setting and maintaining technical standards is increasingly international. The European Commission has a central role in this especially during the run up to the creation of the Single European Market. This is managed through CEN, the European Committee for Standardization, or one of the specialist bodies, e.g. CENELEC, the European Committee for Electro Technical Standardization. Increasing numbers of service and public organizations are recognizing the value of quality standards as summarised in BS 5750.

Operations

Effective, on-going operations rely on the interaction between the product or service and the production system. Manufacturing or service engineering concentrates on these tasks. Choice of location and layout of the factory, bank, hotel, shop or office depends on the access to labour and materials and the working arrangements. Location decisions may be shaped by history: glassmaking in St Helens, caravan manufacture in Yorkshire and furniture in High Wycombe. This means that there will be workers with the right skills and component and raw material suppliers in the vicinity.

Geographically mobile companies are sought actively by inward investment agencies. It is estimated by the Scottish Development Agency that there are 3000 registered agencies chasing the 200 US corporations who relocate every year. Their choice is determined in part by inducements. In making their location decisions, they will relate these inducements to the labour, knowledge, access and material availability factors which will determine how well the business will operate. Most firms recognize that these operational features will ultimately determine success.

The type of building and site is a mixture of function and environment. Some simple rules have emerged. The most basic is that flows should only be in one direction. Natural features on the product or service ought to be exploited. Refining and flour milling illustrate this especially well. The tall buildings use gravity to shift these bulky and awkward materials. Separation for control and safety can be crucial. In the simplest guise, segregation minimizes spoilage and damage. Dirty factories almost invariably mean low quality. Dividing one process or activity from another can increase security especially when dangerous materials are involved.

Retail and office facilities operate under different constraints. The pressure for access and communication dominates. Access to and for clients calls for display and ease of entry. Internal communication is easier if staff can form natural or job-based groups. New technologies have made it easier to open up offices and retail environments. Computer systems enable organizations to move away from separated, hierarchical structures to organic, network-based working groups. Changes in the population structure, allied to higher educational standards, make the quality of labour in industry, especially the service sector, a vital, competitive tool.

People

Success in all types of organizations is built through people. Workers depend on each other for definitions of tasks, delivery of support and achievement of objectives. The recruitment, selection, appointment, development, security, motivation and control policies of the group and the organization affect everyone in the venture. Each has implications for the ability of the enterprise to create the type of working environment which achieves commercial goals while sustaining its internal cohesion.

Recruitment policies are shaped by a mixture of external regulation and internal need. Legislation in recent years has acted to minimize the worst abuses of prejudice and injustice. Most organizations seek to implement equal opportunity strategies of the type recommended by the Equal Opportunities Commission and the Commission for Racial Equality. Both organizations collaborate with employers to support them in their efforts to achieve fair employment policies. In the UK, however, there is resistance to the type of Affirmative Action or Positive Discrimination Programmes used in North America to tackle long established patterns of individual or group disadvantage.

Some groups, notably ethnic and religious minorities and the disabled, suffer from the inability of certain recruiters to recognize their potential. These barriers are made worse in some areas by additional disadvantages such as occur in inner city areas. Projects such as the City Compacts are developed by consortia of firms and education authorities to tackle these problems. In a 'Compact', a group of employers will establish a collaborative arrangement with schools in an area. Employers will guarantee jobs to all those school leavers who achieve specified, attainment targets. The success of the first of these, run through the Inner London Education Authority and the London Enterprise Agency has encouraged other cities to adapt this approach to their needs. The purpose of these schemes is to create opportunities for young people while meeting the needs of firms.

The formal process of recruitment is built around an understanding of the skill needs of the firm, appreciation of specifics of the job plus a mixture of advertising and the use of employment services and agencies. The job description is usually built around:

- the identification of the job, including the title
- description of the job, especially the main tasks
- definition of the job content
- any special features.

It incorporates a mixture of the tasks to be performed and features which allow for change. This description supplies a reference point for training and development. It is the basis for feedback on performance and evaluation.

There is no fixed procedure for selection and appointment. It varies between organizations and people. Recently, there has been some convergence between the bureaucratic, qualification-based routines of the civil service and the technical and individualistic methods of industry. Corporations have established more formal approaches while the public sector is more likely to go into the open market for candidates. This narrowing of the gap is reflected in greater similarities in the terms and conditions of appointment. Civil service jobs are less secure while 'hire and fire' has been reduced by a combination of management policy and legislation.

The shifts in the population structure in most advanced economies place a greater emphasis on skill in recruitment and prior consideration in job choice. The government's employment services are extending their role to encompass longer term 'people strategy' issues and the traditional job placement service. This mirrors developments in the private sector. Employment agencies, headhunters and other similar firms are widening their role to include job counselling and personal development. The type of placement guidance being provided for prospective candidates is indicated below.

Preparing Yourself

- Be selective about applications.
- Know the enterprise by reading the material sent and finding out from libraries the issues it is facing.
- Dress smartly.
- Think through your application and relate answers to it.
- Relate your answers to the firm and illustrate your comments.
- Show you want the job.
- Speak clearly and look at the interviewer.
- Relate past experience to the new post.
- Be honest and candid.
- Review the interview afterwards.
- Get friends to help you tackle any problems, such as the 'er', 'um' response.

The late 1980s has seen a surge of interest in the quality of the managerial labour force in the UK. Two reports highlighted the poor levels of qualifications held by UK managers and the low investment in training by firms and individuals. These findings prompted industry, government and education to seek ways of establishing a more systematic, national structure of management qualifications. The Management Charter Initiative was created to identify needs and develop a scheme for provision. The three key qualifications are: the Certificate; the Diploma and the MBA. Underpinning these is a firm commitment by employers to invest more heavily in personal development. Many leading organizations have expressed their commitment to this area by subscribing to the Management Charter.

Management development is an individual and group pursuit. The most effective learning occurs when people care about the skills they acquire and see some benefit in the knowledge acquired. The notion of the learning organization assumes joint ownership of the process of self improvement. The firm might provide the opportunities. These can occur through public, executive courses, company based training and certificated programmes. The MBA is rapidly becoming the generic qualification for senior management.

Individual achievement and the success of the enterprise are the main determinants of individual security. This is underpinned by the contract of employment. This should be:

- made between two or more parties who are competent to make such agreements
- accepted as legally binding by all the parties involved
- attempting to achieve legal objectives
- based on an offer and acceptance in the same terms between the parties
- backed by 'consideration in an identifiable and recognisable form',[8] e.g. a wage.

The contract is underpinned by a vast amount of law. It covers the terms of appointment, the job itself, the interruption and termination of employment.

Meeting the specific terms and conditions of a post is seldom enough in any job. The maximum benefits for the individual and the enterprise comes from a combination of task competence and motivated performance. Creating a highly motivated workforce is one of the most complex issues facing any organization.

The instrumental view that motivation is achieved through a mixture of reward and punishment no longer carries much weight. Hertzberg[9] indicated that rewarding individuals is not a simple, stimulus–response process. High rewards through pay can be associated with low motivation. Highly motivated workers might be content with low pay. Theories of motivation often emphasize the voluntary nature of motivation. This notion has shaped the 'Expectancy Theory' of motivation.

Vroom[10] emphasized the extent to which behaviour is shaped by a mixture of expectancy, valence and instrumentality:

- *Expectancy* is the belief that a particular level of effort will produce a specific level of performance.
- *Valence* is a measure of the value that an individual places on the outcome.
- *Instrumentality* is the likelihood of a particular outcome.

This means that workers who do not believe that they can achieve high productivity (expectancy) but place a high value (valence) on the monetary rewards associated with high output will be poorly motivated (instrumentality). In sum, the more people feel that their efforts will produce desirable outcomes, for which they will be rewarded in ways they value, the more likely they will try to achieve these goals. Merely changing one variable will have little effect.

The complexity of features that shape performance creates problems for the effective direction of organizations. Control systems exist to link the activities (inputs) of the enterprise to its output. This has to be achieved in ways which reflect the nature of the venture, its environment and the contribution of the various stakeholders. Controls are determined by a mixture of authority, feedback and benefit. These are linked through the information systems which direct authority, provide feedback and allocate benefits. The design of a control system reflects this balance of performance and information. The starting point is an attempt to define the criteria against which effort will be measured. In sport this might be easy. Coming first, breaking a record, are clear indicators of achievement. Success or failure can be seen quickly and a response attempted. This is harder in more complex situations.

It might seem simple to measure the accomplishments of sales staff in terms of sales achieved. Circumstances can, however, affect this. It is harder to sell in some situations. 'Easy' sales to established customers might be less important than 'hard' sales to new prospects. The Return on Investments (ROI) might be emphasized when looking at different operations. Cutting back investment can produce a sharp increase in the ROI in the short term but weaken the venture's long-term position. Share prices are sometimes seen as the best, consolidated measure. But controls work best if they are internalized and people understand how they can contribute. It is hard for most workers to see how they can influence the share price. In the public and voluntary sectors, even this type of measure is hard to identify and relate to a meaningful control system. This is vividly demonstrated in the attempts to assess and manage the performance of universities. There is little consensus about the relative importance of teaching and research. The former is the primary generator of income while the latter dominates institutional and individual appraisal. The notion of a national assessment of teaching is rejected by the University Funding Council. The research review is seen in many quarters as counterproductive. Its emphasis on peer assessment widens the gulf between universities and the wider community. It seems to value established positions at the expense of innovation. Control systems can only work where there is broad agreement about objectives and information linking actions to outcomes.

The people, marketing, operations and financial resources of an organization are drawn together to achieve objectives. These vary within the enterprise and across different type of institution. Most forms of support reflect the needs of particular groups or national priorities. The UK's trading history, especially the dependence on export earnings, has created a comprehensive system of export support.

Exports

The UK has long been one of the world's major trading nations. Towards the end of the last century Britain accounted for over one-third of world trade. A hundred years later this had declined to under 10%. Table 3.1 shows relative share of world trade in 1983 and in 1883.

Table 3.1 Share of world trade

Country	1883	1983
UK	37.1%	7.9%
Germany	17.2%	19.0%★
USA	3.4%	16.9%

★ Federal Republic of Germany.
Source: D. H. Aldcroft and H. W. Richardson, *The British Economy 1870–1939 and British Overseas Trade Board Annual Report 1988/89.*

In some senses, this decline merely reflects the reduction in the scale of the UK economy. The UK still exports a higher proportion of its GNP than many of its main rivals, notably the USA, West Germany and Japan. In recent years, however, both Italy and France have overtaken the UK in terms of share of GNP exported. The task of export support agencies is to help firms arrest this decline and accelerate the increase in total exports that has been seen in recent years.

The lead UK government agency in the export effort is the British Overseas Trade Board. This was set up in 1972 to advise on overseas trade and export promotion. The members of the Board come mainly from industry and commerce. Traditionally, it has delivered its services through the local offices of the Department of Trade and Industry. More recently, it has sought to work closely with the voluntary and private sector. The Active Exporting Programme has been contracted out to the Association of British Chambers of Commerce. It delivers local advice and support through its network of local Chambers and Export Enterprise Centres. This shift of resources reflects practice in France, West Germany and other European countries. The strong Chamber of Commerce movement in these countries has been the primary vehicle for funnelling direct aid to exporters beside using their own resources to support trade development.

Direct government support (excluding staff costs) is dominated by expenditure on overseas trade fairs, export market research, statistics and market intelligence, library publications, overseas projects and publicity. Exhibitions and trade fairs play an important part in market development. Marketing and financial support is available to organizations exhibiting. The Export Market Research Scheme is operated through the Association of British Chambers of Commerce. It is possible to get help ranging from one-third of direct costs for projects involving one enterprise to two-thirds of the costs of collaborative ventures. Most exporting firms are reasonably active in using these services. The public sector is less familiar with the support available. Institutions such as Stirling University are beginning to see the benefits of using fairs to promote their work and overseas market research to identify opportunities. The export market research staff of the BOTB have been willing to classify properly supervised and managed staff and student marketing research, as eligible for the 50% grant provided for in-house research.

The public sector provision is only one element in the extensive network of points of contact with export markets illustrated in Figure 3.5.

This network underpins the commercial export support companies. These range from individual representatives, through highly specialized firms to the giant trading houses notably the Japanese, Sogu Shosa or (General Trading Houses) such as Mitsui and Mitsubishi. Most organizations participating in overseas trade will be approached by people offering to represent their interests in territories ranging from 'the world' to 'my home town'. The quality of service obtained usually reflects the care and attention invested in their selection. The diversity of export environments is matched by the specializations developed by organizations seeking to exploit particular expertise. Barter or counter trade, i.e. the exchange of goods and services without cash is important in some markets. Barter calls for distinct skills. This has led to the emergence of some specialized businesses to bridge the gap between suppliers and buyers.

Public enterprise

The balance between public, private and voluntary support for enterprise has shifted over the last decade. The expansion of the voluntary sector through employment, industrial and enterprise initiatives is perhaps the most marked change. In part, this reflects a desire by firms, such as IBM, United Biscuits, Pilkington, Shell, BP, the banks and the leading accountancy firms, to play a major role in tackling local and

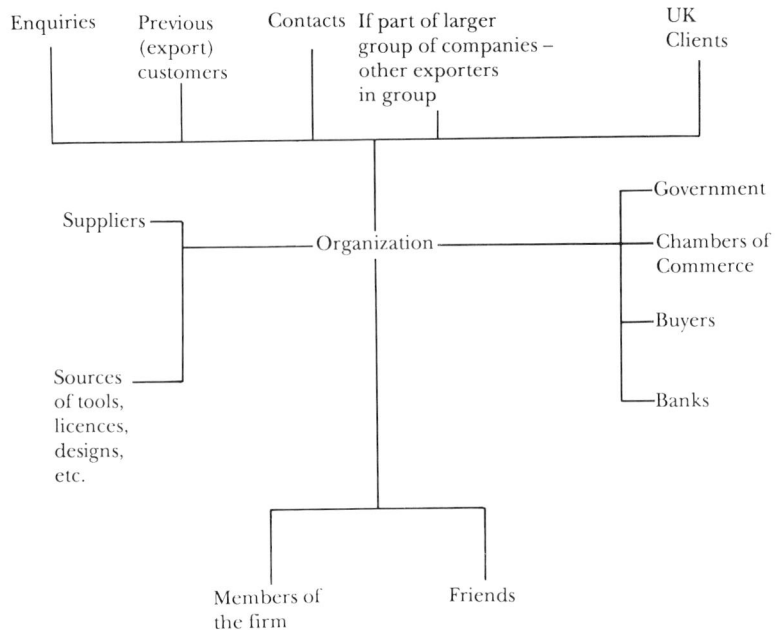

Figure 3.5   An organization's network of contact points

national, economic and social challenges. The willingness of others to collaborate has played its part. Universities, polytechnics, hospitals, voluntary groups and local authorities have generally responded well to the opportunities created. Underpinning these efforts is the determination of government to shift the balance of activity away from the state to greater private and voluntary participation. This move has affected the way government departments work in this area.

The Department of Trade and Industry

The effect of these adjustments has probably been greatest on the Department of Trade and Industry (DTI). It has reduced its direct role in intervention through nationalized industries, regional aid, trade support and agencies. Some of this has been transferred to the private sector. Elsewhere it has been targeted more precisely. Work through voluntary agencies has increased. The wider consultative role has expanded. Much of this reflects external changes. The expanded role of the European Commission has forced DTI to work more closely with Brussels. Greater concern for the environment has led DTI to confer with new bodies. This process of adjustment is most vividly illustrated by the Enterprise Initiative.

Enterprise Initiative

The Enterprise Initiative is the focus for the major strands of DTI support for enterprise development. It is split into two strands – the consultancy initiative and the specialist programmes which focus on marketing, business planning, finance and information, quality, design, manufacturing, exports, research and development, enterprise and education and regional needs. Within each, organizations can obtain consultancy from professional firms to help the venture to realize its full potential. The work can last for between 5 and 15 days. The UK government will pay at least half the cost of approved projects. Through the Initiative, organizations can gain access to collaborative research projects and gain information about proposed innovations and new technologies. A key element in the DTI's strategy is the formation of better links between firms, local schools, universities, polytechnics, central institutions (in Scotland) and other institutions of further and higher education.

The Initiative has features which distinguish it from previous programmes. Its work is more widely distributed than past programmes. The local and regional offices of DTI have greater scope to disseminate and target efforts. Alongside this, there is a powerful commitment to work with other agencies and the private sector. The links with consultants illustrate this. This can be seen in the delegation of aspects of the Exports Initiative to Chambers of Commerce, the Design Initiative to the Design Council and work on all initiatives to the Welsh Development Agency and Scottish Enterprise.

Department of Employment

Much of the early interest in enterprise development reflected concern about the increasing levels of unemployment. Self-employment, business formation and individual enterprise were seen as central elements in any long-term solution. The Department of Employment took a leading role in initiatives to stimulate business development. These included direct assistance to entrepreneurs through the enterprise allowance scheme and indirect support through training and development.

The Enterprise Allowance provides roughly £40.00 per week for the first year to supplement the income from the new business. A number of criteria need to be met to be eligible. Applicants must be:

- aged between 18 and 65 years
- be receiving unemployment benefit or income support
- unemployed
- able to invest at least £1000 in the enterprise
- working full time in the business.

The business should:

- not be trading before an application is made
- approved by the Department of Employment.

This financial support is best viewed as part of a larger scheme of enterprise support.

The Training Agency

Ideally, participation in an enterprise scheme is associated with participation in one of the start-up training programmes sponsored by the Training Agency of the Department of Employment. These include: Firmstart, Graduate Enterprise and the Business Enterprise Programme. Each of these addresses the training needs of distinctive groups of new business starters. These new enterprise programmes are complemented by schemes which provide insights into enterprise for potential workers and existing businesses.

The Technical and Vocational Education Initiative (TVEI) was established to use technological and vocational education to provide job experience and improve the employability of a cross-section of schoolchildren. At first, selected schools were given new resources to enable them to tackle specific technical skill and vocational education issues. The lessons from the study of fields such as computing, business studies, electronics, design, communications and the media are complemented with work experience. The latter takes forms such as:

- work shadowing
- industrial visits
- staff exchanges
- placements
- projects
- young enterprise.

The Enterprise and Higher Education Initiative

This was launched in 1988 to offer graduates the chance to develop a range of enterprise skills. Particular attention is paid to helping graduates create and use opportunities, communicate well, adopt lifetime learning strategies and relate their studies to their future working life. In most cases, the initial emphasis is on staff development in participating institutions. These staff will be responsible for meeting the training needs of the scheme and building bridges with employers.

There is a powerful emphasis on collaboration with employers. They are expected to be involved in programme development, evaluation and long-term funding. The initiative is geared to wider, generic enterprise skills not just those linked to commercial ventures. It highlights the value of enterprise in a public or voluntary enterprise as much as in a private company.

Training and Enterprise Councils (TECs)

The period 1989–93 will see the creation of over 80 Training and Enterprise Councils in England and Wales. These Councils will be responsible locally for directing those government resources allocated for training and enterprise development. In the communities in which they operate they will have considerable discretion in determining priorities and directing effort. The TECs are employer led. This means that the Boards are largely made up from senior executives of local firms or national firms operating in the area. The first TEC (Oldham) was approved in November 1989. Each will be expected to complete a business plan which addresses the main tasks of:

- promoting effective training
- providing practical help to employers
- delivering and developing youth training
- contracting for employment training
- stimulating enterprise and economic growth
- helping local small firm development
- stimulating business education partnerships.

The importance of the TECs lies in several distinct aspect of their remit. First, there is the commitment to local 'ownership' of enterprise and training. The centralizing tendencies which are endemic in the UK are deliberately eschewed. Second, industrial leadership is made central to the management of their activities. Most Board members are leaders of the local business community. Third, latitude is provided to fit performance against resources to improve economic achievement.

Scottish and Welsh Development Agencies

In some senses, the Scottish (SDA) and Welsh (WDA) Development Agencies have provided role models for the newer initiatives. Both were created to address the specific economic development needs of their communities. Their remits were large. This mandate extended originally to include inward investment, factory and commercial development, finance and investment, research, business support, sectoral projects and virtually all non-fiscal aspects of economic progress.

In some aspects of their work, their success is manifest. The success in persuading Japanese companies to locate in Wales and US computer companies to build in Scotland is a tangible symbol of their achievement. Elsewhere the pattern is more mixed. Major environmental improvements such as the Glasgow Eastern Area Renewal (GEAR) are counterbalanced by the continued low rates of growth of new businesses.

Both agencies have been restructured recently. The property and finance roles have generally been cut back with their enterprise, education and training roles reinforced. The creation of 'Scottish Enterprise', linking the SDA and the Department of Employment Training Agency in Scotland, is a tangible expression of this approach. The shift to greater local autonomy reflects the growing awareness of local needs and their evolving remit. The link with other forms of intervention has grown in importance. Their role is normally seen as facilitating other, private forms of provision with the subsidy role reduced or eliminated. Leverage has become an increasingly important feature of their work. This is illustrated in local area renewal projects in Wales and Scotland. The Easterhouse Project in Glasgow and the Valleys Initiative in South Wales bring together a variety of potential funding and support bodies within a framework shaped by the Agencies. These backers include banks and other financial institutions, large and small firms plus voluntary bodies such as Enterprise Agencies. The management problems grow with this type of project but the additional new resources can more than compensate for these new challenges.

Highlands and Islands Development Board (HIDB)

The role of HIDB is broadly similar to that of the SDA and WDA but within the distinctive communities making up the Highlands and Islands of Scotland. The long history of migration, the major problems of scale and the distance from large markets place special demands on those responsible for economic development. The Board was set up to implement government regional policies while recognizing these local features. It has wide ranging powers to tackle problems. Beside these, it can provide loans, grants and equity assistance to new and existing businesses. It weds these to the type of property and sectoral programmes which are needed to provide an infrastructure for industry and back particular initiatives. The role of the HIDB has generally been wider than the SDA and WDA with its tasks of:

- assisting the people of the Highlands and Islands to improve their social and economic conditions
- enabling the Highlands and Islands to play a more effective part in the economic and social life of the nation.

This emphasis allied to the nature of the local economy is reflected in the emphasis given to tourism, fisheries and land development alongside industry in its economic pursuits.

The Board's work has demonstrated the potential for enterprise development in many different situations. The Community Co-operatives or Co-homum have applied the notions of community enterprise to small communities. They address the management problems faced by small local businesses. The community may be too small to sustain the separate managerial overheads of a shop, builder's merchant, fish farm, or crofting supplies store. They can, however, be drawn together under one management, especially if this is strongly rooted in the local community. Typically, initial finance is provided by locals on an individual or group basis. This is matched by the HIDB. Professional management is employed to set up and run the enterprises as a group. In some areas this has been so successful that new activities have been added. These can create jobs while meeting local needs. The model is now being emulated in other parts of the UK where similar patterns of change and outward mobility is seen. Some inner city experiments show considerable promise.

Local Enterprise Development Unit (LEDU)

The enterprise development challenges in Northern Ireland show some characteristics of those in central Scotland and northern England. There is a large but declining base in traditional industries. These include shipbuilding, textiles and engineering. The distance of Northern Ireland producers from the larger markets of Great Britain and continental Europe makes growth hard. Northern Ireland faces some unique difficulties. The threat of terrorism discourages inward investment. This is probably a less serious economic difficulty than the emigration of many of its talented younger people.

LEDU's activities combine the development roles of bodies like the SDA, WDA and the HIDB with a powerful local and educational remit. The cohesion of many communities in Northern Ireland makes these groups the 'natural' focus for projects. The educational institutions, notably the Northern Ireland Institute for Small Business (NISBI) based at the University of Ulster has developed probably the most active education/development agency partnership in the UK.

Council of Small Firms in Rural Areas (CoSira)

There has been widespread debate in England about the potential for an English Development Agency. This has been rejected so far. This is largely on the grounds that the distinctive circumstances which led to the creation of agencies in Scotland, Wales and Northern Ireland cannot be seen across England. The diversity of situations allied to the challenge of allocating resources has dissuaded policy makers to follow this route. The nearest equivalent is CoSira.

CoSira seeks to help the development of small firms and other forms of local enterprise in the rural areas of England and Wales. It employs a group of full-time specialist and part-time advisers to work with new and established firms. Besides this, it can provide limited financial backing. The Council has invested considerable resources in exploring the various ways in which enterprise can play a part in maintaining the health of rural communities.

Local authorities

The specialist development agencies support and complement the services provided across the UK by local authorities. All authorities combine some elements of the education, economic development and environmental planning in their remit. Specific initiatives have benefited from their early backing. The early support for the London

Compact by the Inner London Education Authority illustrates the link between education and enterprise. Authorities like Hackney in London are at the forefront of efforts to break down the racial barriers to enterprise development. Sheffield was an innovator in local venture financing of business through its Local Enterprise Board (LEB). Stirling integrated housing improvements, community enterprise and business advice to locals. Each of these endeavours demonstrates the ability of the authority to provide finance, mobilize educational resources, tackle specific needs (e.g.) housing and implement policies in areas like environmental planning.

Local authorities are unique in their ability to combine these elements. It can mean that the industrial development and the education functions can work together in a co-ordinated way. Local authorities have extensive powers to supply grant aid to promising ventures. Their local responsibilities mean that they can be especially responsive to community requirements.

Voluntary and specialist organizations

The burgeoning spirit of enterprise in the UK has stimulated a wide range of voluntary sector initiatives to support these developments. Some are linked with longer established bodies notably Chambers of Commerce. Others are novel responses to particular issues. The growth of Instant Muscle reflected the needs of younger, manual workers for basic management skills. Project Fullemploy helps members of minority groups. Livewire and the Prince's Trust provide finance for promising new businesses operated by young people.

The diversity of these organizations reflects the heterogeneity of the groups seeking self realization through enterprise. Many express their individuality through particular interests in the Arts, Design and Crafts. The specialist Councils provide professional back-up for these areas.

Chambers of Commerce

The Chambers of Commerce are perhaps the oldest voluntary agencies for enterprise. Some have histories going back over a hundred years. Despite this, their contribution to economic development has seldom matched their potential or the role adopted by Chambers in France, West Germany and other European countries. Only London, Birmingham, Manchester and Glasgow have played a similar part in their local area. Most Chambers have confined themselves to representing their members' interests through disseminating information and tackling specific campaigns (e.g. on rates).

The contrast between the pattern in continental Europe and in the UK has led to efforts to widen the work of Chambers. Many took an active part as Training Agents in the Youth Training Scheme (YTS). The creation of local enterprise agencies was helped by the groundwork done by some local Chambers. The Enterprise Initiative involves a similar, major contribution. This is especially true in exports. The long established provision of export documents and organization of trade missions is matched by a wider export support remit. The creation of the TECs is another expansion of their role.

Enterprise agencies

No organizations more fully represent the enterprise movement in the UK than the Enterprise Agencies or Trusts. They bring together private and public sector resources to support local enterprise development. In early 1989, there were over 300 enterprise agencies in the UK. They ranged from the small like ACE (Alloa and Clackmannan Enterprise) to the large such as Lenta (London Enterprise Agency). They operate under two national bodies: ScotBic (Scottish Business in the Community) and BIC (Business in the Community).

The development of the early Trusts or Agencies highlights key features of their subsequent role. The St Helens Trust was created to tackle the problems created in St Helens by large-scale reductions in the labour force at Pilkington's. It was unlikely that existing businesses could absorb this labour. This meant that there was a serious risk of a rapid increase in unemployment. Pilkington's decided to address this issue directly. A trust was created and financed by the firm. Its remit was to stimulate new business formation and job creation. The model was so successful that it has been replicated across the UK. There are variations on the theme. Lenta (London Enterprise Agency) was established by a consortium of firms. Its work is distributed in many parts of London. It was an innovator in forming links with venture finance and property. Secondments from large firms have played a crucial part in its success. Enterprise North was strongly rooted in the education sector through its links with Durham University. The Scottish Enterprise Foundation adopted a networking and research role in its support for enterprise.

ScotBic

Scotbic (Scottish Business in the Community) and BIC (Business in the Community) have shaped an environment in which these initiatives can flourish. The vision of leading industrialists such as Sir Alastair Pilkington, Sir Hector Laing and Sir Adrian Cadbury showed how potent personal enterprise is today. They helped to shape the early development of these organizations. The willingness of industry to back this work through people and money has encouraged government to expand its commitment to local forms of enterprise support.

Trade associations

The shift towards policy implementation through industry-based organizations has affected the role of trade associations. Normally these represent the interests of particular industrial sectors. The British Plastics Federation (BPF), the Federation of Merchant Tailors and Road Haulage Association (RHA) illustrate the range of associations. Some, like the BPF, have grown up fairly recently to meet the needs of a new and growing sector. Their emphasis on lobbying is matched by technical and library services. The much smaller Federation of Merchant Tailors has existed for over a century. Its members might respond vigorously to specific threats such as the uniform business rate. For the most part their main interest lies in setting standards and maintaining quality. A large and diverse association such as the RHA actively lobbies and campaigns across a range of issues.

The remit of most associations has been influenced by several recent policy initiatives. The restructuring and elimination of the Industrial Training Boards led to a major transfer of training responsibilities to trade associations. This worked well with the Youth Training Scheme. There is less evidence of success in some aspects of technical and management training. The *Directory of British Associations* is the main source of information about trade associations and their work.

Specialist councils

Government has recognized the distinctive requirements of specialist interest or trade groups. In some fields it has acknowledged that these bodies represent wider economic or social concerns. The creation of The Arts Council, Design Council, Crafts Council and Sports Council reflects a wish to funnel resources into key areas of social, cultural and economic life. At the same time, they bring together members of the immediate group and the wider community in shaping and implementing policy. Each has evolved in distinct ways which reflect the resources available and attitudes to their work.

Each operates on several levels. They are responsible for the allocation of government funds to national and regional organization. This raises the dilemmas of achieving the balance between local and national interests or weighing maintenance of the established centres of excellence against innovation and development. The results will vary over time.

The Design Council has recently revised its strategy to reflect new circumstances. It has sharpened its mission to reduce the emphasis on public awareness of design to give greater attention to industrial recognition of the commercial pay-offs from better design. In part, this reflects past success. The public expects better designed products. It sees them on display in stores and exhibitions. This reduces the need for the Council to operate its own shops. Too often, the most popular offerings are 'designed in Britain – made elsewhere' – to quote the title of a successful, recent exhibition.

The Crafts Council and the Sports Council mirror the developments seen elsewhere. They are striving to provide a range of services to a heterogeneous group of users. Some are activists. These will include individual crafts people and sports persons. Some will seek to win recognition for their distinct interests. The artist craftsman or craftswoman will emphasize selectivity and control. Others will advocate more attention to dissemination and access. The framework of support created will try to balance these interests within an overall strategy. Often, this will weigh the calls of the wider community alongside the claims of individuals or specialist groups.

Conclusion

The growth of the enterprise support system in the UK over the last decade is part of a continuous process of evolution. Key institutions such as the Chambers of Commerce are long established. Many of their traditional roles persist. The calls for information and representation are as strong as ever. New circumstances create new demands. Realization of the central role of training has prompted Chambers to become involved in Training and Enterprise Councils. This, in turn, brings them closer to universities and colleges.

Other organizations are new. The network of enterprise agencies that spans the UK was built up over five years. The drive came from the private sector. Endorsement by the government accelerated their growth. This is associated with an acceptance that partnership and collaboration paid dividends in creating a favourable atmosphere for the support of enterprise. Greater maturity has stimulated competition. The top-down provision of support that was *good for you* is being replaced by greater user power. The introduction of training and counselling vouchers puts more power in the hands of clients who can exercise greater choice about suppliers and services.

The growth of the enterprise agencies was a response to the conditions of the 1980s. Circumstances shape the support system. The Royal Society of Arts was founded in the eighteenth century to bring new physical sciences to the service of industry and commerce. For most of its recent history it was probably best known as an examining board. It campaigned during 'Industry Year' to bridge the gap between industry and the rest of the community.

The Scottish Council for Development and Industry was formed in the 1930s to mobilize industry, commerce and government to address the challenges of recession. Its international conferences continue to be a unique forum, bringing together a wide range of Scottish opinion to tackle current policy issues. Many of the most vigorous support agencies display this public backing long before government or other institutional recognition occurs.

The green movement shows this. Friends of the Earth campaigns through its local but autonomous groups. The successful 'home insulation' projects of the late 1970s and early 1980s were designed, refined and delivered through local, community entrepreneurs within Friends of the Earth. The national framework made it easier for their programme to be adopted and disseminated widely. In this case it was a bottom-up initiative. It originated in the north-east of England and grew to a national scheme through a mixture of sideways and central direction.

The strength of voluntary support systems lies is this type of diversity. The Edinburgh Festival Fringe is a specific event which acts as a catalyst for individual and group enterprise. It creates an opportunity for people to translate their desire to perform into action while providing a bewildering variety of role models. Recognition and endorsement can be as important as resources in stimulating and sustaining enterprise.

Resources may be needed. The state, large organizations, trusts and foundations can furnish money and people. These are not substitutes for individual enterprise but complement it. The achievements of the City of Birmingham Symphony Orchestra depends as much on the vision of Simon Rattle as the support from national and local government. The support system creates the environment in which individuals and organizations can realize their potential. Backing can take many forms. Money might be needed from banks. Assistance can take other forms. Secondments of staff from IBM, Arthur Young, and the Scottish Office took the Scottish Enterprise Foundation at Stirling University through its formative years. The aid needed changes with the individual or enterprise. Research into the success strategies of women entrepreneurs highlighted training during the pre-start phase, planning, counselling and finance in early start-up, production skills and networking in the growth phase, and flexible finance and marketing during the mature period. The value of the support system depends on its ability to respond to these different needs and the ease of access for individuals and organizations.

Case study

Anglo Foods Ltd

Introduction

In 1987 Anglo Foods, the co-operative marketing organization for the British Root Vegetable Growers, was under strong pressure to undertake a major review of its activities. It was being accused of failing to respond to new challenges and lacking any answers to the marketing problems facing the growers. This contrasted markedly with the situation which had existed as recently as two years ago. Then it seemed that Anglo Foods had played a major part in arresting the long-term decline in consumption of root vegetables in the UK and even win back markets which were apparently lost for ever.

Anglo Foods had been established by the British Root Vegetable Growers Association in 1976. In many ways its inception had grown from the personal vision of Sir Reginald Abbott, former Conservative Minister of Agriculture and Chairman of Rocar Farms. This was one of the largest farming and packaging companies in the UK. He was convinced that the 'industry' needed to collaborate if it was to succeed in the face of household expenditure on food and a shift in market power towards retailers. His deep commitment, especially to marketing, had been very important in setting up and maintaining the co-operative.

Background

The first few years of Anglo Foods' existence had been characterized by considerable debate and limited success. The appointment of Ian McKennedy as Managing Director in 1980 seemed to transform the situation. The strength of his personality, allied to his understanding of the industry and its marketing problems, produced a unity of vision which coincided with a significant shift in the demand pattern facing the industry. The early 1980s saw decline in overall demand stop and then start moving ahead. The share of total demand accounted for by the UK growers increased. Retailers gave increasing prominence to vegetable and fruit products in their newer, larger outlets. Even the old 'enemy' – diet – seemed to be less of a threat as new writers were more supportive of old patterns of eating.

The current situation

The relatively good situation seen in the mid-1980s had been transformed by a series of separate incidents. A double tragedy occurred in 1986. First Ian McKennedy was killed in a car crash. Within months Sir Reginald had died. These coincided with new shifts in consumption and distribution of food. The pattern of the decline had re-emerged. This seemed to be stimulated by new as well as old factors. Food processors had developed novel systems for producing competitive, substitute products. Their penetration of growth markets, especially fast-food catering, was eroding demand. At the same time, health fears about food had re-emerged. Now there was concern about 'chemicals used by farmers' as well as 'the notoriously bad diet of the British' (*The Green Consumer*, 1986) were reducing demand. Retail buying was changing. Large store groups responding to the lack of growth in overall consumption by attempts to move buyers from cheaper or more expensive lines. The initial indications for 1987 seemed to suggest that 'the bad old days' were back.

The challenge

Peter Andrews, the new Chief Executive was, not surprisingly, very concerned about this turn of events. He knew that large increases in advertising and marketing budgets were unlikely to be forthcoming from an industry which saw itself in financial crisis. In his view the answer must lie in 'thinking smarter'. To achieve this he posed the problems to his more senior managers and asked for their ideas on how best to tackle the problems Anglo Foods and the industry faced.

The developments proposed

At the mid-year management conference it was agreed that each manager would present his ideas on the way forward, especially the contribution his ideas could make in tackling these challenges.

> *H. Sutcliff*: The sales forces in the industry are too small and our merchandizing team is too limited to provide meaningful cover of the industry. Just look at the number the Meat Marketing Board and the Sea Fish people have in the field. We can only cover the market by rushing from location to location. We spend no time thinking about presentation and establishing long-term relationships. The volume is in the stores and we need to be visible. I suggest that we recruit a large team of part-time merchandizers, perhaps retired salesmen, even farmers. Pay them a small retainer with most of their wages coming from some form of commission. This would give us presence and visibility.

> *E. Trainer*: We are failing to keep up with the technologies which are emerging in the field. Root vegetables have such an 'old' and 'traditional' image that fails to reflect their potential. we should break our marketing efforts up. Forget all about 'root vegetables' and focus on other innovatory products. We've just come up with a new curry-flavoured chip. We could concentrate more effort on the more popular lines such as carrots and seek out new variations. Look at the success of the Kiwi fruit and other new lines.

> *G. Briffel*: I really think that approach is wrong. I think the range we are trying to promote is, if anything, too wide. We should concentrate on the major lines. At the same time we need to tackle the critics straight on. People like Geoffrey Green and other health food cranks get away with too much. More aggressive PR is the answer.

Ideas along these lines were reiterated by other members of the senior management team. At the end of the discussion Peter Andrews commented:

> 'Although I have found everything that has been said very interesting and relevant, I don't really think we have really come to grips with the problem. I'd like to bounce these off a few other people.'

Task

1. *Review the present position.*
2. *Highlight the problem areas as you see them.*
3. *Evaluate the suggestions put forward.*
4. *Put forward your ideas on the means to solve the problem.*

References

1. Training Agency. *Enterprise in Higher Education; Guide for Applicants*, December 1989, Moorfoot, Sheffield.
2. Wilson, H. Chr. *The Financing of Small Firms*, HMSO, London, 1979.
3. McLuhan, M. *Understanding Media*, New York, McGraw-Hill, 1966.
4. Deane, P. *The First Industrial Revolution*, Cambridge University Press, 1967.

5. Magaziner, I.C. and Reich, R.B. *Minding America's Business*, New York, Random House, 1982.
6. Woodward, J. *Industrial Organisation; Theory and Practice*, Oxford, Oxford University Press, 1965.
7. Hakansson, H. (ed). *International Marketing and Purchasing of Industrial Goods*, London, Wiley, 1982.
8. Thomason, G. *A Textbook of Personnel Management*, London, Institute of Personnel Management, 1981.
9. Hertzberg, F. (1966), *Works and the Nature of Man*, New York, World Publishing.
10. Vroom, V. (1964), *Work and Motivation*, New York, John Wiley.
11. Carter, S. and Cannon, T. (1988), *Female entrepreneurs: a study of female business owners*, London, Department of Employment, Research Paper no. 65.

Chapter 4
Building an enterprise

There are broad similarities in the processes involved in the creation of virtually every form of enterprise. There is the twin stimulus of need and idea. The creator(s) will have some notion of a deficiency to be met and a way of meeting it. The gap can be explicit and easily recognized. The huge potential that existed in offices for 'dry, good-quality, permanent copies on ordinary paper with a minimum of trouble'[1] was widely recognized in the first half of this century. Numerous companies were formed and products launched to meet this need. It was not until 1959 when Xerox introduced its first automatic xerographic office copier that the opportunity was grasped. Others may not be so obvious. Few predicted that the Littlewoods family would turn a fairly simple form of gambling into a national pastime for millions over more than 50 years.

The opportunity and the originators can be brought together in a slow and relatively indirect way.

> In 1946, everyone still talked about the mother and father of American modern dance, Ruth St Denis and Ted Shawn. She was called Miss Ruth and he was Papa Ted. They had a dance company called Denishawne in the early part of this century in America. Although it was an independent performing company, they also performed as part of the serious act in American vaudeville. A very strange place that was, too, because there on the music hall stage they were inventing what was to become American Contemporary Dance, perhaps the only really American art form.
>
> Cohan, R. 'Contemporary Choreography', *J. Royal Soc. Arts*[2]

Elsewhere, it can occur rapidly. The Manhattan Project drew together a large number of scientists under the leadership of Robert Oppenheimer to build the first atomic bomb. Some developments may be predictable but not acted upon. Kahn and Weiner[3] predicted the creation of fourth and fifth generation expert systems 'as computers become more self programming they will increasingly tend to perform activities that amount to 'learning' from experience and training'. They did not, however, predict the stand alone personal computer. This was created by two high-school dropouts working from a garage in California.

Origins

The origins of most successful forms of enterprise lie in a mixture of need and environment. People provide the catalyst which converts potential into reality. Opportunities to display enterprise occur in a host of situations. Change is probably a more important mother of invention than necessity. The response to opportunity provides some insight into the origins of enterprise. At the core lies a belief that a solution to a problem lies in the hands of a firm or person. Valerie Craine spotted such a situation in the storage of toxic and corrosive materials. She and her partners noted that glass, the traditional packaging material, had many advantages: cheap, inert, transparent. But one major disadvantage: it is fragile. They established Safety Coating Ltd to apply tough, clear, plastic coatings which would retain the contents of a broken container in a safe plastic envelope. Their initiative was based on the classic link between specific problem and technical solution. Often the opportunities are identified from more diverse sources. Sources of new product ideas include:

- Market research
- Gap analysis
- Technology
- Brainstorming
- Customer comments
- Insight
- Neglect
- Foreign search
- Study of use
- Suppliers
- R&D
- Design
- Frustration
- Hobby.

Often these act in concert. A common stimulus to personal enterprise is frustration at the products or services currently supplied. Anita Roddick was frustrated by her inability to buy natural, biodegradable cosmetics that had been manufactured without cruelty to animals. Out of her frustration grew the Body Shop. Many retail outlets are started in small communities by locals who are frustrated by gaps in provision. Student unions have moved into retailing, travel and other services because of their frustration with the services provided by others.

However, frustration is not enough. R&D might be needed to find an effective means of meeting the need. Graham McGrath of Piranha Canoes invested heavily to get the type of manoeuvrability he needed to take on his German rivals. Sometimes foreign search will play a part. McGrath needed a volume product to stand alongside his competition canoe. He turned to a Canadian, rotationally moulded canoe.

Ideas and opportunities surround us but only a small minority try to bring these together. A desire to fill the gap must be wedded to determination, resilience and ability for the project to bear fruit. The successful transputer research at Sheffield's University and Polytechnic indicates the importance of combining pioneering thinking with the grit to see the programme to fruition. The same resolution was shown by the founders of the Terence Higgins Trust. They overcame prejudice and hostility to AIDS to meet an urgent social need. Their successes reflect an ability to combine purpose with effective planning and delivery. The form and scale of these achievements will depend on the environment.

Environment

'*Seize the moment*' could be the motto of enterprise. Opportunities emerge and reflect the environment. This can be illustrated by the openings being created in the food industry today.

The distribution systems for food are experiencing shifts in form and nature. This can be seen in physical distribution systems and channels of distribution. New technologies and the widespread use of more established systems shape the ways that food products can be moved. These, in turn, influence their nature and customer appeal. Food distribution is increasingly international. In the UK, the Europeanization of food distribution can be seen in the origin of food products, the trading policies of distributors and retailers and the new companies emerging to service these needs.

There is evidence that patterns of food consumption are converging at least among Western, more developed economies (Frank and Wheelock, 1988).[4] This trend is likely to be reinforced by the internationalization of major food companies. Examples of this range from the ubiquitous MacDonald's to processors and manufacturers such as United Biscuits and, most recently, UK retailers such as Bejam, Marks & Spencer and J. Sainsbury. There would seem to a progressive shift from a closed to an open system of food distribution in the UK.

Ultimately, the success of this development will depend on the ability of retailers and other members of the food distribution system to respond to the needs of consumers at a time of major behavioural and structural change. Concern with healthier eating is widespread in the economically developed world. This reflects increased choice. At the same time it links food consumption with a range of related market forces. These include the altering role of women in the family, reductions in product life cycles and modified cooking and eating habits. Comparable changes are occurring in the structure of the population. Perhaps the most dramatic is the shift to one-person family units. These have increased from one in ten in 1951 to one in four in 1986. It is reasonable to expect that the proportion will increase to over one in three by the mid-1990s. The transformation of the age structure of the population in the UK will influence both the nature and pattern of food consumption. This is not a local phenomena. It is mirrored in North America and much of Europe (Figure 4.1).

The number of young people entering the workforce is declining rapidly (Figure 4.2).

United Kingdom
Age distribution

	Male			*Female*	
Age	*% of population*			*% of population*	*Age*
70+	3.9%			6.7%	70+
60–69	4.7%			5.4%	60–69
50–59	5.3%			5.5%	50–59
40–49	5.9%			5.8%	40–49
30–39	7.0%			7.0%	30–39
20–29	7.9%			7.7%	20–29
10–19	7.6%			7.2%	10–19
0–9	6.4%			6.0%	0–9

4600 2300 0 2300 4600

(in thousands)

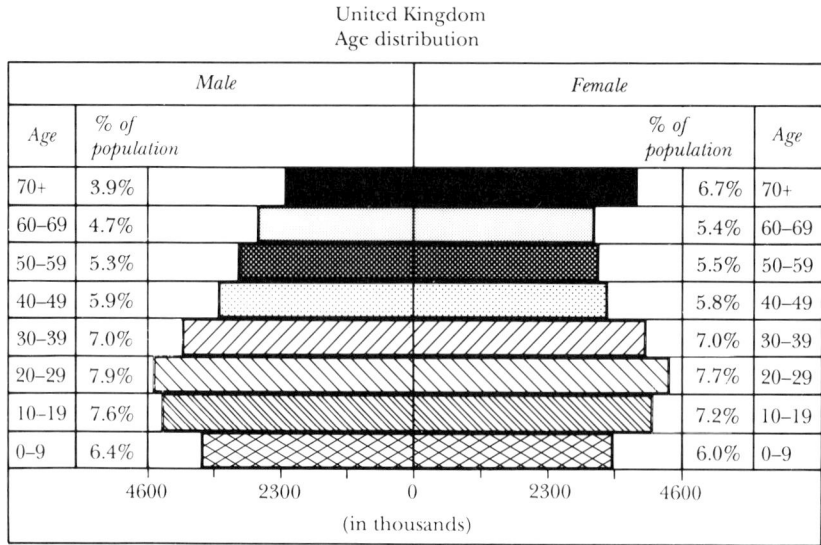

Total population: 56,936,000 (1988)

Figure 4.1   The age profile of the UK economy

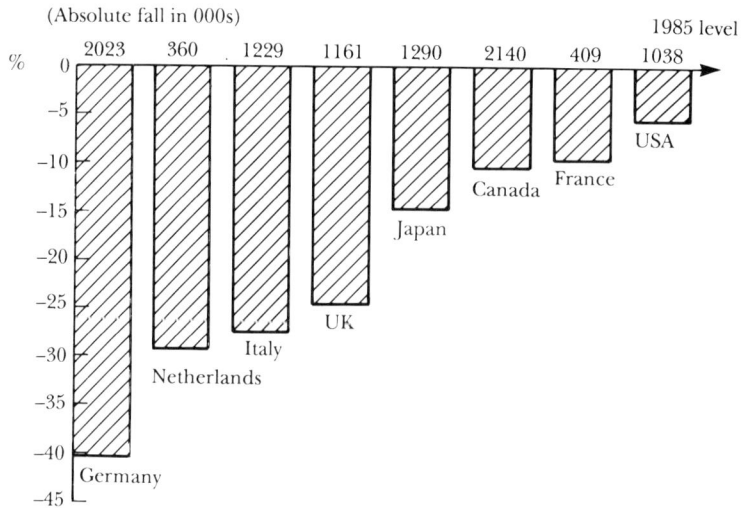

Figure 4.2   The fall in numbers of 15- to 19-year-olds. The percentage between 1985 level and projected numbers for 2000
Source: Eurostat/Data Resources

The forces which underpin the patterns described above range from the highly individual to the global. In the UK and much of the developed world, prosperity has prompted increased demands for choice and freedom. The shift towards a healthier diet is affecting the stocking policies of major retailers besides opening up new market opportunities in retailing and catering. This turmoil is being reinforced by media and political pressures. Slattery (1986)[5] suggests that 'many consumers face a new problem: that of deciding which "healthy" products are genuinely useful in a healthy diet'. Other writers are more sanguine: 'present policies artificially raise consumption of either potentially harmful products, such as sugar, whole fat milk and butter or less healthy products, such as white bread' (Black, 1986).[6] The most likely outcome will be increased innovation and enterprise as firms and individuals experiment in the face of ignorance to respond to market change.

It is useful to counterpoint these alterations at the individual level with wider environmental concerns. Few human activities are more closely linked with the physical environment than food production and allocation. The shape of the landscape largely reflects priorities in these areas. It is unlikely that society will give producers the type of freedom of action that has been enjoyed in the past. In part, this reflects the successes achieved in boosting production which in turn creates opportunities for greater restraint.

The FAO World Food Report in 1986[7] indicated that more food had been produced than ever before leading to large surpluses in food grains, butter, milk powder and animal products. These surpluses have helped to keep prices down. This has enabled domestic consumers in Europe and North America to exercise more choice and spend less of their family budget on food. Retailers and wholesalers have been able to sustain their profits, even increasing margins in some areas in a static market. It is hard to see this pattern being sustained in the long term. Widespread concern exists in the West about the costs of intensive, chemical-driven farming. These are matched by worries in developing economies about the price being paid in those countries in the face of price and production imbalances.

The move towards the Single European Market in 1992 is the most wide-ranging and tangible expression of the commitment by policymakers to market mechanisms to enhance competition and consumer choice. The highly concentrated nature of grocery retailing is often seen as a major constraint on the workings of the free market. Mintel, basing his work on DTI data (1988) showed the percentage shares of grocery sales for 1986–7 to be:

Major multiples	57.0%
Other multiples	14.0%
Co-op	12.6%
Independents	16.4%.

Similar patterns of concentration have not been especially effective at preserving the *status quo* in the face of skilled and determined new entrants. The personal computer market illustrates how quickly market position can be lost. The collapse of one-time market leaders such as Sinclair and Acorn and the rapid loss of market share by IBM indicates how established positions can be eroded.

The cost of entry into markets is an important element in the competitive process. Traditionally, the food distribution system was characterized by relatively low entry costs. The classic 'Wheel of Retailing' model, describes the shift made by most entrants from small, low-cost units to large units with wide ranges. This could reasonably describe the evolution of several of the leading UK grocery retailers. Tesco developed this way in the 1940s and 1950s. Kwik Save is using the same approach today. A number of recent changes in the food distribution system may change this.

The location and service opportunities which were exploited by earlier generations of entrepreneurs are shrinking while existing traders recognize the importance of 'the service edge'. Ease of access to outlets is increasing. It is estimated that even in London, the most expensive and least developed area for superstores, there is 1 to every 350 000. Outside London, the ratio drops to 1:150 000 in the more developed areas. This type of saturation reduces the opportunities open for new entrants adopting the classical strategies.

The favourable financial environment of the last decade has supported the investment strategies of the large retailers. The effects of this go beyond support for expenditure on new technology. The value of the larger acquisitions in the UK during the period 1986–7 exceeded £1700 million. The food sector generally has found access to capital for acquisition and investment relatively favourable. In the UK the Nestle/ Rowntree take-over was merely an extreme example of a process which has seen firm like Northern Foods spend over £225 million on acquisitions over the decade. There is, however, nothing rivalling the KKR $25 billion leverage buy-out of Nabisco. The interest in placing a stock market valuation on 'brands' is likely to enhance the value of many leading food producers and distributors.

A number of producer groups have achieved considerable success in building up trade and customer loyalty through effective marketing. This has been achieved with established products, e.g. the success of French apple producers. Innovations, notably the introduction of Kiwi fruit, have benefited from the same improved understanding of marketing. Among retailers, the same learning process has occurred. The creation of a clear identity built around an understanding of customer needs is shaping location, size, store design, presentation and merchandizing decisions. The emergence of marketing as a central element in policymaking coincides with major structural changes in the population and its food-buying habits. These reflect movements in work patterns, population structure and social attitudes.

Throughout Europe and North America the role of women in the workforce, hence their domestic role, is changing. In the 1980s, growth in the numbers in employment in the UK was largely a function of the rapid increase in women entering employment. In North America it is estimated[8] that 'More women in the workforce will mean more dual career families – as many as 75% of all families by the end of the decade vs. roughly 55% now'. In Europe, much of this expansion in the female labour force is accounted for by relatively low skill, low wage, casual employment. It is unlikely that this will continue.

Two contrasting phenomena highlight the dynamics within the female labour force which are likely to change its nature. The first is the change in the structure of the population, notably the reduction in the numbers entering employment for the first time. This contraction will force employers to seek out new sources of labour for higher skill jobs. The largest underutilized group with real skill development potential are women, especially those between the ages of 35 and 55 years. They are likely to have a higher terminal education age than their older compatriots. Investment in education and training for higher skill tasks will be worthwhile as their working life is relatively long. The dual career family may emerge as the norm in the mid-1990s. This will have a marked effect on shopping and domestic catering arrangements. Established providers will find traditional ways of doing business challenged by new conditions.

The second feature partly reflects the same reshaping on the female role in the economy. Women are increasingly important as members of the entrepreneurial population. It is estimated[9] that women-owned business accounts for one in three of all new formations in the UK. In the USA, business receipts from this type of enterprise increased dramatically during the 1980s. This can be seen in most of Europe. In Scandinavia, over a quarter of all owner managers are women. They are breaking out of the retail and services sectors where women business ownership was concentrated. Rates of start-up and ownership are growing in light engineering, new technologies and business services. In the medium term, this type of change is likely to produce supply side changes to match the shifts in buyer behaviour.

The nature of the adjustments which will be required in supplier behaviour are harder to estimate. Some appear to be emerging already. The troubled recent history of convenience store retailing is not likely to prevent the long-term growth and success of the sector. Seven-day, long-hours retailing seems inevitable. Increased levels of customer services, especially at the point of purchase are already demanded. Improved standards of food hygiene and production controls are certain to be expected by an increasingly affluent and discriminating buyer. There may be a change in the food shopping profile. One possibility is a switch away from 'bulk' buying of food towards 'top-up' shopping especially among young married couples and those with mature families.

The pattern may be reinforced by adjustments in the purchase behaviour of other members of the family unit. The drop in the birth rate is likely to have an immediate effect on sales of child- and youth-orientated food products. Volume consumption seems certain to drop significantly. The shift to healthier eating in the wider population may be even more marked among this group as increased purchase discretion and better health education have an effect. The catering industry may be earliest beneficiaries as smaller numbers with more disposable income enter the market. Niche retail outlets targeted on this group have grown in importance in North America. This is likely to be matched in Europe. The problems seen by groups like Sock Shop are not likely to reverse this trend.

The dual career, smaller family environment is modifying the male role in food purchasing. Until recently this was largely an indirect or support role. This is not likely to persist as economic power within the family unit varies more widely over time and between households. The choices men make and the ways in which these are expressed are likely to increase the pressure for improved service and better customer information.

The analysis so far has concentrated on the traditional family unit. The food production, processing and distribution system will face a rapidly evolving client base. The most marked example of this is the increase in number of single unit households. As noted above, it is estimated that one in three households will consist of a single member by the mid-1990s. This may be an underestimate as a combination of later marriages and an ageing population may have a more marked effect on household size. The move towards larger pack units and higher expenditures on each purchase occasion may be reversed.

Changes in population structure are closely related to shifts in social attitudes. The preoccupation with youth which has characterized much of the last 30 years, following the two baby booms of the mid-1940s and early 1960s may be replaced by a preoccupation with maturity or age. The greater prosperity of older age groups which is allied with higher wages as well as better pension and assurance provision will increase their purchase discretion. Trade structures will adapt to meet the new challenges.

Increased scale of operation has been recognized as one of the most distinctive features of the UK food distribution system. The shift towards smaller numbers of larger outlets has characterized the business development strategies of the majority of UK food retailers. In the 21 years to 1982 the number of food retail outlets was halved. There is some evidence that the increased buoyancy of specialist, niche retailing and convenience stores is slowing this rate of decline and stimulating new forms of provision.

Inner city areas redevelopment, allied to a growing interest in 'lifestyle' shopping, has created a major opportunity for the development of niche-orientated food production and retailers. Specialist producers such as California Cake and Cookie and Derwent Valley Foods have emerged to cater for these needs. The revitalization of inner city areas through projects such as the Waverley Market in Edinburgh and the Albert Dock in Liverpool create favourable environments for newly emerging and growing companies to establish a stable commercial base.

Alongside new opportunities there are threats. The future of the convenience store is not likely to be assured through such favourable external developments. The high levels of access to large food retailers which characterizes most of the UK undermines their basic commercial advantage outside inner urban areas. Restrictions on trading hours and a poor image have added to their problems. The right mix has not been achieved in the UK by any of the recent entrants. It would seem that the impasse will only be broken when the image problems are overcome and a clear and distinct customer benefit is achieved.

New approaches may present some answers. Franchising may provide the organizational framework for this type of development. There are presently about 4500 franchised, food and drink outlets in the UK. Their combined turnover exceeds £1 billion

(Ayling, 1988).[10] Much of the early growth has occurred through catering outlets such as Wimpy and Spud-U-Like. So far, none of the UK-based convenience store franchises has achieved a breakthrough in terms of customer awareness.

In the short-to-medium term, choice in the food sector is likely to be dominated by the type of concerns which have been to the fore over the last decade. Innovation and New Product Development activity is likely to increase as producers and retailers respond to changes in eating habits. Wheelock (1986)[11] vividly illustrated the reductions in consumption of established 'basics'. He outlined the problems faced by producers and retailers in adapting to these needs. Producers cannot easily shift from production of potatoes to tomatoes or other growth products.

New product development remains primarily in the hands of the producer/processor. This poses increasing demands on their resource base. The costs of innovation are growing but the likely returns are declining. Very few, new food products are reaching the type of £7–10 million a year turnover need to sustain marketing and development costs. Niche markets almost inevitably mean small volumes. This is unless ranging can be built in or the niche itself expands, e.g. through internationalization. This is an international problem. In the USA only *eight* new food products launched in the period 1982–7 achieved annual sales in excess of $100 million. The contraction in product life cycles can be seen in food markets across the world.

Innovation is an important aspect of the business development of all members of the food production and distribution system. The success of Marks & Spencer in collaborative new product development and positive purchasing is an integral part of the growth of the firm's retail food operations. Other food retailers are likely to follow this route. This will involve greater integration of the retail chain as well as providing a framework for greater differentiation between outlets.

The rapidly changing nature of food industry R&D is a crucial aspect of this. The costs are increasing and the technology is becoming more complex. Biotechnology developments will enable growers to change key features of their crops. These developments are long term and involve high risks. Established new product development, test and launch strategies will need to be re-examined. The nature of these changes will increase wider public concern about the workings of the food industry. Geoffrey Cannon (1987)[12] is not alone in calling for changes in trade practice. Major manufacturers are playing a crucial part. In the USA, H.J. Heinz ordered its suppliers to cease the use of 12 named chemicals on crops grown for its use (Elkington and Hayes, 1988).[13] New enterprises and innovation within existing businesses will emerge to meet many of these demands.

The same pattern of environmental change and the creation of opportunity can be seen in most parts of society. Traditional defences based on cost of entry can be challenged by new types of organization or better management. KKR managed their successful take-over of Nabisco despite the apparent scale advantages of the latter. The growth of Quick-Fit under the leadership of Tom Farmer illustrates how a traditional industry can be reshaped by skilled entrepreneurs. Bob Scott's success with the Palace Theatre in Manchester had an effect beyond the confines of this theatre and the city.

People/personality

Most approaches to the examination of personal enterprise attempt to address the question, 'Can we predict whether someone *has what it takes*?'. This is both an individual and a group issue. Before venturing on a programme or project it is necessary for the initiator to assess her or his capacity to see it through. A simple checklist, based on the US Small Business Administration's criteria,[14] can be used. Score between 0 and 5 depending on strength of agreement. A score of less than 100 suggests that major personal development is needed to cope with the demands of individual enterprise.

	High (5) (4) (3) (2) (1) Low (0)
1. Do you like to make your own decisions?	☐☐☐☐☐☐
2. Do you enjoy being self reliant?	☐☐☐☐☐☐
3. Do you relish competition?	☐☐☐☐☐☐
4. Are you a self starter?	☐☐☐☐☐☐
5. Do you have willpower?	☐☐☐☐☐☐
6. Can you build teams?	☐☐☐☐☐☐
7. Do you plan?	☐☐☐☐☐☐
8. Can you take advice?	☐☐☐☐☐☐
9. Can you adapt to change?	☐☐☐☐☐☐
10. Do you establish schedules of activities?	☐☐☐☐☐☐
11. Do you keep to them?	☐☐☐☐☐☐
12. Can you keep others to schedule?	☐☐☐☐☐☐
13. Do you deal with complex issues well?	☐☐☐☐☐☐
14. Can you deal with ambiguity?	☐☐☐☐☐☐
15. Are you capable of adapting to change?	☐☐☐☐☐☐
16. Can you work long hours?	☐☐☐☐☐☐
17. Are you single minded?	☐☐☐☐☐☐
18. Do you have the physical stamina to deal with the project?	☐☐☐☐☐☐

19. Do you have the emotional strength and resilience to handle the strain? ☐☐☐☐☐☐

20. Will you make sacrifices to achieve your goals? ☐☐☐☐☐☐

21. Are you capable of identifying the skills needed for success? ☐☐☐☐☐☐

22. Do you have them? ☐☐☐☐☐☐

23. Can you fill in any gaps in your skills from elsewhere? ☐☐☐☐☐☐

24. Can you deal with the risk of failure? ☐☐☐☐☐☐

25. Are you skilled at networking? ☐☐☐☐☐☐

26. Can you keep your objectives in view despite distractions? ☐☐☐☐☐☐

27. Do you know your goals? ☐☐☐☐☐☐

28. Can you communicate them to others? ☐☐☐☐☐☐

29. Can you handle several tasks at once? ☐☐☐☐☐☐

30. Do you separate *need to's* from *nice to's*? ☐☐☐☐☐☐

Underlying the questionnaire is a series of propositions about individual enterprise. At the core lies a notion that the person is self reliant, and can make personal decisions, enjoys being self reliant and is not intimidated by competition. Alongside these ought to be the capacity to be a self starter. The enterprising individual does not wait for others to give a lead. This reflects a well-formed and strong will.

Enterprise and closed-mindedness are not the same. Success is likely to depend on the ability to build a team, plan, take advice and adapt to changing circumstances. The ability to realize the potential of a group as well as oneself often separates the winning leader from the failure. The same talent for managing people may come to bear on situations. Schedules of activity are needed and their value lies in keeping to them. This is crucial where some client group is involved. The skill to deal with complexity, ambiguity and change marks the successful out from the competent. It might call for very hard work as the entrepreneur needs to be the backstop capable of carrying-on when others flag. Physical stamina is not enough. Pressure will produce stress. Clients, colleagues and others will look to the leader to resist the pressure to buckle under the strain.

Coping with these challenges calls for a range of personal and organizational skills. Foremost among these is the ability to recognize true priorities. This issue has been emphasized by different writers in various ways. Peters and Waterman[15] talk about successful firms 'sticking to their knitting'. By this they mean that the firm has recognized what matters for its success and making this its overriding concern. Most studies of failure have highlighted the extent to which initiatives which fail lose sight of the main purpose of the effort, pursue secondary goals and run into the ground.

After General Foods lost $100 million on its Gourmet Foods project, Berg[16] commented

> The Gourmet Foods case illustrates the consequences of a failure to understand the true nature of a company and to define its basic purpose and essential needs. The Gourmet Foods failure was primarily the result of General Food's neglect first to codify and then adhere to product policies which would delimit diversification activity and guide the firm into fields where full advantage could be taken of its unique strengths.

It is a view echoed in many of the analyses of the US defeat in Vietnam.

Priorities will change over time but these should be understood and communicated to colleagues. Shaping policy requires time. The process of establishing priorities benefits from time and openness. The greatest gains occur when schedules are established well in advance and the procedure is understood by those involved. Once this is completed 'most management situations benefit from being explicit and decisive'.[17] Sacrifices may be needed to achieve these objectives. They might be personal or institutional.

Assets and liabilities

Some skills are important for success. Often they are personal. Harold Greenen of ITT had a phenomenal memory. The football manager Bill Shankly was able to inspire deep loyalty. Giuliana Benetton of Benetton stimulates creativity. Microsoft's Bill Gates gets the best minds to work together. Marcus Sieff (Marks and Spencer) established and got others to maintain a core business philosophy. President John Kennedy was able to communicate his political vision. Richard Branson of Virgin stimulates enthusiasm. Understanding the key skills needed for success in a venture is the preamble to employing them. Gaps will exist and need to be filled. The Benetton family illustrate how a group can come together naturally: Gilbert Benetton deals with finance, Carlo Benetton production and Luciano Benetton management.

More often, however, external recruitment is needed. Recruitment into any activity involves a commitment on both sides. Many entrepreneurs find this to be the hardest aspect of management. It inevitably involves transferring authority and tasks. Only responsibility cannot be transferred. The failures of others need to be absorbed and accommodated. One of Japan's most successful firms, Matushita Electrical has as its core philosophy: 'If you make an honest mistake, the company will be very forgiving. Treat it as a training expense and learn from it'.

A badly managed response to risk-taking can stifle creativity and enterprise. The fear of failure is a plausible explanation of key aspects of the UK's relative decline this century. It is reflected in an education system in which the vast majority of young people are required to fail in order to sustain the equilibrium of higher education. The banks have been accused of transferring their fear of failure on to the businesses to which they lend. Failure is the ultimate sin under this regime, not an opportunity to learn. This is despite the evidence that restarts have the highest success rates of any type of enterprise. This perspective can permeate the individual's view of him or herself and the enterprise. Fear of failure can explain the low comfort level which persuades British organizations to stop growing and leave markets and opportunities to others.

Need driven

The examination of the reasons why some individuals overcome these barriers while others fail, lies at the centre of research on enterprise. Some authors suggest that the explanation lies in a distinctive feature which exists in a sub-set of the population.[18] Others[19] suggest that most people have the potential but it shows itself in different circumstances. They will respond differently to environmental barriers and opportunities.

Psychological theories of enterprise tend to concentrate on the notion that there is a single trait, group of traits or characteristics of personality which differentiate enterprising individuals from others. McClelland[20] emphasized the high achievement needs of these individuals. They were not content to accept a situation as given. They seek to express themselves by tackling problems and resolving issues others might neglect. In some cases this mirrors their need to lead or achieve prominence. Elsewhere, enterprise and achievement is a response to anxiety. It provides a mechanism for transferring problems and resolving dilemmas. This need to achieve can be realized through all forms of enterprise.

Conclusion

In part the value of these theories to different situations reflects underlying similarities in the processes involved in starting an enterprise. There is the recognition of a need or opportunity. It can be for a new business service. Mrs Steve Shirley started F International because she recognized the need for business services based on 'distributed office work'. This matches Lord Olivier's belief that it was absurd that a nation with the UK's theatrical tradition did not have a national theatre. Bob Geldof stimulated the creation of Live Aid out of a determination to do something about famine in Ethiopia.

These opportunities surround us. They are usually recognized by others beside the initiators. The creators go beyond recognition to action. They are not deterred by rejection.

They are recognized because they act successfully. This calls for individual and group skills. Dr Land took his Polaroid process to Kodak. Their rejection spurred him to create his own business.

The determination of the individual is a necessary precondition for the creation of an enterprise but no guarantee of its success. Mistakes will be made. Unforeseen problems will occur. External challenges will be mounted. The venture will require the drive and the resilience to overcome these. The more effectively resources can be accumulated, integrated, managed and directed the more likely it is that the project will survive and prosper.

Case study

Clearwater Fishfarms

Clearwater Fishfarms was established in 1973 as one of the pioneers in the fish-farming industry. It was founded by Bryan McLain. He had seen fish farming as a new and emerging industry with considerable long-term potential. His first farm was based in the West of Scotland. Initially he had concentrated on brown trout; later he had used his acquired expertise to move into salmon ranching. During the early years of his business he had developed a strong link with a number of important external agencies. These included the Highland and Islands Development Board, the Institute of Aquaculture of Stirling University and the Scottish Salmon Growers Association. The pattern of innovation, flexibility and effective networking helped Clearwater to become one of the largest independent fish farmers in the UK.

The market today

The marketing chain for farmed trout and salmon is divided into several key sectors as described below (R=retail; C=catering; E=export).

Clearwater has generally been very successful at spotting opportunities and developing its business. It was one of the first farmers to build up strong links with a major retailer (Tesco) and has been very active in the Salmon Growers Association. Its links with the university bring in new ideas and bright people. Recently, it has led to opportunities in consultancy. This is largely linked with the expansion of fish-farming in other countries. A project to introduce salmon ranching in the Falklands was the first of these. More recently, work in Tasmania and Malaysia has been won.

Clearwater is now facing a major challenge to its ability to survive and thrive as a major independent concern. This has been caused by a combination of rapid growth in production, increased concentration among processors and slower than expected growth in demand. Farmed salmon output in Scotland increased ten-fold over the decade 1976–85. This was paralleled by a growth in output of trout, albeit at a slower rate. This was not a uniquely Scottish phenomenon. In Norway, in particular, heavy investment in the late 1980s had created an industry which was four times the size of the UK markets. Meanwhile export sales were being hit by greater competition.

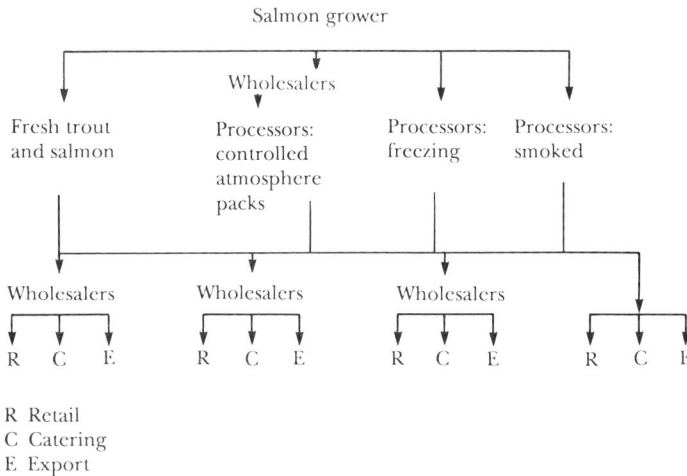

Salmon grower

Wholesalers

| Fresh trout and salmon | Processors: controlled atmosphere packs | Processors: freezing | Processors: smoked |

Wholesalers   Wholesalers   Wholesalers

R C E   R C E   R C E   R C E

R Retail
C Catering
E Export

Figure 4.3

The entry of firms like Unilever, Booker McConnell and Norsk Hydro into the market as farmers and processors had led to significant increases in concentration in the 'industry'. Some observers saw this as an inevitable outcome as the trade moved from the early, rapid growth stage of its life cycle to a more mature slower growth phase. There was a general view that an increase in the rate of failure allied to increased merger and acquisition activity would characterize the industry over the next few years. This type of comment had prompted Bryan McClain to comment, *'Well, we had better be one of the survivors then'*.

Growth in consumption had occurred but at steadily lower prices. Research indicated that:

● most people still do not buy trout or salmon
● higher social groups contain higher percentages of users
● buyers liked what they were currently getting
● buyers saw trout and salmon as occasional purchases.

Among non-buyers:

● over one in three simply did not like fish
● others did not like the 'mess' associated with fish
● others thought trout and salmon were expensive
● they saw all fish as an occasional, not a regular purchase.

Major problems were seem to persist at the wholesaler, distributor and retailer level. Among the most marked were the pressure from the larger retailers for assured quantity and quality. This required significant capital investment. At the same time many processors and traditional wholesalers disliked long-term contracts: *'It's not the way we do business in the fish trade'*.

The current situation

The combination of these events poses special problems for a large independent like Clearwater. They cannot re-trench and revert to farm gate and other informal channels. At the same time they cannot afford costly mistakes if they get their longer-term strategy wrong. They have been approached by one of the large conglomerates about acquisition but the price is far worse than was offered just two years ago. Just last week several small producers approached Clearwater about setting up a joint marketing operation. Their view is that 'if we don't get together we cannot survive'. Bryan had dinner recently with the professor from the university. Although they agreed the market was depressed, his friend argued that he should stick it out and diversify into other fish types and new activities like consultancy.

The task

Advise the board, chaired by Bryan McLain, on the business strategy and related tactics. Go through each of the challenges and make recommendations about the future direction of the enterprise. The recommended choice should be backed by clear recommendations on implementation and likely returns.

References

1. Brooks, J. (1971) *Business Adventures*, London, Penguin, p. 155.
2. Cohan, R. (1989) Contemporary choreography, *Journal of the Royal Society of Arts*, October 1989, pp. 709–12.
3. Kahn, H. and Weiner, A.J. (1969) *The Year 2000*, Toronto, Collier Macmillan.
4. Frank, J. and Wheelock, V. (1988) International trends in food consumption. *British Food Journal*, January/February 1988, 90, no.1, pp. 22–9.
5. Slattery, J. (1986) Current diet and health recommendations – the response of the food industry, *Food Marketing*, **2**, No. 3, pp. 180-6.
6. Black, Sir D. (1986) *Diet, Nutrition and Health*, London, British Medical Association.
7. Food and Agriculture Organization (1986) *World Food Report 1986*, Rome, Italy.
8. Managing now for the 1990's, *Fortune*, September 26, p.34.
9. Carter, S. and Cannon, T. (1988) *Female Entrepreneurs: A Study of Female Business Owners*, Department of Employment, Research Paper No. 65.
10. Ayling, D. (1988) The universe of franchising, *Management Today*, April 1988, pp.115–21.
11. Wheelock, J.V. (1986) Coping with change in the food business, *Food Marketing*, 2, No. 3, pp. 20–45.
12. Cannon, G. (1987) *The Politics of Food*, London, Century.
13. Elkington, J. and Hayes, J. (1988) *The Green Consumer Guide*, London, Gollancz.
14. Small Business Administration (1984) *Feasibility Check-list for Starting a Small Business*, Washington, US Government Printing Office.

15. Peters, T.J. and Waterman, R.H. (1982) *In Search of Excellence*, New York, Harper & Row.
16. Berg T. (1970) *Mismarketing*, London, Nelson.
17. Pascale, R.T. and Athos, A.G. (1981) *The Art of Japanese Management*, London, Penguin.
18. Kets de Vries, M.F.R. (1977) The entrepreneurial personality; a person at the crossroads. *Journal of Management Studies*, February 1977, pp. 34–57.
19. Cannon, T. Creating Entrepreneurs. Proceedings of the Third International Conference on Technical Innovation and Entrepreneurship, IC Institute, University of Texas, Austin.
20. McClelland, D.C. *The Achieving Society*, Princeton, N.J., Van Nostrand.

Chapter 5

Managing an enterprise: the first steps

Enterprise and the risk of failure are inseparable. Initiative would have little meaning if success was guaranteed. Much of the value of enterprise lies in an acceptance that outcomes cannot be predicted perfectly. This requires the individual or the group to take a step which involves risk. There is, however, a difference between calculating the chances of success and taking a foolhardy gamble. The skill lies in underpinning each venture with sound management.

The danger of failure will never be eradicated. The Department of Employment's Training Agency has created a number of enterprise training programmes. Participants have a failure rate of 40%. This compares well with an overall failure rate of 80% among all new businesses within the first three years. This can be compared with the failure rate of new products and brands by large firms. Most contemporary studies[1] put the new product or brand failure rate at between 30% and 60%.

The same pattern can be seen in the Arts. The well-publicized failures of films like *Heaven's Gate* and plays such as *Inadmissible Evidence* are the tip of an iceberg. It is likely that over 90% of all plays, films and other artistic endeavours fail to generate sufficient return to pay off their initial investment. The sciences and engineering show a similar pattern. Although 85% of all doctoral dissertations *that are submitted* pass, less than 20% of all PhD courses started are ever submitted. The UK's history of spectacular research failures is neither unique nor unexpected. These débâcles include the linear induction engine, hydromatic power and fuel cells.

None of these difficulties are arguments against innovation. They serve to illustrate the dangers involved and the gains from better management and early identification of the difficulties. Research into the new product development problems of large established firms illustrates the nature of the difficulties in this area and some of the solutions. Ansoff[2] has indicated the extent to which familiarity is a defence against failure. The risks are greatest in areas in which the firm has least knowledge and familiarity with conditions. *Ansoff's development matrix* identifies an increase in the probability of failure as the organization moves from existing markets and products to new fields.

Products

		Existing	New
Markets	Existing	Market penetration (.3)	Product development (.5)
	New	Market development (.5)	Diversification (.8)

The features which distinguish successful new products from others can be analysed in terms of product and price benefits. Those innovations offering potential customers superior products and lower prices are far more likely to succeed than those which do not deliver these gains. Improvements can take many forms. The item can be easier to use, provide extra features, be more reliable or be better designed. Price advantages include lower unit costs, reduced maintenance, added features for no increase or volume discounts. The less the client gains the lower the likelihood of success. The benefit matrix illustrates this.

Product advantage

		High	Low
Price	High	Radical innovation	Bargain product
advantage	Low	Novel product	Me-too offering

Pioneers often fail to gain the benefits of their originality. The advantage may go to followers who learn from the mistakes of innovators and manage their relationship with clients better. In marketing, the notion of 'poisoned apple marketing' or 'let the other person take the first bite' has been conjured to describe this. It highlights the importance of getting a development right rather than let someone else learn from your mistakes.

Pre-Training

The simplest way to minimize start-up and business development problems is to undertake a programme of pre-training. Surveys of entrepreneurs undertaken by the Department of Employment's Training Agency suggest that this can reduce the probability of failure in the first three years from 80% to under 40%. Studies of different groups and type of enterprise endorse this conclusion. Carter[3] found that the completion of a programme of pre-start training was a clearly identifiable 'success strategy' for successful women entrepreneurs. A solid grounding of research training is widely seen as a crucial factor in successful doctoral study.

The opportunities for enterprise training in the UK are extensive and varied. They range from short courses run by Enterprise Agencies, through the more intensive programmes arranged by the Training Agency, to the enterprise or small business electives included in many undergraduate and postgraduate courses at universities and polytechnics.

Most short courses of the type that last one or two days are more valuable as information or awareness raising sessions. They identify the sources of help or assistance. Longer programmes can be identified and their distinctive features highlighted. Some short courses are designed on a modular basis. This enables the participant to take some of the concepts, apply them and get feedback.

The notion of 'learning through doing' is an especially important feature of enterprise education. It highlights Argyris's[4] notion of the double cycle of learning. Figure 5.1 indicates the way in which the two cycles interact. The first concentrates on the acquisition of knowledge. The second emphasizes its application.

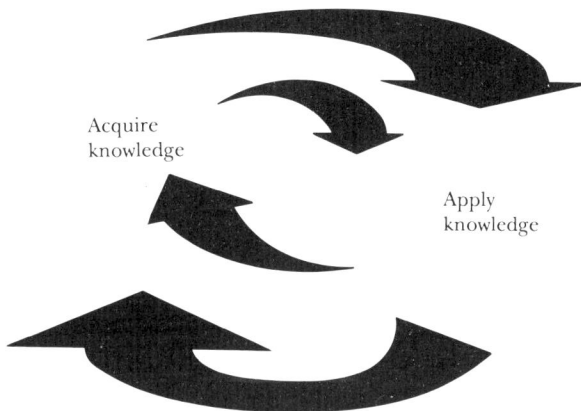

Acquire
knowledge

Apply
knowledge

Figure 5.1   Argyris's double cycle of learning

Longer programmes such as those sponsored in the UK by the Department of Employment's Training Agency include Graduate Enterprise, Firmstart and the Business Enterprise Programme. The surge in interest in self-employment, allied to high levels of employment, led British policy makers to emphasize immediate pre-start-up training. This contrasted with policy in North America and Europe. Programmes in these countries tended to concentrate on early preparation or on-the-job training. The Small Business Institute programmes in the USA helped undergraduates to build up an awareness of the business problems of small- and medium-sized firms through project work. Students were used to undertake specific assignments for firms. These helped the company while providing a learning opportunity for students. The strength of the Chambers of Commerce in Europe has encouraged training bodies to focus on the needs of existing companies.

The last few years saw a convergence of these programmes. The danger of leaving training too late has been recognized in the UK. New venture programmes highlighted the value of early awareness of enterprise and long gestation periods. Research[5] on business formation among graduates indicated:

1. The higher the overall level of awareness, the more likely it is that young people will consider starting their own business.
2. The longer the potential entrepreneur had been considering starting a business the less prone it was to early withdrawal and failure.

A range of initiatives have been introduced to increase this awareness. They include the Technical and Vocational Educational Initiative in schools and the Enterprise in Higher Education Initiative in higher education.

In Europe, the Social Fund of the EEC has endorsed immediate pre-start programmes such as Firmstart. Most countries in the Community have similar schemes underway. In the USA, Small Business Development Centres (SBDCs) have been established in most states. They have taken the lead in shaping short courses for new and existing companies. India and other industrializing countries have tended to concentrate efforts on rural businesses and co-operatives.

More recently, the emphasis has shifted to help for technology or knowledge-based companies. A similar pattern can be seen in much of Asia. Malaysia has used a combination of specialist educational institutions such as MEDEC and development bank finance to shift resources in the same way. Often this is linked to national development plans. Bank Bumiputra and the different institutions of higher education in Malaysia have shifted resources away from rural and co-operative enterprise towards manufacturing to meet the needs of the latest development plan. The same pattern can be seen in other newly emerging countries.

Elsewhere, a broadly similar pattern of training linked to finance can be seen. Often these face difficulties because of the gap that exists between practitioners and educators. Australia has a long record of successful pre-start and new company courses. The Enterprise Workshops project has been particularly effective at bridging the gap between students and practitioners. The Young Achiever Programme (called in the UK, Young Enterprise) has worked with success in many countries.

The appropriate form of training for individuals depends largely on their existing knowledge base and the nature of the enterprise. The projects most likely to succeed are those which have evolved over some time. The formal training should:

- fill in knowledge gaps
- subject ideas to review and peer group assessment
- be focused on implementation
- cover key areas
- lead to a coherent outcome, e.g. a business plan.

A typical course will cover the traditional business management areas of marketing, finance, production and personnel. These should combine with the more immediate concerns of the new business:

- where can I raise start-up finance?
- how do I get the right premises?
- what are my tax liabilities?
- how do I get my bills paid?

- where do I find my first customer?
- should I buy or lease?
- why isn't anyone buying?

The better programmes draw these elements together through the completion of a business plan. The plan itself is useful but secondary. The crucial process is planning. This forces the prospective entrepreneurs to sort and organize their ideas in a coherent form. This will normally be subjected to external appraisal from a combination of tutors, peers, practitioners and intermediaries. The latter two are especially important. Practitioners have been through this process. They know the pitfalls and risks. Intermediaries can be bankers, accountants or customers. They deal with similar proposals daily and have learned to spot the flaws and the wishful thinking. They are, however, only advisers. The ultimate decision in any form of enterprise lies with the individual. Many notable successes were rejected by experts. Most leading authors can point to leading publishers rejecting their work. Galileo was neither the first nor the last scientist to see his ideas rejected by his peers. Entrepreneurs soon learn to shop around for advice, weigh it and make their own decisions.

The sources of ideas/projects

The central decision concerns the nature of the enterprise, the underlying idea and project to be completed. There are many sources of these ideas. Often, they reflect long-standing preoccupations or concerns. Hunter Davies describes the process which led to him writing his book *A Walk Along The Wall* in the following terms:

> I was brought up at one end of the Wall and educated at the other, even to the extent of taking a course in Roman Britain Archaeology. I have to admit that I always found the subject incredibly boring ... Slowly with age, I've come to appreciate that it was a living wall, then as well as now, as this book will try to show.

Much of Hugh MacDiarmid's poetry was shaped by his lifelong love of Scotland.

> Yet thinkin' o' Scotland syne's like lookin'
> Into real deep water whaur the depth
> Becomes sae great it seems to move and swell
> Withoot the slightest ripple, yet somehoo gie's me
> An unco sense o' the sun's stability
> And fills me, slowly, wi' a new ardour and elasticity.
> > MacDiarmid, *A Change of Weather*, 1966

Lloyd Morgan described the process of scientific creativity in terms which would find many echoes elsewhere, in saying 'saturate yourself in your subject and wait'. This view echo's Pasteur's comment 'Fortune favours only the prepared mind.'[6] Edison created his businesses out of the same type of lifelong dedication.

The same pattern is continually repeated. Hobbies, interests, curiosity, research, travel and opportunity spotting provide the base load of ideas from which each enterprise emerges. The discipline which turns an interest into a venture is a mixture of systematic search, adaptation, testing and modification. The base load of ideas from which to draw can be derived from a host of sources. These range from identification of research and development outcomes or foreign search to more informal methods such as brainstorming (Figure 5.2).

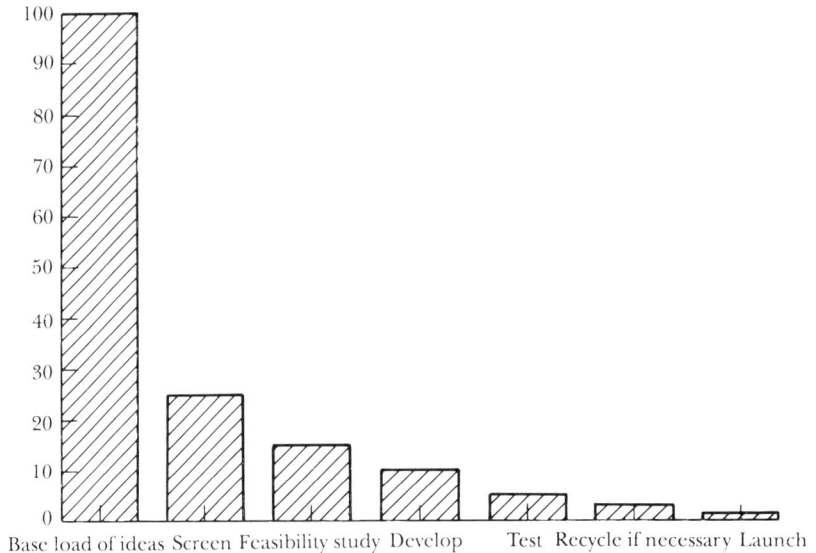

Figure 5.2   The innovation process

Brainstorming and other search processes

In many fields of endeavour the benefits of foreign search illustrate the gains from a relatively formal and systematic approach. On each occasion that social scientists read the foreign literature, they are undertaking a form of foreign search. It might lead to a replication study of US findings or an offer to collaborate on a joint study. This is similar to the company which visits an exhibition in Germany and offers to act as UK agent or licensee for a product seen at the show. The low cost of travel and the ease with which ideas cross borders has accelerated this process over the last century.

Brainstorming and other informal approaches tackle the problems from a different angle. The challenge is the identification of novel projects or developments. Setting up and managing a brainstorming session sheds light on many features of the internal generation of ideas. Rickards[7] has highlighted the extent to which an early stage in all creative activity involves breaking down the mental blocks which inhibit free thinking. De Bono[8] suggests that the barrier lies in a tendency to give either a standard response regardless of circumstances:

> Message to deep-sea diver: '*Surface at once. The ship is sinking*'.

or believe that the solution to a new problem lies in repeating past actions.

> You cannot dig a hole in another place by digging the same hole deeper.

Brainstorming is one of a number of approaches to seeking out novel solutions. Typically it is undertaken in groups with a facilitator. His or her role is to help the group work together and break down any barriers.

The initial requirement is a suspension of disbelief. The process will not work if ideas are criticized or attacked. It is useful to have some technique for achieving this, e.g. Bob Newhart's recording of *Introducing Tobacco to Civilization*. The humour relaxes the group while the product illustrates the curious behaviour which can build markets. Who else but 'Mad Walt' would believe that people could be persuaded to put leaves in their mouth and set fire to them. Participants are then encouraged to produce as many ideas as possible, quantity counts and 'breeds quality'.[5] The group is encouraged to build on the ideas of others. Pace is important. The facilitator will encourage members to expand in both a linear and lateral way. Word associations, themes or radical shifts in direction can be exploited. All judgement is suspended until the session is ended. Only then does the process of selection start. Confidence grows with familiarity. One-off sessions are not as effective as the formation of a regular group.

Screening

The creation of the base load of projects is a low cost activity. Costs grow as projects are developed. The initial screen is typically a fairly arbitrary, elimination process. The criteria must be determined in advance. The organization might be looking to diversify. It would be wrong under these circumstance to reject ideas because they did not fit with existing operations. Elsewhere, the task might be the opposite. There can be absolute criteria. High-cost projects, unethical activities or schemes involving certain risks might be included in the initial screen. The criteria will be developed in parallel with the generation of ideas. The purpose is to identify those projects justifying further investment.

Feasibility study

The identification of a potential project provokes the question; can it be progressed? Research projects often founder because the investigators simply could not hope to complete the work with the resources at their disposal. It is common to see undergraduates identify final-year projects which attempt to measure:

- the effect of advertising on sales
- the impact of sponsorship on political attitudes to cigarette advertising
- sexism in recruitment to senior political posts
- price leadership in the oil industry.

The projects are commendable but each fails to meet the most basic criterion for Normal Science: *is it researchable with the time and resources at our disposal?*

Ideas for new enterprises face the same feasibility barriers. A community group might suggest that there is a need for a community printing service. It would supply similar groups with low-cost printing, perhaps branching out into a community newspaper. Unless the group had access to the capital for equipment and the skills to operate, it is not feasible. Even with these resources, the group might find that the risk of hurting other local printers and costing jobs dissuades them from take-up of the project in the future.

The dominant criteria for a feasibility study are:

- is there a market?
- can we get help from outside?
- is the necessary information available?
- do we have access to the finance?
- do we have the skills to complete the project?
- is the equipment available?
- can we house the scheme?
- can it be completed in the time?
- will it affect other work?

A graduate student might find that no-one will fund the project on 'Lasers in Surgery'. It might be equally hard to find a supervisor. A scheme to publish a directory of current scientific research in universities in West African countries might founder because the information is impossible to gather. A plan for a new science park next to a college might demand far too much money to complete. Consultants might be invited to tender for projects outside their field of expertise. A pioneering product may need specialized equipment that the company cannot afford. A site might not be available for a new shop. An initiative attached to a particular event might be impossible to complete before the occasion takes place. Research could show that the innovation will take most of its sales from the company's existing products. In each case desirable initiatives must meet the test of practicality.

Development

The development process is best viewed in terms of making mistakes in private at low cost. It allows the initiators to adjust the external circumstances while providing the scope to withdraw with the minimum cost. Development gains from a relatively open environment in which information moves on a 'need to know' basis not along lines determined by formal, institutional structures. Burns and Stalker[9] associate this with an organic organizational structure rather than a mechanical or bureaucratic system.

A strong external perspective is useful in the development process. This can involve some form of the technological gatekeeper. This role highlights the importance of extensive, environmental monitoring. The gatekeeper explores extensively the wider context especially parallel or similar work. This is fed into the current initiative on a regular and systematic way. Lessons learnt elsewhere are internalized and mistakes avoided.

The research environment of the technological gatekeeper mirrors the market networks highlighted by Hammarkvist.[10] This work drew out the development benefits which could be gained from active involvement of prospective users and buyers. These yields included lower costs and better adaptation to user needs. Prospective users were willing to share their knowledge. Customer loyalty was increased because they were involved, not merely presented with a *fait accompli*.

It is important to use the development period as part of the selection process. It may be necessary to call a halt to a cherished development. Circumstances might change. Concorde was still under development when it became clear that the Jumbo from Boeing had changed the nature of air travel. Research might highlight a fatal flaw. Early customer research into Corfam, the leather substitute, made it clear that customers found the shoes made from the material very uncomfortable because it did not mould to the shape of their feet. The notion that the 'wish is father to the thought' has deluded many into persevering when withdrawal or a thorough re-examination was needed.

Testing

Pilots and pre-tests are stages in the development of a project which are easily and often fatally dropped. Sometimes, time pressures discourage those involved. Elsewhere the costs and perceived risks are used to justify the neglect of this stage. This does, however, mean that an invaluable opportunity is missed. The costs and risks involved can be controlled through the design and implementation of the test. The experiment gives the initiator the chance to test the idea, project or product in a limited way in a microcosm of the total environment. It provides insight into:

- the go/no-go decision
- the likely level of performance
- possible problems
- the composition of the offering.

The go/no-go decision focuses attention on avoiding total failure. The trial might show that assumptions about wider interest are completely false. The easy confidence shown by many potential entrepreneurs who say *everyone will buy* is often shattered once money is involved. Performance in the field tests may fall far short of the levels predicted in the laboratory. Unexpected barriers can occur. The organizers of an expedition might find that there is no support from sponsors. The test might highlight changes that are necessary for success.

The value of the test depends on the skill with which the experimental situation is constructed. The location, timing and resources should be controlled to replicate the final setting as closely as possible. The performance criteria should be established before the experiment. Adherence to these is important to the integrity of the test and the value of the findings. A thorough review is necessary on completion and before moving to the next stage of the programme.

Recycle and introduce

The test results will produce three types of outcome – cancellation, recycle or launch. Recycling is needed if major adaptations offer real prospects of success. The recycle usually means further work at the development stage. The launch introduces the individual, the project, the business or the product to the wider community. They may be colleagues listening to a presentation. It could be a supervisor judging whether to back the proposal. It might be bankers deciding whether to lend money or a retailer choosing to stock. In each case the decision has two distinct stages. The first is the initial reaction: people are often open to newness and novelty. The follow-up is crucial to long-term success. Continued support and repeat buying must be assured for the survival of an enterprise.

Preparing the ground is vital. Internal and external forces will determine success. All those likely to be affected will need to be involved. The potential entrepreneur will need family and other support over the long haul.

> *Ken*: 'When I started this firm, I started it with twenty-five pounds, a hand-cart and a good woman. Well, over the years the money's devalued, the cart's disintegrated and Gracie? – well, Gracie, God bless her, has departed. Only her name lives on in the firm, Ayres and Graces'.
>
> Alan Ayckbourn, *A Small Family Business*

The individual deciding to leave his job to do an MBA needs the same type of financial and family backing.

There are options about the nature of the introduction. A product might be launched regionally, not nationally. Many small businesses start on a part-time basis. The principals keep their jobs while setting up the enterprise. The legal status of the project should be resolved early. Most small businesses start as sole traders, others as partnerships, while some create limited liability companies. The legal implications extend beyond the nature of the enterprise. A part-time business which tries to use an employer's facilities, money or clients without permission is breaking the law.

The title, name or identity provide clues to the nature and desired outcome. This may be original. 'One Price Clothing' stores combined originality with a very clear description of its basic proposition. Others look to established names. A product might be relaunched under an established brand name. Some new businesses start by purchasing an existing firm. It might be a company they know. *The Times, Guardian,*

Financial Times, Dalton's Weekly and *London Weekly Advertiser* regularly advertise businesses for sale. Business transfer agents and estate agents have details of companies for sale. Resources will need to be mobilized to maximize the chance of success. The 'window of opportunity' is often quite small. Publishers estimate that 70% of the sales of a novel will occur in the first three months. A fad might pass through its entire life-cycle in less time.

Planning

Planning is the process of shaping priorities and programmes to achieve specific outcomes. Plans provide the coherent framework against which decisions can be measured. All those involved in an operation can use the plan to assess their performance and seek policy guidance. Underpinning the plan are the strategies and tactics that will be used to direct the enterprise. Generally, there is a need to weigh different interests and make choices about resource allocation. The strategic plan will call for the acceptance of certain options and rejection of others.

> 'In the meantime,' he continued, 'formulating policy means making choices. Once you make a choice you please the people you favour but you infuriate everyone else. This is liable to end up as one vote gained, ten lost.
>
> Jay, A. and Lynn, J., *Yes Minister*, Vol. 2,[11] p. 430

Plans have several common characteristics:
- they are working documents
- they gain their value from use
- they benefit from simplicity especially in execution and communication
- they incorporate strategic and tactical elements
- there are three core components – preparation, implementation and evaluation.

Within this framework the precise form depends on the nature and complexity of the enterprise and the particular needs and skills of those involved. Planning tends to be hierarchical; the plans for parts or activities within the enterprise deriving from the overall project or business plan. The following structure has been found to work in many situations.

The audit of resources reviews the capacity which exists to create the enterprise or complete the project. It surveys the *Strengths* and *Weaknesses* of the venture and the *Opportunities* and *Threats* facing it. This type of *SWOT analysis* defines the objectives which can be realistically achieved. It identifies the strategies which best match the capabilities of the enterprise and the needs of the environment.

Few organizations can handle many objectives. Most find four or five primary goals enough. They should be actionable, communicable, quantifiable (if possible) and consistent. The strategy describes the overall approach that will be adopted to achieving these objectives. The tactics are the specific tools that will be employed to deliver the strategy.

Expenditure is needed to convert plans to action. The budgets indicate how much

The audit of resources

↓

Statement of objectives

↓

Define strategy

↓

Identify tactics

↓

Allocate budgets

↓

Schedule activities and expenditure

↓

Research

↓

Evaluate

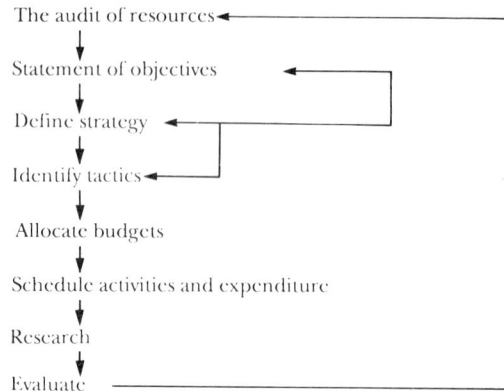

Figure 5.3   The planning process

is being spent, for what and when. The ubiquitous spreadsheet has made the process of budgetary planning simpler and more flexible than in the past. The effective enterprise is likely to be the learning enterprise. Research into future needs and evaluation of past performance are integral features of this type of organization.

Failure!

Plans reduce risk but provide no guarantee against failure. Recognition that the initiative might fail is an aspect of all enterprise development. Withdrawal strategies should be considered at an early stage. Normally, these will minimize the risks of catastrophe and maximize the opportunities to gain from the experience. The warning signs of failure are easy to recognize. They include: persistent failure to meet schedules; refusal by suppliers or helpers to provide more aid; increased rejection or failure rates; over-exposure of assets and increased reliance on panaceas.

These can be recognized in the students who will flunk their projects and entrepreneurs whose businesses will fold. The student will start running out excuses for missing tutorials. The entrepreneur will be juggling his or her production to satisfy the most vocal customer. Suppliers will cease delivery and tutors will stop rescheduling meetings. The papers which are presented will be thin and full or error. Reject rates will increase. The massive new order which will turn the business around is as unlikely to occur as the extension on the project.

The enterprise going into liquidation has several options. Ideally, the process is recognized in time. The activity can be terminated with creditors paid off and some assets retained. This may arise when the entrepreneur recognizes change early. The enterprising individual who produced compilation records, i.e., LPs made up from previous 'hits', closed this business and moved into skateboards when record companies stopped selling the rights. He made a large profit. There was even more profit when the skateboard business was closed at the first sign of falling demand. In each case the end of the fad was recognized for a timely withdrawal. Scott has suggested that over two-thirds of all business closures are voluntary and leave no bad debts.

The voluntary liquidation of a limited liability company requires the assent of 75% of shareholders. The insolvency of a sole trader or partnership makes the individual responsible for all the liabilities of the enterprise. In all cases, the best strategy for reducing risks and costs is to seek the best advice possible from outside sources.

Enterprise and the risk of failure are inseparable. Initiative would have little meaning if success was guaranteed. Much of the value of enterprise lies in an acceptance that outcomes cannot be predicted perfectly. This requires the individual or the group to take a step which involves risk. There is, however, a difference between calculating the chances of success and taking a foolhardy gamble. The skill lies in underpinning each venture with sound management.

Conclusion

Success in any enterprise is largely shaped by the early groundwork and initial set-up. Personal preparation through training and research dovetails with the groundwork invested in the venture. There may be an element of luck which can surprise others.

> Behind every successful man there stands an amazed woman.

Effective preparation depends in large part on the skills which are applied to learning from others. This partly explains the high start-up and success rates of businesses founded by people with a background in small business. Large firms, notably Hewlett-Packard, deliberately nurture an enterprise culture. Their former employees have high success rates. The ability to learn from others and take advice lies at the centre of effective networking. Extensive networks provide the best source of early opportunity spotting and danger avoiding. The danger of failure will never be eradicated. But a secure foundation for the initiative minimizes these risks while providing the underlying strength to withstand difficulties and exploit opportunities.

Case study

A new product for Promex

Company background

Soon after the War four young men met together to discuss the commercial possibilities of a range of measuring and recording instruments. All had been concerned in the development and use of these instruments in the forces.

It was at this meeting that Promex Ltd, was born. The company went into production in unpretentious premises with a limited range of products. In a year it had a select reputation amongst the cognoscenti for producing instruments of exceptional quality.

The four founders of Promex – Peter Arrow, John Mortar, Bill Crown and Edward Hargreaves – had come together in the first place because they liked one another and had many values in common. As the firm developed and they learned more of each other's abilities, it became apparent to them that in many ways they formed an exceptionally well balanced team. John Mortar was a creative research man of the highest order – as the firm grew, he was naturally made Director of Research. Peter Arrow and Bill Crown were respectively interested in production and engineering problems, and later became Production Director and Director of Engineering. Edward Hargreaves had exceptional commercial flair, and was, from the beginning, very much interested in problems of administration. These abilities, together with the fact that he had some private money, ensured that by common consent he became Managing Director.

Hargreaves wanted Promex to grow, and he continuously sought to increase sales and to develop new products, Growth, to him, meant creating a healthy organization full of opportunity and challenge. He was not seeking great profits, but he was profoundly interested in establishing a vigorous company which could break new ground in a difficult technical field, and which would offer the possibility of real achievement to all who joined it. Products of the highest quality were an essential feature of such an organization. Similarly, Hargreaves' fellow directors could see that an organization of the sort he hoped to build would foster the high standards they demanded.

For a few years, Promex's visions were limited by lack of funds. Then, however, Hargreaves inherited a considerable fortune. He at once invested £100,000 in the company and for some years afterwards enabled the company to obtain overdrafts on his personal guarantee. With this, the first big strides in expansion and product development became possible. The market was certainly there. The demand for the type of instruments which Promex made was growing rapidly and seemed likely to expand almost as fast as customers became aware of the potentiality of these instruments.

However, in this field both expansion and the development of new products were costly. True to Hargreaves' vision, Promex began to grow – but it did not begin to distribute large profits. There has never been any change in the company's broad financial policy of devoting as much money as possible to research and development.

The developments of the next few years were extensive in many directions. Thus, for example, as the engineering work increased the machine shop grew and then began to accept outside contracts to make use of any temporary spare capacity. In turn, these contracts warranted purchase of machines in anticipation of Promex's own needs.

In the 18 months after the company came into money, two senior appointments were made. Sam Gorringe joined as Company Secretary. As a chartered accountant, he brought with him the expertise to help in the application of Hargreaves' financial policies to the different phases of Promex development. Then Edward Pettifer joined as Marketing Director with the specific assignment of developing marketing policies and the sales department. Hargreaves saw that much must depend on developing sound long-term marketing policies and he went to considerable trouble to persuade

Pettifer to join the organization. In fact, he had to persuade Pettifer that Promex, which then employed 150 people, could offer him a more interesting future than the senior job in a large organization which he then held. By the time Pettifer joined, he was convinced of this, and he brought great enthusiasm to his task of developing marketing policies and creating the sales department. He soon appointed a Sales Manager, Jim Left, who shared his ideas, and the two of them set about developing a distinctive selling policy. Under their guidance, Promex has undertaken only a little prestige advertising and has relied mainly on a force of highly qualified technical salesmen who develop almost a consultant relationship with many customers. From the beginning, these salesmen have been kept well informed of plans for new products, partly through regular briefing sessions and partly through informal discussions which their technical ability has enabled them to maintain with the company's research men. To create the market for completely new product lines, they arouse customers' interest by discussing with them well in advance of their appearance – and often, indeed by explaining their function and potential – and by directing attention to the exhibition at which Promex models will appear.

The salesmen's technical knowledge of company products and of customers' needs has meant that they have sometimes been able to contribute new ideas for development, and both Pettifer and Left are given to referring to the sales staff as the company's 'antennae'. Another feature of Edward Pettifer's marketing policy is the store he has always set on the company's ability to show interesting new models at important exhibitions.

In passing, it may be remarked that Pettifer and Left were highly typical Promex appointments. Wherever possible, Hargreaves and the other founder directors used to bring in people to tackle particular assignments for which they could be given considerable responsibility. They would define the assignment carefully, take great pains over the selection of the applicant who seemed most able to undertake it, and then give him as free a hand as possible. In general, delegation was carried to great lengths and managers were judged to a large extent by results. Those who succeeded were generously rewarded by promotion and salary increases.

This policy, which tended to appear in appointments throughout the company, was an integral part of the general atmosphere of challenge and interest in rapid and effective development which the directors sought to foster in all departments. Thus, whilst Edward Pettifer and Jim Left were developing the Sales side, Production and Engineering were working immensely hard to meet orders for established products, and Research was at work on a flow of new ideas, most of which poured from the fertile brain of John Mortar.

In particular, Mortar's method of working furthered the Promex philosophy. He would pick up suggestions for new products from all sources, and work furiously on any which involved some technical problems which intrigued him. As he saw the solution to the problem, he would prepare a case for the development of the product.

If he obtained the Board's approval of the new product he would hand the whole idea, with the solution to any technical difficulties broadly indicated, to one of his research staff. This left him free to work on the next idea and meant that his research staff still had a good deal of creative work to do.

An early suggestion of his was for the development of a uniscan.

Development of the uniscan

The suggestion that Promex might develop a uniscan arose out of John Mortar's post-war experience. In the Services he had worked briefly with an instrument known as a multiscan. This instrument recorded, in the form of dial readings, information from three sources simultaneously. It was manufactured by one company, Gradalls, which held a Government contract to supply all multiscans to the Services. Gradalls had begun production of multiscans in the early 1930s. The means by which the multiscan collected information from three sources simultaneously had been discovered by Gradalls' research engineers and was still protected by patent.

By the end of the War, Gradalls had accumulated much valuable experience in the production of multiscans, whilst the many uses to which these instruments were put by the Services indicated their commercial possibilities. Gradalls set out to develop the commercial market and did so with considerable success.

It was John Mortar's conviction, however, that the multiscan was an unnecessarily elaborate instrument for many of the tasks which it was required to carry out. He had considered the functions performed in the Services and in commercial organizations, and had concluded that a much simpler instrument, capable of recording information from only one source at a time, would perform the great majority of these functions just as well. At the Board meeting soon after Promex began expansion in earnest, John Mortar raised the question of challenging Gradalls' multiscan monopoly by producing and marketing a simpler instrument which he proposed to call a uniscan. He discussed the uses of a uniscan and pointed out that where a multiscan would represent a major advance in complexity on the general range of products the company now produced, the uniscan would not be nearly so great a change. It would, however, be somewhat more complicated than many current products and so would provide the company with valuable training for the future.

The directors debated the many difficulties involved in challenging Gradalls, but they were impressed by Mortar's analysis, and also by his statement that the Government was now considering a plan for the gradual replacement of multiscans in service use. They agreed that he should try to obtain a Government contract to develop a uniscan for the Services.

Mortar succeeded in doing this and with such outside assurance of the potentials of the uniscan, Promex went ahead. For a year the company worked under Government contract producing an instrument which performed a simpler task then the multiscan, but which improved it in various ways. The directors were sufficiently happy with the design to negotiate with the Government for the commercial rights and then to put the instrument on the market. Their optimism seemed justified, for two years later Promex sales had mounted to one-fifth of Gradalls. This was a remarkable achievement in view of the fact that Gradalls still had the name and was selling the multiscan at a price below that of the uniscan. The uses found for the uniscan seemed ample justification for John Mortar's view that a simpler instrument could perform many of the tasks previously assigned to the multiscan.

Nevertheless, the sales department was not entirely happy. Jim Left, in particular, kept pointing out that Promex's sole advantage lay in the quality of the uniscan design. Although results so far had justified the directors' policy of maintaining high standards of design, there was no saying how long the success would be maintained. It was very surprising, he insisted, that even when Promex had entered the commercial market with the new instrument Gradalls had not attempted to make any improvements in the design of the multiscan. They must still be presumed liable to do so at any time and meanwhile the low price of the multiscan did not help Promex's sales staff. It was not at all easy to sell a relatively simple instrument for a higher price than its more complex and versatile competitor. He was soon urging that Promex should make its own multiscan. At Board meetings, Edward Pettifer supported his subordinate's views to the extent of insisting that uniscan costs must be brought down, and periodically raising the question of a Promex multiscan. But at first the other directors agreed with John Mortar that sales so far only demonstrated that there was still a big market for the uniscan. Besides, the Research Department, which would initially be most affected by any decision to develop a multiscan, was fully occupied with other promising projects. The company was still growing fast and there were many other matters to preoccupy the Board.

Development of the multiscan

Jim Left did not give up, however. He and his sales staff began a campaign to interest people in the possibilities of a multiscan, which took the form of steady lobbying in all individual encounters. At first the Research Department staff resisted it because they shared John Mortar's opinion that since the uniscan could do most of the work of the multiscan, the latter was largely unnecessary. Moreover they pointed out that the only established method for developing a multiscan was protected by Gradalls' patent. Anyway, all the personnel and resources of the department were fully committed for the time being.

However, Mortar's attention was caught at last when a member of his staff returned from America with news of attempts to develop a multiscan by a new method. Theoretically, this method would make possible the development of a multiscan which could receive information simultaneously from a number of sources. The difficulty lay in developing receptors capable of maintaining very fine discrimination over acceptable periods of time. If this difficulty could be overcome, it would make possible the development of a multiscan with great market potential which would in no way infringe the Gradall patent.

It was the kind of difficulty which intrigued John Mortar and he was turning it over in his mind when rumours reached him of British attempts to develop new types of multiscan. These were dramatically confirmed when one company displayed a new type of multiscan at an exhibition. Mortar and Jim Left went to see it together. Its performance was poor, and Mortar came away convinced that Promex could do better. A month later he arrived at a Board meeting with a well-argued case for the development of a Promex multiscan and with the suggestion that it should be shown at a forthcoming international exhibition. This exhibition would be the first important exhibition to be held after the display of the multiscan produced by the rival company, and the directors were particularly impressed by the advantages of showing a Promex multiscan on such an occasion. John Mortar outlined some ideas he had for tackling the technical problems involved in producing an instrument which would not infringe the Gradall patent, and suggested that it was now reasonable for the company to think in terms of producing this more complicated type of instrument. Although he had hitherto consistently argued against the development of a Promex multiscan, the new circumstances provided a reason for his change of view. His current arguments were in line with Promex general policy and he was of course strongly supported by Edward Pettifer. After some discussion, Hargreaves and the other directors agreed that he should go ahead. This time, however, his assignment was to produce, not a simplified version of a well-known instrument, but a model of a highly complicated instrument involving a still experimental technique, in time for an international exhibition just six months away.

He tackled the project with the enthusiasm he always showed for a challenging new venture, setting all the other plans aside, and in four weeks he did, in fact, produce a design which overcame the major difficulty in the instrument's receptors. Following his usual procedure, he then handed everything over to one of his senior research staff, Andrew Munro, and told him to pick a team from the department and go ahead and produce a working model within five months.

In order to do this, Andrew Munro had himself to lay aside all other work. But he, too, saw the multiscan as an exciting challenge. He and his team entered on a gruelling schedule of work in an effort to produce the multiscan in the required time.

When the project came his way, Munro had been with Promex for nearly two years. He was a man who particularly appreciated the company's (and John Mortar's) habit of throwing people a challenging task and rewarding them according to performance. Working in such circumstances, he had built himself a reputation as a talented and thorough designer and he intended to turn out a first-class instrument. In the course of working on Mortar's design he saw several ways in which it could be improved. He appreciated Mortar's skills in overcoming the major technical difficulty but felt that in other ways Mortar had kept too closely to the uniscan design. He mentioned these points to Mortar, expecting to be told to effect the improvements. Mortar, however, was aware of the importance placed on making the exhibition date and defended his own design on the grounds that its resemblance to the uniscan would facilitate production. For example, the operatives were used to working on the uniscan, but a radical change in design would involve problems of retraining. Everyone outside the small team actually working on the multiscan emphasized the need for speed, and indeed, Munro had barely time to assemble the instrument, let alone modify its design, in the period allotted to him. He worked with an increasing feeling that he was having to subordinate engineering integrity to the demands of expediency.

Nevertheless, he and his team did produce a working model in time for the exhibition. They knew very well that it was untested and had many limitations. One general fault of the design became particularly apparent the night before the exhibition and during the exhibition itself – it was that some of the parts were very difficult to reach for repair and maintenance. The engineers who remained with the model at the exhibition kept it going when various snags developed only with great difficulty. As the exhibition date had drawn nearer, and when it finally came, Munro had kept insisting to everyone he talked with that many difficulties had still to be worked out, and reminding them that the multiscan was a very much more complex instrument than the uniscan had been. He frequently said that he wanted the exhibition over so that he could perfect the design.

Although these statements seemed to be accepted, they did not detract from the fact that the Research Department had produced a working model of a multiscan which represented a technical advance on any other multiscan currently available, and had done so within six months, in time for the exhibition.

It was hailed by the company as a great achievement, and all the directors came to see it. Munro found that he and his team were receiving general acclaim, in the Promex tradition, and that he himself was being held responsible, and indeed highly praised, for producing a model of which he did not entirely approve.

The directors were greatly impressed by the model and so too were potential customers, many of whom had heard advance news of the multiscan from Promex technical sales staff. After the exhibition, Andrew Munro was extremely surprised to learn that in spite of his exhortations a number of orders had been accepted for the multiscan. It appeared that John Mortar had indeed expressed some doubts about this, but the other directors, in particular Hargreaves and Pettifer, had overruled him by emphasizing the importance in terms of prestige and finance in accepting orders. It also appeared that when customers inquired about prices and delivery dates, Peter Arrow had made some calculations based upon the time and money it had taken to produce the present model and upon the normal uniscan production times. As a result he had tentatively offered delivery in three months and had similarly fixed a price. Thus it happened that Munro, hoping to overhaul the multiscan design slowly and thoroughly, was told to go ahead and overcome any remaining difficulties there might be as fast as possible.

Production of the multiscan

The news that orders for the multiscan had been accepted, and that he was required to produce a trouble-free model as quickly as possible, seemed to Andrew Munro to be yet further proof that factors of expediency were receiving much more consideration in decisions about this project than were the principles of sound engineering and development. He felt that his warning had been ignored even by John Mortar, who was best able to understand the situation, and that if he went back to Mortar now he would only be reminded once again of the importance to company prestige of producing the instrument on time. Meanwhile, the multiscan, with all its headaches, had become associated with his name. Thinking he could get little help from his director, he decided to try to cut himself and his team off from the outside harassments as much as possible, and to work steadily on the basic design problems which remained in the multiscan.

In two months, he and his team had produced some important modifications in the basic design. But they had not solved all the problems and they had not worked without interruptions. The works manager, Ted Carrington, with his eye on Peter Arrow's delivery dates, had begun asking when he could expect the model a fortnight after Munro had begun work, and his inquiries had grown steadily more frequent and insistent. After a month, George Drew began asking if he could take over the design to prepare it for production. George Drew had joined Promex some months previously as manager of the new Production Development Section in the Production Department. This section was to prepare models for the production line, and George Drew was anxious to prove its value to Carrington. Besides, he was an experienced development engineer and his admittedly brief examination of the multiscan as shown at the exhibition had convinced him that his section could alter its design in various ways which would simplify production.

At first, Andrew Munro took little notice of these requests. They came from people whom he felt could have little understanding of the problems of the multiscan, and he was persuaded that he must turn out a first-rate design of an instrument which was very much more complicated than anything Promex had tackled so far. He realized that this instrument was going to make quite new and different demands on the department involved in its production, and this made him dismiss without discussion as entirely unrealistic any idea of trying to keep to the original delivery dates.

Meanwhile, however, George Drew had convinced Carrington that he could improve on the design to help production, and Carrington, when he felt he could not wait another day, took the problem to Peter Arrow. This was on a Tuesday. John Mortar had left for Scotland the previous day to address a conference and visit some research establishments. Arrow spoke to Hargreaves, who agreed the problem was urgent, but did not wish to bring Mortar back if this could be avoided. There then began a series of phone conversations between Mortar and Arrow and Mortar and Munro, as a result of which Mortar concluded that Drew might indeed be able to do some work on the general design, while Munro carried on with his present work on certain components. Munro was therefore ordered to hand over the design to Production and Arrow immediately gave Drew instructions to make any alterations he saw fit to prepare it for production. Munro continued to work at the problems of the components. He had commented in his phone conversation with Mortar that the final form of these components would affect the design of various neighbouring parts, but had the feeling that once again Mortar was underestimating the implications of this in the interest of expediency. Altogether he was in no mood to take his problems to Mortar when the latter returned from Scotland. Meanwhile, George Drew and his team began the task of preparing the designs for production, and when they had worked on it for a month Carrington decided production must begin. It was now four months after the close of the exhibition.

Production thus began with Research still working on the design of components and Production Development still struggling with production problems. Drew himself very soon became well aware of the complexities of the multiscan: he and his relatively inexperienced team ran into great difficulties and at last he came back to Munro for help. Thereafter Munro or one of his team was often working with the Production Development Section.

All these design problems greatly added to the difficulties of producing an instrument which was in any event much more complex than other Promex products. The Production Departments were having to accept modifications even as they learned to undertake quite new operations. Work was accordingly very slow and labour costs extremely high. The first batch of multiscans began coming off four months after the date Peter Arrow had given for delivery. The design was insufficiently proven and in use revealed a number of shortcomings. In fact, a large number of the first 150 multiscans broke down within a month of delivery to the customer and they all had to be recalled for modification at considerable cost and inconvenience. Only customers' tolerance of Promex's difficulties in producing a new design prevented cancellation of orders. Fortunately thereafter matters began to improve. This was partly due to Production's increasing familiarity with its task, and partly because the design problems were at last being settled. Munro's own work was bearing fruit and he was now aided by other engineers in the Research Department who had been assigned work on the development of a multiscan for Service use. John Mortar had begun negotiations for this second Government contract soon after Promex had shown its multiscan at the exhibition. He had traded on the success of the uniscan and the new principles embodied in the Promex to gain a contract gradually to replace all the obsolete multiscans at present in service use. The Service specifications arrived as the Promex multiscan was going into production and work on the Services model resulted in some important modifications which were fed into the commercial design.

None of the improvements, however, could be said to have resulted from experience of the instrument in use. Nothing was being learned from the many difficulties which customers were experiencing with the early models.

At Promex, customers' requests for help had always been dealt with by whoever seemed most appropriate for the particular task. When the multiscans began to break down, engineers might be sent from Munro's team, from Drew's section or even from the Production Department, depending on the type of problem the customer described. In informal discussion, these men mentioned many causes of trouble, ranging from basic design to customer's ignorance.

The discussions made it clear that a great many things could go wrong with a multiscan, but they did not point to any common or general problems. When Munro complained to Carrington that he could not get any systematic information about how the machines were working, Carrington listened sympathetically and instructed all in his department to send Research full reports of their visits to customers. Munro began to receive varied and sometimes lengthy reports which he found of very little use.

Sequel

Edward Hargreaves and all the directors and managers involved took a serious view of the difficulties which developed in the course of producing the multiscan. They considered themselves lucky not to have had any orders cancelled, and did not assume that customers would show the same tolerance if they should run into comparable problems with other instruments in the future. Hargreaves instigated a careful analysis of how the situation had arisen, and held a series of meetings about it. The conclusions arrived at contributed considerably to the making of the following decisions:

(a) To concentrate the attention of the Research Department on applied research and the preparation of basic designs and models.
(b) To take the Production Development Section out of Production and make it an independent Development Department responsible for the development of all models received from Research up to the first batch of production models.
(c) To establish a separate Service Department responsible for handling all customers' queries and complaints and also for maintaining adequate servicing records.
(d) To prepare estimates of time schedules for research and production much more carefully and systematically.
(e) To set up training schemes to improve knowledge and working performances of all production workers to facilitate the introduction of changes in working methods.

So many developments, in fact, could be linked with the multiscan experience that, looking back on it, all the people concerned are inclined to describe it as a milestone in the development of the company.

Published with the generous permission of The Acton Trust.

References

1. *State of Small Business; A Report of the President* (1983), US Government Printing Office.
2. Ansoff, I. (1968) *Corporate Strategy*, Harmondsworth, Penguin.
3. Carter, S. and Cannon, T. (1988) Women in Business, *Employment Gazette*, vol. 96, no. 10, October, pp. 565–71.
4. Argyris (1952) *Reasoning, Learning and Action: Industrial and Organization*, San Francisco, Jossey-Bass.

5. Cannon, T., Rosa, P. and McAlpine, A. *Career Orientation Towards Enterprise*, Stirling Scottish Enterprise Foundation, Working Paper no. 05/89.
6. Koestler, A. (1966) *The Act of Creation*, Pan.
7. Rickards, T. (1988) *Creativity at Work*, Gower.
8. De Bono, E. (1978) *Opportunities*, London, Penguin.
9. Burns, T. and Stalker, G. (1966) *The Management of Innovation*, London, Tavistock.
10. Hammarkvist, K. O. (1983) *Markets as Networks*, Marketing Education Group, Annual Conference.
11. Jay, A. and Lynn, J. (1984) *The Complete Yes Minister*. London, BBC.

Chapter 6

Managing the enterprise: the on-going process

The creation of an enterprise, the shaping of a strategy, the production of a plan – together they mark the end of the beginning in management. The true test of the individual and the group lies in using these, to link internal operations to an external environment, in ways which are mutually beneficial. This will need to be achieved against a background of constant change. The movements can be global such as the shift in economic power from Europe and North America to East Asia or the widespread recognition of the threat to the environment. These affect all types of individual or institutional enterprise. Locally, changes in the pool of available labour or shifts in attitudes to art and design can have a similar influence on a programme or activity. Ventures adapt and respond to endure.

Survival depends on the success with which the enterprise meets the needs of those people with a stake in its existence. These stakeholders can include owners, investors, employees and customers. All put something into the undertaking and expect some form of return. Investors look for a cash return through dividends or increased asset values. Employees will seek job satisfaction and wages. The leader or manager's task involves balancing these interests 'while creating a true whole which is greater than the sum of its parts'.[1] The more complex the organization, the greater the number of stakeholders, the harder it is to balance these interests and meet these demands.

The private tutor helping a student work for an exam has a limited number of stakeholder responsibilities. The parents will expect their child's performance to improve. The tutor and her dependants require a certain level of pay. The student probably wants to balance interest and enjoyment in the study with better grades. The challenge facing a Vice-Chancellor and his or her colleagues is very different. There are many stakeholders. They include government, other members of the community, academic peers, students, industry, academic staff, non-academic staff, political and social groups, banks and the media.

In some areas of work the interests of most will coincide. All should be committed to ensuring that students realize their full potential through the studies they follow.

There are, however, many areas in which conflict can occur. It can happen between groups. Academic peers may place a powerful emphasis on the research being undertaken. They will give prestige to those staff with the largest number of publications in academic journals. Students might place a far higher premium on teaching, tutorial support and willingness to help them. The renown of the professor might be less welcome than his or her availability. The graffiti, referring to a famous local professor, found at one university epitomizes this.

> 'What is the difference between ... and God? God is everywhere, ... is everywhere but here!

Discord may exist between sub-groups within a body of stakeholders. Some academic staff might emphasize the importance of traditional academic publications while others will highlight the value of patents or income generation. Similar debates affect all types of organizations.

The enterprise life cycle

Organizations evolve over time. The broad pattern can be related to the life cycle of the enterprise as it shifts from the individual or entrepreneurial to the corporate (Figure 6.1).

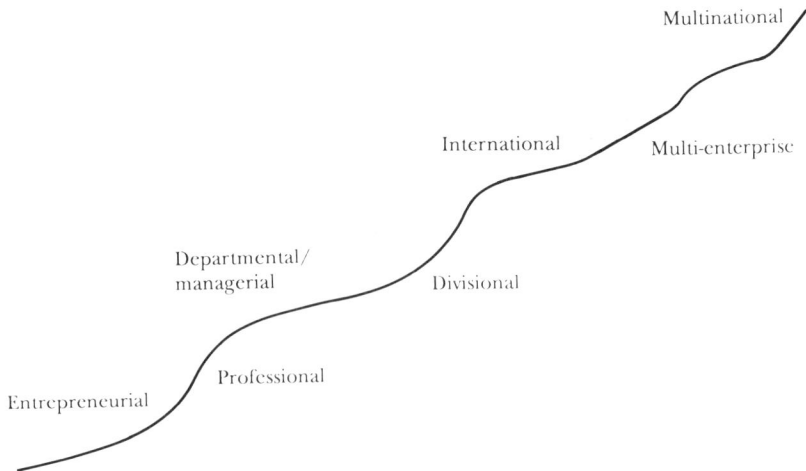

Figure 6.1   The enterprise life cycle

The entrepreneurial phase occurs when the enterprise is shaped by the drive and commitment of one person or a group. Their ideas and energy shape its work. The venture centres on them. Growth poses problems. Issues arise which are outside their competence. In order to survive, new expertise is needed. The process of professionalization involves bringing in outside skills in fields such as finance. Often, the immediate stimulus for this is the requirement to meet statutory or legal obligations. The accounts may need to be published. VAT registration may be necessary.

The use of professionals does not require significant delegation of authority. The creator(s) of the enterprise usually retain control of policy and implementation. Further growth makes this hard. Parts of the organization require delegated authority to operate effectively. Their operations have an inner cohesion. Departments emerge and managers require control of their operations. Further development might see internally coherent sub-divisions emerge. This can occur because new activities develop which require operational autonomy.

The benefits of greater independence might outweigh the gains from scale. ERF, the lorry maker, found this in its dealings with its plastics operations. Orginally, plastics production was introduced to produce panels for lorry cabs. After several years, two sources of tension emerged. The department responsible for manufacturing claimed that it was possible to buy panels on the open market more cheaply than the unit prices offered internally. In part, this reflected the 'overheads' imposed by head office. The plastics division claimed that they were getting better prices when selling spare capacity outside than were offered inside. This reflected the different pattern of production. The unit-by-unit production of trucks did not fit neatly into the process production of plastics. The firm resolved this by creating two separate operating divisions. Each was expected to be a profit centre in its own right.

Further expansion may lead to a greater international dimension to operations. This, in turn, may require the creation of separate enterprises within the one organization. In many countries the pressure for this comes from government. Joint ventures and local affiliates are created to meet these demands. Eventually, this can loosen the links between the organization and its original home. The multinational firm seeks to operate in most markets as if each is a 'home' market. The nature of the enterprise, the expectations of its stakeholders and its objectives, evolve and change to reflect these changes. Two issues are consistent. The first, is the need to adapt to change. The second, is the importance of those people who interpret the different signals and shape the vision of the enterprise.

Change

Change dominates modern society. It affects most aspects of the venture. It can be large, external and complex. A new technology might emerge which transforms the environment. It can be small, local and simple. A new grading scheme might be introduced on a course. Each case call for the same broad disciplines. These are:

- the existence of change is recognized
- the features of the adjustment are diagnosed
- the implications for those involved are acknowledged
- a strategy for managing change is developed
- the adaptations called for, are spelled out

- consultation is used for feedback, local ownership and response
- implementation takes into account the need for staff development and modification
- all recognize that if anything can go wrong, it will go wrong.

The features of change

Lewin[2] was among the first writers to suggest that managing change is best viewed as a multi-stage process. He emphasized three basic steps: 'unfreezing,' 'change' and 'refreezing'. Unfreezing involves those activities designed to break down the barriers to change and identify the part people and groups play in easing through the change. Change is 'the movement from an old state to a new one'.[3] Refreezing is the creation of the new *status quo*. This is usually accompanied by some reassurances about the future.

Breaking down the barriers to change depends on an understanding of the obstacles that exist and the forces that are provoking the innovation. Force field analysis[2] is employed to map out these pressures and examine the ways to achieve the desired outcome. In Figure 6.2 the forces prompting and holding back proposals for the

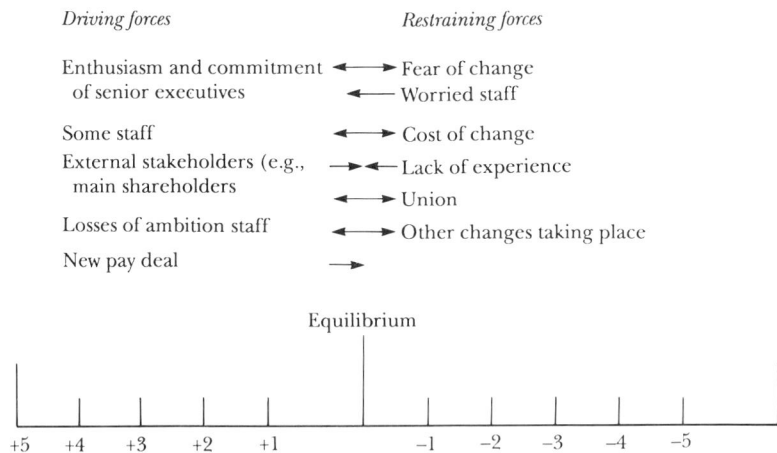

Driving forces   *Restraining forces*

Enthusiasm and commitment ← → Fear of change
    of senior executives ← Worried staff

Some staff ← Cost of change
External stakeholders (e.g., → ← Lack of experience
    main shareholders ← → Union

Losses of ambition staff ← → Other changes taking place
New pay deal →

Equilibrium

+5 +4 +3 +2 +1   −1 −2 −3 −4 −5

Figure 6.2   Staff appraisal. Force field analysis

introduction of a new staff appraisal scheme are presented. Once the system is in equilibrium, change can only be achieved by reinforcing the driving forces or reducing the restraining forces. A change agent may play an important role in disturbing the equilibrium and creating the opportunity for change. He or she can be from inside or outside the enterprise. Their presence, however, creates an opportunity for change while symbolizing the development taking place. The existing forces for change can be strengthened or new pressures introduced. External shareholders might make continued support conditional on the introduction of the appraisal scheme. The University Funding Council indicated that part of the increased salaries offered to university staff in 1989 was conditional on the introduction of staff appraisal. New driving forces can be added. Further promotion might be conditional on systematic appraisal. The restraining forces can be weakened, even eliminated. Training reduces the lack of experience in using appraisal. Union resistance might be eliminated with safeguards.

Change agents help with both aspects of these developments. Their value derives from a mixture of status, trust, expertise, credibility and focus. Status derives from their role as leaders. Trust is important as it provides leeway for the inevitable break-downs in communication. Expertise provides the change agent with a series of templates applied to situations to minimize costly errors and achieve results with a minimum of effort. Credibility reassures other players that the results will justify the effort. The agent will provide a useful focus for those members of the organization advocating and backing change. Continued support for the developments and those shaping their implementation is necessary from all members of the leadership group. This needs to be shown through deeds and words. Perhaps the easiest way to undermine change is for members of the leadership group to undermine those responsible for change.

> McGuinness had been put in charge of several players nearing the ends of their careers who had managerial ambitions of their own. It was easy for them to mutter how they could have done things better. The close contact that some kept with Sir Matt – Denis Law, Pat Crerand and Willie Morgan, for instance – on the golf course or in restaurants on Saturday nights maintained a channel for discontent, perhaps more imagined than real. 'I didn't mind other players going behind my back,' McGuinness said recently. 'What I did mind was that he accepted their side of the story rather than mine.'
>
> Crick, M. and Smith, D., *Manchester United*, p. 754[4]

Resistance to change occurs at an individual and organizational levels. People oppose because the proposals challenge existing ways of behaving and provoke fears of the unknown. Some threats are real. People recognize they may be unable to adapt and find their position under threat. The innovations challenge their past behaviour and raise questions about its value. These hurdles are reinforced by organizational resistance. Established power and authority systems may be challenged. Change costs money. The proposals may not sit well within the current structure. Success will turn on the manager's ability to overcome these obstacles while retaining organization coherence and prosperity.

Progress is likely where:

- the need for change is recognized and internalized
- communication and participation are high
- innovation is endorsed
- early successes are recognized and disseminated
- the leadership group acts together
- change is underpinned with training and development
- a holistic view of the enterprise is adopted.

Difficulties occur when:

- goals are unclear
- conflict appears to exist in the leadership group
- change has too narrow a focus
- support systems are weak
- reinforcement is delayed or obscure.

The work of the leadership team is central to the process of managing change. Their task is to work out the strategy and find ways to identify their roles in ways which sustain momentum. Timing is critical. The introduction of new equipment often makes staff responsive to changes in work practice. It helps them to make the best of the new resources.

Communication, participation and agreement underpin the programme. Widespread awareness of the reasons for the development is an important factor in gaining support. Extensive programmes of communication throughout the process ought to be underpinned with a strong sense of participation. Resistance increases with a sense of lack of control. Training and development reassure participants while giving them the skills to respond to new challenges. Feedback and response reinforce local confidence while building a stronger sense of agreement and ownership.

The first and subsequent employees

The first employee taken on by an enterprise signals one of the most profound alterations in its operations. The venture will need to employ a variety of skills to ensure the success of this innovation. The purpose behind this move will be analysed and the implications and role understood. The job description provides the initial remit. It should cover skills needed, length of appointment, experience, responsibilities, authority, remuneration, and other terms and conditions. All those now involved will be affected by the new appointee. A day nursery might, until now, operate through voluntary workers. They can make the salaried new appointee's introduction easy or hard.

Recruitment may involve a mixture of advertising and use of recruiters. The local Job Centre can provide advice as well as prospective candidates. The effective recruitment advertisement is based on a mixture of basic information and modification to suit circumstances. Advertisements and further particulars should encourage and help serious candidates and discourage others. No-one gains from large numbers of inappropriate applicants. They are misled and the advertiser wastes time. Note should be taken of similar advertisements placed by comparable employers. This can influence the overall style. The core information included is company name, details of firm, location, job title, work involved, requirements (e.g. experience), how to apply (especially by when and to whom) and any other special conditions. It is important to ensure that the law is complied with throughout the hiring process. Recruitment policies quickly enter the public domain. Others involved in the venture should be kept fully in touch to minimize concern and ensure that all aspects of the work are appreciated.

The interview is still the most common and popular device for choosing between candidates. Most research[5] suggests that the interview is not a reliable tool when used on its own. The team involved in selection require prior training, agreement about objectives and information about other performance measures. The candidates may be expected to give some indication of typical performance in a relevant task and some other form of examination (e.g. aptitude test). The selection process should be based on a clear appreciation that a long-term relationship is being created. The implications and costs of the relationship and the work ought to dominate the process.

The growth of the workforce will impose various strains on the enterprise. Human resource policies turn on the skills with which people, tasks and the organizational needs are wedded to create a successful operation. The way people work will determine the ability of the venture to meet its goals. In part, this is a function of the way the role or job they undertake is designed. In the early part of this century, the work of Taylor and others[6] led some managers to believe that job design could be used to devise a mechanistic system of determining the ways in which work was performed. This has not occurred. Subsequent investigation showed how much individual or group behaviour shapes performance.

There is, however, a growing body of knowledge about the ways in which work can be developed and enhanced to give greater individual satisfaction and improve performance. Job enrichment is employed to increase skill variety, task identity, task significance, autonomy and feedback. The more skills the person can use, the less chance tedium or lack of challenge will impair effectiveness. A strong sense of identity with the work, allied to recognition of its value increases motivation. Autonomy linked to feedback reinforces the desire to do well. Each of these is built up through communication, training and development.

Management by Objectives (MBO) extends this practice of integrating the individual, her or his objectives and the goals of the enterprise. MBO is a procedure for gaining acceptance of goals and accountability by collaboration in objective setting by managers and subordinates. Typically, the objectives of the total enterprise are broken down into the goals for particular units or individuals. Those responsible for achieving these are given an opportunity to respond, adapt or agree their targets. There is a negotiating system during which manager and subordinate explore their goals and the resources needed for their achievement. Once the objectives are finalized, a method and schedule for monitoring and rewarding performance is established. The success of this technique highlights the value of winning acceptance of the goals set for individuals and groups.

Markets and marketing

Management by Objectives is widely used in sales and marketing. Those responsible for winning business play a major part in establishing the sales targets they will be expected to achieve. Its value is enhanced by the insight those close to the customer can provide on market needs and competitive conditions. These may bear little resemblance to the assumptions held by the producer.

Parker Pens gained an important insight into this. Traditionally, they saw themselves in the business of making pens. The product, its promotion, its distribution and price reflected this view of their business. Product development concentrated on improving writing quality. Promotion was constant over the year and concentrated on the use of the pen. Distribution was centred on specialist outlets. Pricing policies reflected a constant struggle to compete with cheaper rivals. Over time, the firm found costs of product development and promotion increasing. At the same time, retailers were looking for larger discounts and prices were dropping. Eventually, they were forced to step back and look at the market and their assumption in order to survive.

Research highlighted several crucial facts about their market. The most important reshaped the way they saw their business. They found that the vast majority of their pens were bought as gifts. They were not in the pen business but in the gift business. They followed this with a revision of their marketing effort. Product development concentrated on features which enhanced the product as a gift. This included styling, presentation and packaging. Promotion was reorganized and concentrated on the two main gift-buying times of the year. Distribution was widened to include department stores, gift shops and many other outlets. Pricing reflected the priorities of gift buyers, not users. Profits and market share grew.

This type of review and adaptation lies at the centre of marketing. It prompts modification of offerings to meet client needs. The notion of the extended product has emerged because suppliers recognize the different satisfactions sought by users. A producer of heavy-duty hiking boots can use the reputation created to introduce lighter walking shoes, gloves or capes. This makes it easier to sell into some outlets while using up spare capacity at times in the year. Museums and art galleries have adopted a policy of augmenting their service through shops, lectures, leasing items or production of replicas. These generate additional revenue while adding to the pleasure gained by visitors. The success of the Assembly Rooms during the Edinburgh Festival persuaded the owner to expand his product by using the facility over more of the year. This approach to marketing combines a determination to meet customer needs with recognition of the value of improved productivity.

Production

Wickham Skinner once described manufacturing as 'the missing link in corporate strategy'.[7] This fairly reflected the neglect of production, the dangers of which are only now recognized through the success of Japan. Improvement turns on a combination of strategic direction, innovation in approach and improved operations.

Shifting production into the centre of strategic planning reflects the long-term competitive benefits that can be won. The production edge can win businesses for manufacturers who have low failure rates. Hoteliers have discovered that hard-won business is easily lost through poor service. Universities find that expensive recruitment visits overseas can be wasted because colleagues at home are slow to process applications. Theatre groups can play at home to empty houses because posters were not sent out. Each case reflects a failure to place the total production effort at the centre of policy. This involves a recognition that design for efficiency and quality is called for in all operations.

This strategy is underpinned by a constant up-dating of systems and operations. Standardization is perhaps the best established technique for improving overall productivity. It involves the identification of the key components in an activity. A method is established for producing these as separate items, to a fixed specification. Henry Ford's fame reflected the skill with which he introduced this approach into automotive production. MacDonald's have achieved the same in the production of fast food.

Value analysis is used to ensure that the facilities built into an item or service reflect the customer requirements. An engineering firm found that the reduced cost of air transport meant that they could ship certain items by air rather than sea. It was only three years later that the packaging was modified to reflect the lower risk of damage. Value analysis teams drawn from a variety of functions can analyse each aspect of a product or service to identify ways of reducing costs without affecting customer satisfaction.

Research, development and investment provide the keys to progressive improvement in operations. Research provides insight into the ways others are facing the same challenges while seeking out ways of improving output. Development adapts existing operations to current conditions to get the best from existing capacity. Investment upgrades and improves systems and skills. Each of these affects the underlying procedures. These are purchasing, materials management, inventory, handling, production, engineering, logistics and distribution.

Finance

The finances of a firm provide an insight into the workings and health of an enterprise. Money is both a means of exchange for the organization in its dealing with the outside agencies and a crucial source of information and control. The finances of all enterprises are best viewed in terms of flows of resources. For every flow of goods and services in one direction, there is a flow of money in the other. This creates the three types of money that can be identified in an enterprise:

- *Money outflows*: The money required to finance the running of the organization. This pays for wages, raw materials, energy, etc.
- *Cash*: This is needed as a buffer between income and expenditure. It permits the enterprise to balance the inflows and outflows and adjust for any lags between income and expenditure.
- *Money inflows*: These are the payments and other revenues from clients, lenders and grant-aiding bodies.

Most organizations try to achieve some broad balance between these flows. An enterprise with excessive outflows will find it cannot meet its bills, credit will dry up and it will not be able to operate. Too little cash might mean that it cannot satisfy short-term calls on its resources. In the short term, borrowings might fill the gap but the costs and inconvenience can hamper effectiveness. Excessive inflows probably reflect excess demand. This can overwhelm the organization's ability to supply, irritate clients and encourage new entrants into the market. High profits can encourage competitors and give clients the impression of overcharging.

It almost impossible for an enterprise to achieve this balance without some recourse to outside finance. There is a variety of different sources of money to an organization. Credit can be provided by suppliers. This can be voluntary. Payment will not be required for 30, 60, 90 or 120 days. This is not free money. The supplier will be adding 'the costs of credit' somewhere into the account. Involuntary, extended credit may be forced on suppliers especially by large customers. This can poison relationships and lead to long-term problems.

Banks provide credit in several forms. The most common is the overdraft. Equity or investment finance means transferring some element of control of the enterprise to a third party. The sources of this range from Local Enterprise Boards to a listing on the Stock Exchange. Grants are available from a host of organizations. The nature of this type of support reflects the character of the enterprise seeking backing. Voluntary and charitable organisations can look to *The Directory of Grant Making Trusts*, individual philanthropists, large organizations or more public sources. Commercial concerns can turn to local government or one of the head government departments.

The struggle for finance is so intense that planning and professionalism are vital. This means:

- *Deciding exactly the purpose for which the money is needed.* Nothing is more irritating to a trustee or public affairs manager of an enterprise than the vague or ill-thought through request for help. The approach should convince the donor that the finance will be used well and thoughtfully. There are roughly 180 000 charities operating in the UK so competition for funds is tough. The same discipline is required from the commercial enterprise. A business plan, outlining why the money is needed, how it will be applied and the returns is essential.
- *Getting the presentation of the case right.* Good presentation makes it easier for the donor or lender to respond positively. It creates an image of responsibility and professionalism which can reassure those responsible for the funds that the money will be well spent.
- *Providing clear indications of performance, return and how the project will be monitored.* Follow-up reassures lenders and creates a favourable long-term environment for later requests or approaches.

Profits are the primary, long-term measure of the success of an enterprise. These can be retained in the organization to finance new activities or distributed to owners. The profit and loss (P&L) account measures activities of the organization over a specific period of time, usually one year. The P&L account will identify total revenues over the period. Against these will be put direct costs, overheads, interest payments and depreciation. Taxes due should then be indicated. The resulting outcome will be net profit after tax. Direct costs are materials, energy, supplies and services and labour. Overheads are those items which cannot normally be allocated to specific items. Rents, rates and certain fees are usually placed in the overhead account. Depreciation is the mechanism employed to ensure that the enterprise is capable of renewing its plant, equipment and capital resources. A specific amount of money is allowed each year to represent the deteriorating 'value' of purchases. A company car costing £10000 might be expected to depreciate at the rate of 33.3% per annum. It is assumed that it has no value at the end of three years.

Accruals are used in accounts to relate expenses to the period during which an activity will take place. It is common for an organization to accrue a sum of money in a particular year even if the bill has not been received or paid during this period. This allows the P&L account to give a fair picture of true activity.

Similar conventions are used when a new project is evaluated. Costs and revenues are calculated and the point at which the activity 'breaks even' is estimated. This helps to determine the feasibility of a project. Break-even charts relate fixed and variable costs to likely income. Fixed costs are those which do not change with the level of activity while variable costs change with work. A community co-operative

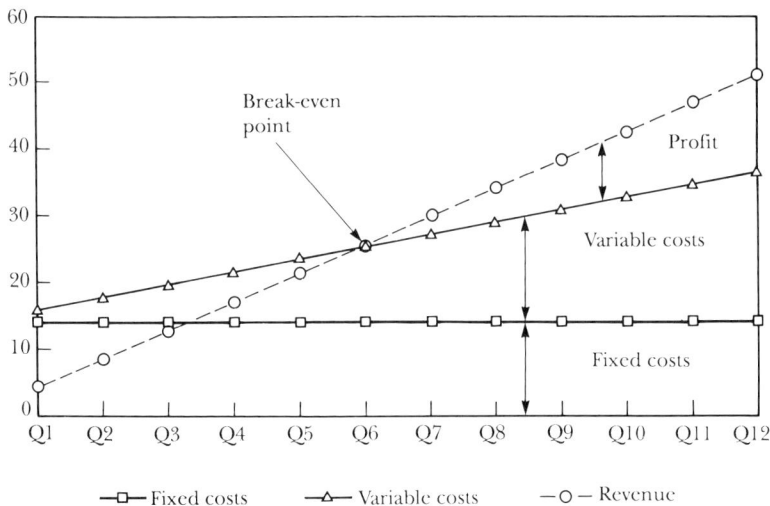

Figure 6.3   Break-even chart

in the Western Isles used this technique to evaluate the proposal to buy a tractor and trailer for use by themselves, hire to local crofters and refuse collection on contract to the Western Islands Council. This is described in Figure 6.3.

The fixed cost is the £14000 for the purchase of the tractor and trailer. The variable costs include wages for the driver, fuel, service, insurance, some allowance for depreciation and miscellaneous charges. The income comprises the contract from the Council, hires and project work. Break-even occurs at the start of the sixth quarter.

Periodically, an enterprise will need to produce a statement of its assets and liabilities. This is the Balance Sheet. It describes what the organization owns and owes. It can own property, equipment and cash. Its liabilities are bills due for payment, loans and any taxes due. A small engineering company might find itself faced with the situation outlined in Table 6.1 at the end of its financial year.

Table 6.1 The Balance Sheet.
XYZ Engineering
Balance Sheet 31 March 1989

	1989 (£,000)	1988 (£,000)
Fixed assets		
Land and buildings	450	400
Equipment	150	100
Fixtures	300	125
	900	625
Current assets		
Stock	240	150
Debtors	75	50
Investments	30	30
Cash	75	75
	420	405
Current liabilities		
Due within a year	475	450
net current liabilities	50	45
total assets less current liabilities	850	580
Due after more than a year	35	30
Other provisions		
deferred taxation	10	10
Net worth	805	540
financed by share capital	300	300
Retained profit	305	120
Loans	200	120
Total capital employed	805	540

The data in the balance sheet, especially when related to other performance data, teaches the trained observer a great deal about the enterprise. It is possible to arrive at an understanding of how well the capital employed in the venture is employed by relating balance sheet information to profits. The net profits of XYZ Engineering in 1989 were £250000 on sales of £2.5 million with costs of £2.25 million.

$$\text{Return on capital} = \frac{\text{Net profit}}{\text{Capital employed}}$$

$$\text{For XYZ Engineering} = \frac{250}{805} \times 100 = 31\%$$

The ability of the enterprise to finance its day-to-day activities depends on the amount of working capital or liquidity ratio. This is the relationship between current assets and current liabilities.

$$\text{Liquidity ratio} = \text{current assets: current liabilities}$$

$$\text{For XYZ Engineering} = 420:475 = 0.9:1$$

Generally, it is better for a manufacturing enterprise to have more current assets than liabilities. The situation facing XYZ will require some attention especially given the little movement in this figure over the last year. In other sectors, notably retailing, this is less important. It is useful to link this review of current performance with an examination of the extent to which the organization is self reliant. This is analysed in terms of a series of gearing ratios. Usually, these measure the contribution of the owners, shareholders or proprietors against providers of loan capital. The proprietor's ratio indicates the extent to which the venture is dependent on loans to operate.

$$\text{Proprietor's ratio} = \frac{\text{Capital employed}}{\text{Total liabilities}}$$

$$\text{For XYZ Engineering} = \frac{605}{675} = 0.9:1$$

This is significantly better than the 0.7:1 situation seen in 1988. Shareholders will be especially concerned about the capital gearing ratio. This measures the extent to which the value of the shares held in the company are assured in the case of difficulties.

$$\text{Capital gearing ratio} = \frac{\text{Share capital}}{\text{Fixed interest loans}}$$

$$\text{For XYZ Engineering} = \frac{300}{200} = 1.5:1$$

This means that the risk to shareholders if the company gets into financial difficulties is quite low. This is despite the fact that fixed interest loans are paid back before share capital. The requirement to pay interest before distributing profits highlights the importance of the income gearing. This is the relationship between interest and trading profit.

$$\text{Interest gearing} = \frac{\text{Trading profit}}{\text{Interest paid}}$$

$$\text{For XYZ Engineering} = \frac{250}{30} = 8:1$$

In some highly geared firms the ratio can be much lower. This means that a small decline in trading profits can have a devastating effect on net profits.

Each of these and other ratios gives some insight into the performance of the firm. They flag warnings. An enterprise which is overtrading can go bust simply because it does not have enough cash to pay its bills despite trading at a profit. High asset values sometimes encourage predatory take-overs especially when the assets are easily realized. There are dangers in the ratios. They are snapshots at moments in time. An image taken at another time can give a different picture. Patterns vary widely between industries. Some businesses have different structures to others in the same sector. Ratios do, however, provide an insight especially when related to performance over time.

Facilities

Almost any type of venture requires accommodation. This can range from the filing cabinet, kept in the flat of the secretary of the local dramatic society but containing its records, to the corporate headquarters of a multinational. These 'facilities' shape most aspects of the enterprise. Their location and accessibility will determine the audiences served and the employee base. The price placed on them will be a crucial element in the financial base of the venture. The quality and character of the facilities will influence the satisfaction gained by workers and clients. The mix of facilities will determine the types of activities undertaken. Control of the property can mean control of the venture. The facilities of an enterprise include land, buildings, lay-out, fixtures, fittings, furniture and equipment.

An enterprise can employ its property to support directly its own activities or to enable someone else to trade and gain indirect benefit itself. Universities adopt the former route where they use buildings and land for teaching, research and adminis-tration. The property portfolio of most higher education institutions is large and valuable. They are, however, hard to convert to cash. This can have a direct effect on their work. A university based in Central London is sitting on some of the most valuable property in the world but can face a financial crisis.

> The Universities Funding Council may send management consultants into the University of London following concern about the university's growing financial crisis.
>
> *Times Higher Educational Supplement*

The value of the property owned by a venture is based partly on its stability and the tendency for the value to increase over time. This has to be balanced against its inflexibility.

Most ventures start from the home. The political group, voluntary body or leisure activity is likely to depend on the willingness of people to store equipment or host activities. A similar pattern can be seen in small business. The back bedroom, garage or stable have been the starting points for many companies. The developing concern will soon grow out of these facilities. The host will tire or the neighbours will complain. Even if this does not occur, the need for proper insurance, demands for extra space, even the call to put the link on a more formal basis, will make the purely informal relationship hard to maintain. The secretary of the drama club might need the back bedroom for a child. He or she might not be willing to give the Chair access whenever it is requested. A facility 'owned' by the group or the venture may be the sole means of ensuring access and proper control.

The choice of facilities tends to centre on function, availability, cost and access. A brief specification of purpose in terms of the activities planned and numbers involved is needed at an early stage. A rock band will want somewhere in which the volume of noise can be accommodated. A chemicals plant needs to minimize risk to locals and endure safe disposal of waste. Generally, it is better to cater for the worst case in defining function. The first meeting of the local pressure group might only attract small numbers but no-one will want to turn down members because they cannot be accommodated. Premises can be found from talking to acquaintances, advertisements in local newspapers, estate agents and direct approaches to organizations with property. Costs can be deceptive. The rent might be small but rates high. Other charges can soon mount. Repairs and refurbishments can be expensive. This is especially true when the insurers impose requirements for security and safety.

Property once chosen, requires regular investment and revaluation. The investment is needed to maintain its value while ensuring that it continues to meet needs. Technological changes can transform space requirements. This is vividly illustrated by the contrast between the traditional, tall, multifloored mill or similar factory and the modern single-storey operation. The modern emphasis on continuity of flow and separation of process has redesigned the industrial landscape. Continuity of flow encourages planners to seek out buildings which minimize operations which go back to early stages of the process. Separation of process highlights the value of keeping distinct activities separate.

This emphasis on separation of process differs from traditional notions of division of labour by emphasizing the importance of internally coherent work groups. People work better when they can relate to others and the physical environment is supportive. Technology provides many more opportunities for reshaping the environment than existed in the past. Noise can be reduced, temperatures controlled and dirt minimized. Technology eliminates many of the more obvious barriers to operational efficiency for the enterprise. This is especially true in those fields in which the traditional barriers between pursuits are breaking down. In the computer industry, for example, the division between manufacturing and services is blurred. Another feature of this can be seen in higher education. Institutions are using science parks to gain indirect financial benefits while benefiting directly from the research and teaching links with companies on the 'parks.' The underlying assumptions are simple. These are:

- economic activity is increasing, driven by the ability of communities to exploit knowledge
- institutions of higher education have access to talented people with access to knowledge
- the creation of an environment in which the transfer of knowledge to economic gain is easier will benefit both communities.

Science parks exist to ease the move from laboratory to the factory. Ideally, they are on the same site as research and teaching. This helps people to meet and exchange ideas. In practice, there are a number of dilemmas and difficulties. The initial quandary is the same as that faced by every socially aware developer. The gains, even rents and links, will emerge some time after the costs – disruption, loss of amenity, etc. Science parks are now recognized as a long-term development. Even in the most favourable circumstances[8] these two processes can take time and resources to integrate effectively.

Conclusion

The nature of the challenges facing an enterprise evolve with the venture. Some entrepreneurs find that their original interest in making a product or providing a service is overwhelmed by the needed to acquire property. The real estate might be more important to bankers and investors than the product or service. This may not be part of the original intention but plans need to be shaped which can accommodate these demands.

It is sometimes asserted that these changes devalue planning. Why bother when so little is predictable? In part this reflects a confusion between plans and prediction. It also views plans as epistles or testaments, the value of which lies in that they are immutable. It is, however, the process of planning, the time and thought invested and the re-examination of the ideas and assumption behind plans that gives them value. Plans are organic not mechanical.

Change derives from the interaction between the pressures of the environment and the demands of stakeholders. The expectation that the physical environment is attractive and comfortable forces design companies to reshape the physical environment. Levi's found that their new 'functional' office block for their California HQ reduced morale, undermined creativity and increased staff turnover. The move to a less austere, older and more sympathetic building generated the attitude and performance improvements that functionality failed to generate.

Stakeholders impose on a venture a variety of demands. The primary task of those seeking to shape the enterprise is to balance these needs while managing the overall performance of the venture. Sometimes there are inherent contradictions in role.

The members of a social club perform two roles. They are managers when acting as committee members and customers when using the facilities. As buyers they want low prices, as committee members they are responsible for club profits.

The long-term viability of the organization turns on its ability to establish systems for resolving the questions provoked by conflicting needs. These methods can be behavioural. Public authorities establish priorities through debate and political choice. The party which wins an election gains a mandate to impose its framework for decision making. Quantitative techniques are used extensively in management science to problems including; how much to invest in a new project; the choice between different advertising media and establishing the best way to distribute a product. These have been used with mixed success in public and voluntary enterprise. Durham County Council experimented with the use of decision analysis to allocate part of its social work budget. The police use programming techniques to design routine patrols. The great value in the use of these techniques lies in helping those responsible to specify problems, identify decision criteria, formulate alternative solutions and describe the outcomes of choices. The more complex the problem, the greater the gains from this type of approach.

The responsibility for these decisions lies with specific people. They will relate their choices to the situation faced by the enterprise. Their knowledge of the main areas of activity and the impact of their selection will shape their action. The impact on the viability of the enterprise will be shaped by the extent to which the needs of suppliers, members of the enterprise and customers are met. This is not done in a vacuum. A depressed market can persuade component suppliers to extend credit. Suppliers of funds, such as the banks, will be more willing to be patient if they expect a market to pick up. Voluntary workers on an issue are easier to recruit and enthuse if the topic affects them and their families. Employees make less wage demands during periods of high unemployment. Voters (the customers of politicians) are impatient if they see no hope for economic improvement. The interaction between these forces and its internal operations will determine the long-term prosperity of the enterprise.

Case study

Donnington City Polytechnic

Donnington City Polytechnic is one of the larger of the UK polytechnics. It has grown significantly since its opening in 1963. This has been a result of both merger activity and natural growth. In 1972 it merged with Donnington College of Commerce. Five years ago Adamshaw College of Technology and the Central College of Art and Design were incorporated. It is now dispersed over six sites which straddle the city centre.

The college has 16 000 students of whom 9000 are full time and 7000 part time. The programmes include City and Guilds, BTech Diploma and Certificate, CNAA degrees and postgraduate and professional courses. There is a post-experience centre linked to the polytechnic.

Structure and management

The college is organized on the basis of five faculties: Humanities; Professional Studies; Art and Design; Science; and Technology. The heads of departments and Deans of the faculties are answerable to the Governing Council through the Director. There are several central services units in the college. These include Library Services, Computer Services, Learning Services, and Physical Education. Last year the polytechnic introduced a system of rolling plans. Each department produced an annual plan which is agreed with the faculty, then the council.

The challenges

Donnington City Polytechnic is in many ways a very successful institution. It does, however, face a number of challenges which could threaten its prosperity or act as a severe brake on the growth it has enjoyed in the past. The main threats to its current position are:

* increased competition especially from the local university
* shifts in the local industrial and economic structure
* changes in demand for its portfolio of courses
* demographic changes
* technology
* staff shortages in certain key areas.

These are balanced, at present, by clearly identifiable strengths:

* national and international potential for its courses
* co-operative ventures with other institutions
* reputation
* innovative and enterprising staff
* a secure resource base.

The Director of the polytechnic is determined that the new constitutional position of the poly will lead to the creation of a strong, successful and highly competitive institution. He believes that

> 'each department must learn that to survive, it must innovate and grow or it (and eventually the whole poly) will be left behind.'

He wants to build up a culture in which there is

> 'rivalry between departments to be the best in its field and attractive to its clients, while working to the benefit of the college. The success of any department should have a cascade effect on the others – success breeds success'.

The Governing Council support this approach and is especially anxious that this leads to success in the marketplace. The council is especially anxious to increase the take-up on courses, reduce the dependence on public funds and cut back on costs. The latter is seen to be an increasing problem. The large number of new courses introduced over the last five years by all faculties have increased the scale of activity but led to smaller numbers on each programme.

The Director has invited several heads of department to advise him on:

1. Whether to establish a new Marketing Services Unit.
2. The contribution it might make to improving marketing organization at a polytechnic, faculty and department level.
3. The marketing goals he should set.
4. The specific ways in which their faculties/departments can contribute to these.

Task

Take on the role of these advisers. You should concentrate on points (3) and (4).

References

1. Drucker, P.F. (1982) *Management: Tasks, Responsibilities and Problems*, New York, Harper and Row.
2. Lewin, K. (1951) *Field Theory in Social Science*, New York, Harper and Row.
3. Griffin, R.W. and Moorhead, G. (1986) *Organizational Behaviour*, Boston, Houghton Mifflin.
4. Crick, M. and Smith, D. (1989) *Manchester United: The Betrayal of a Legend*, London, Pelham Books.
5. Thomason, G. (1981) *A Textbook of Personnel Management*, London, Institute of Personnel Management.
6. Taylor, R. (1911) *The Principles of Scientific Management*, New York, Harper & Row.
7. Wickham, S., Production – A Link in Business Policy. (1981) *Management and Production Readings*, London, Penguin.
8. Segal Q. (1985) *The Cambridge Phenomenon*, Cambridge, Segal Quince & Partners.

Chapter 7

Management and the larger enterprise

Richard Dawkins[1] opens his analysis of the complexity of existence by commenting:

> Complicated things, everywhere, deserve a very special kind of explanation. We want to know how they came into existence and why they are so complicated
>
> *The Blind Watchmaker*, p. 1

Here, this concern centres on actions which shape a particular type of complex entity – the large enterprise. A simplified picture of its development from the entrepreneurial and the professional concern was given in earlier chapters. From these stages emerge the departmentalized, divisionalized, or other form of large complex enterprise. Working for these poses a specific set of challenges.

Is there any real difference?

It is possible to argue that there is no real difference between the larger and the smaller enterprise. Many of the disciplines which are required for success are the same. The need to manage finance, property and people is the same. Success in meeting client needs is the ultimate determinant of success. There are, however, substantial differences. These change the nature of participation in the venture. Small enterprises are shaped by generalists. The jack-of-all-trades is as important to the amateur dramatics group as to the small company. The producer is likely to be asked to sell tickets and write press releases. The owner-manager can find her/himself packing cases, or driving the van, beside negotiating with the bank manager.

Specialists shape the larger venture. They manage and work in its main activity areas. They have expertise and acquired knowledge to apply to problems. The value placed on this know-how influences the quality of the relationship with client groups.

> Specialisation, in turn, promotes expertness among staff, both directly and by enabling the organisation to hire employees on the basis of their technical qualifications.
>
> Blau, P. and Scott, W., *Formal Organisations*, p. 32

The complexity of the challenges facing the larger venture requires both this expertise and access to the management skills to integrate and direct their work. Knowledge alone is not enough when faced with complex signals from the wider environment which must be interpreted if the venture is to survive.

Karl Weik describes an experiment by Gordon Sin:

> ... If you place in a bottle half a dozen bees and the same number of flies, and lay the bottle down horizontally, with its base to the window, you will find that the bees will persist, till they die of exhaustion or hunger, in their endeavour to discover an issue through the glass; while the flies, in less than two minutes, will have all sallied through the neck on the opposite side ... It is their (the bees) love of light, it is their very intelligence that is their undoing in this experiment. They evidently imagine that the issue from every prison must be there where the light shines clearest; and they act in accordance, and persist in too logical action ... Whereas the feather-brained flies, careless of logic as of the enigma of crystal, disregarding the call of light, flutter wildly hither and thither, and meeting here the good fortune that often meet the simple, who find survival where the wiser will perish, necessarily end by discovering the friendly opening that restores their liberty to them.
>
> Quoted by Charles Handy in *Understanding Organisations*, p. 302

The combination of scale, specialization and the need for integrating and directing activities distinguishes both the experience and nature of work in the larger enterprise.

Scale

In most industrially advanced countries, the majority of the working population work in large organizations. In the UK, the broad pattern of employment is outlined in Figure 7.1.

This excludes the public sector which is mainly organizations and the voluntary sector which is mainly small scale.

Working for large organizations places several distinctive demands on people. In part, these reflect the need for some degree of integration: common standards and a system of authority and control. Some responsibilities reflect the power that large ventures exercise. Other duties mirror systems of accountability, control and power that go beyond the specific venture. Each can operate at the level of the individual, the group or the enterprise.

The effectiveness of large organizations depends on their ability to bring together an array of resources to achieve a common purpose. The material available can be people, capital, equipment, values, images, etc. In a small venture it is possible to achieve a high degree of consistency and uniformity. Graduates from the same university might decide to set up a software co-operative. Initially they will share very similar qualifications, skills and values. The growth of the venture will force them to recruit new staff. Some will lack their skills. They will have different sets of experiences. Their values will differ. The task of integrating these various skills will increase in importance. It will no longer be possible to assume a common purpose.

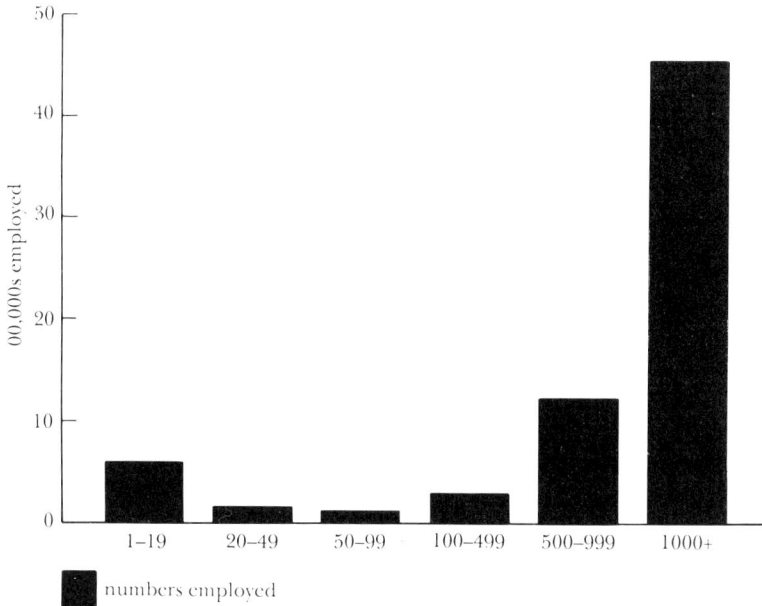

Figure 7.1 The pattern of employment in the UK

Integration

There are a variety of integrative devices. Handy[2] identifies:

- rules and procedures
- direct managerial contact
- appeals to the hierarchy
- temporary cross-functional teams
- permanent cross-functional teams
- individual co-ordinators
- co-ordinating departments.

These can play an important role especially during periods of change and where debate or disagreement exists. There is some evidence from the work of Lawrence and Lorsh[3] and others[4] that the extensive use of formal integrating devices indicates poor integration. The best forms of integration derived from shared values, good internal communication, a clear understanding of organizational goals and an acceptance of individual roles.

Integration of a large venture involving substantial numbers of people calls for the creation of common standards for communication and performance. In the past this was often achieved by bringing all the workers together in a single location or drawing them from a common pool. The mining communities that grew up in Australia or America frequently mirrored similar communities in Europe. Town names like Newcastle (New South Wales) reflect these origins. The mills of Lancashire normally drew their workforce from the local community. In some senses, Oxford and Cambridge performed the same role for the British civil service. Common standards of behaviour, similar values and shared values made the process of building a unified civil service easier.

Organizations which draw large numbers from diverse backgrounds require mechanisms to cultivate the common standards which help the members of the enterprise to work together. Education and training can play a major part in this. Some large firms have emulated the civil service by drawing their recruits from a common pool. The BBC is often accused of hiring the vast majority of its graduates from Oxbridge. These universities are, in turn, charged with basing their recruitment on a small number of public schools. The induction courses run by companies will usually seek to introduce an understanding of the firm's expectations of its employees to new workers. The failure to achieve some common standards leads to fragmentation, poor communication and discipline problems. A special form of this problem occurs when two independent activities are merged. The creation of a pattern of common standards is necessary if reward systems are to be effective. Methods of reward and punishment underpin the creation and maintenance of common standards.

Authority and control

The authority and control which the firm exercises to mobilize resources are based on roles of those involved in the activity and the ways they work together. Chandler[5] chronicled the shift from kinship-based authority to competence-derived power in large organizations. The basis of the manager's authority lies on a combination of position and assumed competence. Other sources of authority – hereditary, kinship, force – are less important. There is, however, a suggestion that personal charisma can sway key decisions and win personal authority beyond the confines of a specific role. This is linked to Etzioni's[6] suggestion that the combination of personal and positional power places the manager in the best position to achieve her or his goals.

The allocation of power to individuals is seldom the primary aim of an enterprise. This power is deployed to help the organization achieve its goals. This poses twin challenges.

- How can the control systems support the deployment of this authority?
- How can the institution ensure that application of power is managed without undermining personal enterprise?

Hershey and Blanchard identified three basic types of control system. The first is based on personal direction of all primary tasks. The manager controls by being on the spot and directing behaviour. This can work in quite large, unitary operations. The mill manager with an office on a gantry can overlook the entire operation. Subordinate managers can reach and be reached quickly and easily. The second is based on task completion. The outcome is understood and all agree on the results to be produced. Craftsmen, outworkers, contractors and writers operate under this regime. The publisher will agree the title, content and completion date with the prospective author. Direct supervision is minimized. The third system is devolved authority to collaborators. This can operate within the venture. Peters and Waterman[4] describe this as the 'tight–loose' organization. There is tight control over strategy but implementation is left in local control.

It is increasingly common to find devolved authority shaping the pattern of development for large ventures. The 'creative disintegration' of the large enterprise can be seen in those ventures which break their activities into smaller, more internally cohesive operating units. This approach has characterized the evolution of the electronics industry. Firms avoid taking on activities that are outside their main field of competence. The development of Channel 4 TV in the UK was based on the extensive use of external production companies. Other organizations seek to identify strategic business units around which they build their business.

Strategic Business Units (SBUs)

Strategic Business Units are those units in a business which have a distinct internal and external coherence. Internally, this means that SBUs can be managed as a unit without being dependent on other parts of the enterprise or affecting the effectiveness of these parts. Externally, it means their client or market base can be distinguished from the rest of the venture. They are, in effect, mini-enterprises within the organization. The identification and creation of SBUs has major implications for the control systems of the organization. It means the entire venture:

- should be managed as a portfolio of ventures
- is shaped by the interaction between the strategies of the SBUs and the overall approach of the organization.

The concept was originally developed at General Electric in North America. GE sought to identify the 'natural business units'[7] that made up the organization. The performance and potential of each can be measured and evaluated. Investment is directed to those SBUs with the greatest potential. Others might be viewed as sources of this finance while the organization may decide to withdraw from some businesses. This approach is being employed in some parts of the public sector. Institutions of higher education are reviewing their subject mix along these lines. It provides a mechanism for concentrating in some areas while devolving operational management away from the centre.

Responsibility

The resources, power and wealth of large organizations impose heavy responsibilities on them. These include the traditional roles society has provided. Companies have an economic role. Universities transmit knowledge and values. Voluntary organizations help to bridge the gap between state and commercial activities. Within these there are specific tasks. Firms are expected to generate sufficient profit to encourage share-holders to maintain or increase their investment. University staff write to disseminate the findings of their research to their peers and the wider community. Charities direct their efforts to help the needy.

There is some debate about the extent of these responsibilities. Friedman has argued that corporations have a sole responsibility to perform their economic role. This means maximizing the returns to investors while remaining within the law. Wider social roles should be left to the state, its agents or voluntary bodies. Recently, bodies like Business in the Community have challenged this vision. They see companies as full members of a community, performing a wide range of social roles. These include the provision of specialist expertise, funding charitable and other activities, care for the economically and socially disadvantaged and accepting a responsibility for protecting the environment.

The case for this more extensive approach is built around several related arguments. There is simple self interest. This takes two forms. The private sector can keep the compulsory demands of the state to a minimum if it acts earlier and voluntarily. Commercial interests are further satisfied if the prosperity of the community generates more and richer customers. Actions on behalf of the economically and socially disad-vantaged satisfy both these criteria. Serious and systematic attempts to employ more people from disadvantaged groups will reduce the risk that the state will act. Govern-ment intervention may occur in ways which do not wed the needs of the firm to the needs of the groups. Success in helping more people to start their own businesses creates wealth and stimulates healthy competition.

Access

The routes into and through large enterprises are a mixture of discipline, skill and luck. The conventional point of access is the job application. For students this is a mixture of using 'the milk round' (the process by which organizations sell themselves to students) and applying for advertised jobs. Supply and demand shapes this market as much as any other. Large numbers of graduates from a host of disciplines pursue jobs in the media, publishing and parts of the civil service. Competition is tough. Unless the graduate has an edge, winning a job will be hard. This is especially true if the biases of certain recruiters are recognized. Getting the edge needed to win a job can be hard.

Differentiation is an approach which works well in other markets in which supply exceeds demand. Some graduates substitute the business news pages for the jobs pages in their search for work. A letter to a senior executive responding to a positive news story might win an interview when a 'cold application' fails. In part, this reflects one of the primary sources of a competitive edge – better intelligence. Recruiters expect applicants who are keen to join them to know something about the firm. This is especially true if the enterprise has some distinctive feature.

> There is the story of the Oxford graduate who applied for a job in the Foreign Office. He was interviewed. The Chairman of the Panel asked 'You do realize that this is the Foreign Office?'
> 'Of course', said the candidate.
> 'But, you don't have any foreign languages', commented the Chairman.
> 'But I'm not a foreigner', replied the candidate.

A well thought through and presented curriculum vitae (CV) can be the difference between a simple rejection and an interview. The availability of modern word processors means that there is no longer any excuse for poor presentation or lack of updating. The basic design principles are:

- establish a clear and logical framework built around sections, e.g. voluntary work
- concentrate the reader's attention around key achievements
- use a chronological structure to guide the reader
- avoid gaps and the risk of misunderstanding
- find ways to make it easy for the reader to say 'yes'
- never misrepresent yourself.

The basic strategy is the same as that which shapes successful enterprise elsewhere: decide on the goal, assess capacity, seek an edge and project well in terms that the client understands.

Management training and development

In competition between large ventures, it is the way resources are used which determines success. Productivity gains based on the better use of resources are crucial. The quality of the management responsible for deploying these assets is a major concern in the UK. The creation of the Management Charter Initiative (MCI) followed the publication of a series of reports initiated by the British Institute of Management, The Confederation of British Industry and the National Economic Development Office. They found that UK managers were far less likely to have a first degree than their rivals in the USA, Germany, France and Japan. They were, however, far more likely to have a background in accountancy. Expenditure on management training is much lower especially if on-the-job training is included.

The figures in Table 7.1 provide a narrow view of the pattern of management education, training and development in the UK. This can be viewed in terms of a matrix which relates competency to source (Table 7.2). Managers are expected to combine specific task competencies with more general capabilities. It is assumed that the finance director can recognize and use a spreadsheet. No such presumption will be made about the sales director. All share a need for some basic 'managerial'

Table 7.1 Education and training of managers

Country	Top managers with degrees (%)	Number of qualified accountants (,000s)	MBAs per annum
Britain	24	120	120
USA	85	300	70 000
FRG	62	3.8	0
France	65	20	0
Japan	85	6	60

Source: Handy, C. *et al. Making Managers.*[8]

skills in working with people. Proficiency comes from a mixture of formal certificated education plus executive training and development.

Beside these, there is a steady growth in the study of business and related topics in schools. These subjects include 'A' levels (Cambridge), 'Highers' in Scotland and the Technical and Vocational Educational Initiative (TVEI). The creation of the National Council for Vocational Qualifications (NCVQ) has led to the creation of a comprehensive framework for study in this area. Further education qualifications offered by BTech, ScotVec, City and Guilds, RSA and other providers encompass both specific and general competencies. The proposal for an introductory 'certificate' in business and management envisages a programme based on a mixture of these skills. The numbers studying business and related subjects at polytechnic and university has grown rapidly over the decade. These normally concentrate on general competencies. The links with professional societies in disciplines like accountancy, marketing, distribution can lead to more specific skills.

Table 7.2 The development matrix

Level	Competency	
	Specific	General
Further education Higher education Postgraduate Post-experience On-the-job		

Postgraduate education in the UK is split between specialist studies in fields like Marketing, Operational Research, Management Science and courses in General Management. The dominant qualification is the Master of Business Administration (MBA).

This has emerged as the most widely recognized international qualification for managers. The leading providers of MBAs such as Manchester Business School, London Business School and Cranfield often undertake extensive post-experience programmes with industry and the public sector. These include 'Open' courses which any firm or manager can follow. Some programmes are 'restricted' to certain firms or consortia of organizations. The bulk of management training takes place within firms or on-the-job. Progressive companies link the progress of managers with appropriate training and development. The Department of Employment's Training Agency co-ordinates or leads the UK Government's activities in these areas.

Conclusion

Large and small enterprises depend on each other. The scale of resource that the former can apply to an issue cannot be matched by their smaller rivals. The latter depend on their speed, creativity and flexibility to win. Both require people and systems capable of gaining advantage from the better use of resources. In larger firms, the major challenge is to deploy resources in a co-ordinated way to maximize productivity and value. The issues faced and the appropriate responses depend on the environment in which the company operates and the company culture.

The organizational culture is the mixture of attitudes and values which determines the ways in which managers will respond to specific situations. The devices employed to integrate the firm or allocate authority and responsibility are shaped by the same factors which create the firm's culture. The ingredients are:

- history and ownership
- technology
- objectives
- wider social values
- size
- people
- rewards.

Managers work within this culture. Change is possible but normally requires an external crisis or a well designed and implemented change strategy. In either case the costs can be considerable especially in terms of disruption and distraction from the primary business aims.

References

1. Dawkins, R. (1986) *The Blind Watchmaker*, London, Longman.
2. Handy, C. (1985) *Understanding Organisations*, London, Penguin.
3. Lawrence, P. R. and Lorsh, J.W. (1967) *Organization and Environment*, Harvard University Press.

4. Peters, T. and Waterman, R. (1982) *In Search of Excellence*, Harper and Row.
5. Chandler, A. D. (1977) *The Visible Hand: The Managerial Revolution in American Business*, Cambridge, Mass., Harvard University Press.
6. Etzioni, A. (1961) *A Comparative Analysis of Complex Organizations*, New York, The Free Press.
7. Hall, W. K. (1984) SBU's hot, new topic in the management of diversification. In Weitz, B. and Wensley, R. *Strategic Marketing*. Boston, Kent Publishing.
8. Handy, C., Gordon, C., Gow, I. and Randlesome, C. (1988) *Making Managers*, London, Pitman.

Chapter 8
Public and voluntary enterprise

The public and voluntary sector accounts for between 40 and 50% of all jobs in the UK. This is a pattern which is repeated in most advanced industrial societies. The tasks which are allocated to the public sector range from the traditional 'core' responsibilities of external and internal security to new roles which reflect society's present needs. The pattern of activity shifts significantly over a relatively short period of time. In Figure 8.1 the reduction in state ownership in a wide range of industries during the 1980s can be seen.

The virtual disappearance of state ownership of airlines, car production, gas distribution and oil exploration reflects a shift in government attitudes to industrial involvement.

The last decade saw a parallel growth in interest in the contribution that modern management techniques play in the more effective operation of the public sector. This affects the civil service, local government and large government agencies. Lord Rayner was a business efficiency expert invited in by the Government to look at its operations. Local authorities have experimented with new forms of investment appraisal, restructured their operations around 'business units' and tried using marketing, new technology, etc. to improve their effectiveness. The Health Service, Police, Prisons, Education, Social Services are among the major arms of government to be affected. They have responded to reports such as *The Griffiths Report* on the Health Service and re-organizations like replacing the University Grants Committee with the Universities Funding Council.

The voluntary sector and other forms of enterprise have been affected by the same pressures. In part, these changes are responses to dissatisfaction with traditional approaches to their organization and management. The large number of registered charities in the UK raises questions about the value and viability of the smaller units. Their operations range from large, permanent and complex ventures such as Oxfam and Trinity House to smaller, temporary responses to particular initiatives. Most have found that their resources have not kept pace with the demands placed on them. Better management is seen as an essential feature of improved use of resources. This

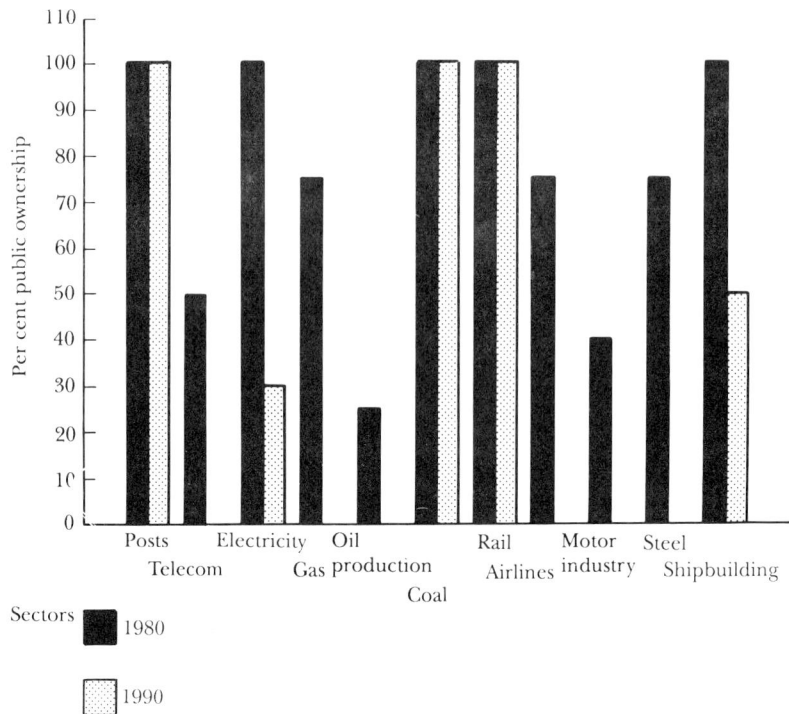

Figure 8.1   State ownership in the UK

affects most parts of their operations. The problems of moving tents, ambulances and support to a disaster area call for logistics skills of a high order. Investment managers are expected to get the best return possible from funds raised. Marketing can reinforce the relationship between the charity and its supporters.

National government

The work of central government influences the life of almost everyone in the UK. Those managing its operations are directly responsible for spending about 40% of the Gross National Product. They influence how the rest is allocated. Management in the public sector shows fundament differences from the private sector. In the former, policy formulation is specifically separated from its implementation and administration. Politicians are responsible for policy. They seek a mandate. Once elected they are expected to interpret and implement the wishes of the electorate. Implementation, administration and information are among the key responsibilities of the civil servant. This shapes behaviour. Top managers in industry might spend 10% of their time reporting to shareholders and bankers on their actions on performance. In the public sector this can increase to 50 or 60% of their time spent reporting on actions taken. It means that the time spent 'attending to the job' changes dramatically.

Each of these differences raises issues of individual and group enterprise. An example can be seen in overseas trade policy. The UK is highly dependent on exports. The British Overseas Trade Board (BOTB) has the task of advising ministers on the best ways to expand exports and control imports. Priority is generally given to expanding the range of services to meet identified problems. Evidence that British exporters were poorly informed about market opportunities prompted the creation of the Export Intelligence Service. Reports that UK companies spread their efforts too widely and failed to concentrate on key markets encouraged the BOTB to launch the Market Entry Guarantee Scheme. The proliferation of these initiatives led some critics to assert that the BOTB was more interested in schemes than exports. The core problems lay with a preoccupation with quick, publicly demonstrable, transaction-based reactions, not a strategic response.

The 'quick fix' is the archetypal, transaction-based response. The stimulus might be evidence that UK exporters are short of overseas market intelligence. This can mean that the information is not available, exporters do not know how to get it or the nature of the need is poorly defined. The immediate reaction is to launch a scheme. The same pattern of reaction rather than response recurs in public administration. In part, it reflects the pressure on politicians for a quick fix. Elsewhere it can derive from a belief that the state must act even when alternative suppliers and different responses are more effective.

Local government

Local government faces the same problems. The challenge is increased by the immediate and local nature of the areas of responsibility. These include social services, education, housing, environmental health, recreational services, property, planning and some aspects of economic development. In each, there is the difficulty of satisfying demands which increase faster than resources while responding to local pressures. Some features of modern management have an immediate relevance. Information technology permits social workers to build better databases on clients. These can be more accessible, better referenced and lead to superior reporting systems. The same technology assists housing managers to deploy resources and education to match pupils and needs. Poor communication especially in highly stressed areas is the besetting sin of 'public administration'. People are too busy to invest time keeping colleagues and juniors fully informed. The result is greater inefficiency and less time.

Major changes have occurred in recent years. The Local Authority Training Board and INLOGOV, the specialist training centre at Birmingham University, work with local authorities to improve standards. Their work reflects wider developments. The unions and professional bodies in social work, housing administration, education and other aspects of local government have increased the emphasis on better management. Most professional qualifications include some aspects of management. The approach taken reflects the immediate concerns on the profession. Recreation management emphasizes marketing. Education places a premium on communication and human resources. Social work and housing administration courses highlight information. This skewed approach is slowly giving way to a more comprehensive and wider ranging view of enterprise.

Quangos

Key aspects of public administration in the UK fall under the aegis of QUasi Autonomous National Government Organizations (quangos). Generally, they are formed to deal with three situations:

- Areas of government interest which do not fall neatly within the remit of a specific government department.
- Programmes which call for a range of outside expertise in policy and implementation.
- Work which requires a level of discretion or freedom which cannot be obtained within a conventional departmental structure.

Put more simply, they are set up to tackle issues which call for enterprise and freedom of action. Their success depends on an ability to mobilize resources, cut through barriers and exploit this freedom. Effective management is based on skills in establishing a clear strategy and using this to overcome traditional barriers to change. The 'hands off' approach by government is not complete. Specific activities will be closely scrutinized while the overall work of the unit will be subject to periodic review. The efforts to encourage inward investment by the Welsh or Scottish Development Agencies are examined regularly by the Welsh and Scottish Office. The change of the University Grants Committee into the Universities Funding Council emerged from a review of its work. The recent change in direction and funding of the Design Council occurred because of an assessment by the Department of Trade and Industry of their work. Others will be evaluated by their sponsoring departments.

The autonomy of quangos is relative. Policy shifts by government can change their role. Other participants can withdraw support. A mixture of these led to a major reform in the structure and approach of the Training Agency recently. Those working in these organizations need to be flexible enough to respond to change while sustaining their commitment to broad goals.

Trade unions

The 1980s saw increasing pressure on the trade union movement. The recession in Western Europe was accompanied by reductions in union membership in most countries. In the UK this has been especially severe. During the period since 1980 it has been estimated that the net loss has been of the order of 15%. The same period has seen a parallel increase in the demands placed upon the unions as government pressures have grown and the position of many members worsened. Trade unions are faced with the classical management dilemma of balancing increased demands with reduced resources in a generally hostile environment. This places tremendous strains on the management resources and skills of the full-time and voluntary officials of the unions. They have coped surprisingly well. Their performance compares well with many sectors of commercial management.

However, the skill base within which trade unions operate is very limited. The amount of research into the management of trade unions is very small. Programmes of management education and training for officers and officials are small in number, diverse and often very limited in range and coverage. This is especially true in the newer, more commercially oriented fields of business and management skills. Areas such as marketing, logistics, finance, management information systems have as much relevance for unions seeking to survive and prosper as for commercial concerns and public bodies. New technologies are having a direct impact on the operations of unions. Skills in database management and micro-computing are increasingly important for organizations with widely scattered and diverse memberships.

Co-operatives

Perhaps the most interesting alternative to manager and managed as a form of working arrangement is the co-operative. Co-operatives have existed in the UK since before the nineteenth century. Over their history they have tended to be either producer or consumer based. The early producer co-operatives in the UK were prompted by the writings of Robert Owen. He saw the creation of self-contained, self-supporting communities as the natural antidote to the exploitation of workers by capitalists. A number of experimental developments were tried during the nineteenth century. Very few survived even when backed by powerful consumer co-operatives.

The history of consumer co-operatives can be traced to the 'Rochdale Pioneers' who created a successful retail and trading operation in the 1840s. Their success, the growth of other Co-operative retail societies and the achievements of the Co-operative Wholesale Society dominated thinking about co-operative enterprise in the UK until the 1970s. In the Western Isles crofters and fishermen had created successful consumer co-operatives. They were, however, small. They were generally seen as marginal, economic activities. Although co-operative production played a major part in the work of the CWS and specific societies, few producer co-operatives survived. Variations on the theme developed in some parts of the UK.

Renewed interest in co-operatives stemmed from several sources. 'Phoenix' co-operatives emerged as a specific response to the proposed closure of business. The three most famous were *The Scottish Daily News*, Kirkby Manufacturing and Engineering (KME) and Meriden. Each of these eventually failed through a combination of high start-up costs, adverse market conditions and inadequate management. Despite this, enough was achieved to suggest that co-operative enterprises have a part to play in local economic development. This view is reinforced by the achievements of the Mondragon Co-operatives in Spain. They have stimulated economic growth and generated jobs.

A series of small-scale variations on the co-operative theme have made significant headway in parts of the UK. Community co-operatives were formed in some of the islands of Scotland with the support of the Highlands and Islands Development Board. Local resources were mobilized behind them. They play a significant role in providing local services and creating new jobs. Similar successes can be seen elsewhere.

Underpinning these specific initiatives are wider social and economic developments. The increased popularity of co-operatives reveals a preference among some people to work in this type of collaborative environment. This is made easier by the growth of some commercial sectors (e.g. software development). In these, co-operative enterprise seems to suffer from no major disadvantages. Those forming co-operatives can get help from a variety of sources including Co-operative Union, Industrial Common Ownership Movement, Co-operative Development Agency and Community Enterprise. Those local authorities which are politically sympathetic to co-operatives may give local backing.

The characteristics of a co-operative are:

- *Ownership* – should be vested in the members of the co-operative
- *Control* – is exercised through the members, typically on a one member, one vote basis
- *Profits* – are distributed among the workers in proportion to their involvement, not their financial investment
- *Interest repayments* – can, however, be made to investors but will normally be limited in some agreed way
- *Dissolution* – is possible on a basis agreed at formation by the members. The assets should not be distributed to members.

The chequered history of co-operatives prompted the Co-operative Bank and PA Management Consultants (*Workers Co-operatives; Past, Present and Future*, Manchester, PA Management Consultants, 1985) to examine the factors which determined the success or failure of co-operatives. This study found that:

- co-operatives need access to sufficient start-up funds to take them through initial teething troubles
- seed-corn finance needs to be supplemented by longer term and adequate funds
- products and services must be intrinsically attractive to customers
- products and services will need to be delivered to clients on time, to agreed quality standards and at a profit.

The management of co-operatives calls for skills which can only be acquired through formal training and experience.

> Too many of the co-operatives ... had managers ill equipped for their role. The same union members who insisted that a tradesman must have served an apprenticeship, arro-

gantly assumed that anyone could be a manager. Where such attitudes persist co-operatives will not be well managed and will almost certainly fail.

Workers Co-operatives; Past, Present and Future p.141

In Spain, the Mondragon experience of successful co-operatives confirms the importance of sound management, enterprise and adequate finance for the long-term success of co-operatives. Experience in Spain adds further insight to the advantages and disadvantages of the greater worker involvement in decisions and operations. It can lead to higher levels of quality, improved output and greater job satisfaction. Elsewhere, it has led to resistance to change, excessive delays through protracted decision making and factionalism. The challenge facing those working in the co-operative is to achieve the benefits without incurring the costs.

Case study

Queen Elizabeth Polytechnic

Queen Elizabeth Polytechnic is one of the smaller polytechnics in the UK. It has 12,850 students (3,850 full-time equivalent students) and 290 staff. It has a largely urban catchment of 140,000. This centres on the northern industrial city of Meltwood. The college operates through seven divisions each containing several areas of study. The broad division structure is:

- Business and management
- Hotel and catering
- Electronics and computing
- Media and cultural studies
- Construction and environmental studies
- Mechanical and production engineering
- Social sciences

The subjects taught include Accountancy, Business, Law, Secretarial Studies, Catering, Hotel Management, Tourism, Electrical and Electronic Engineering, Computer Science, IT, Media Studies, Music, Communications, Environmental Studies, Recreation, Building, Manufacturing Sciences, Mechanical Engineering, Sociology, Psychology and Economics.

The employment patterns and industrial structure of the region around Meltwood is broadly similar to the UK as a whole. Recently, however, trends in the overall pattern of employment and industry in the UK seem to be having a more marked effect in Meltwood. There has been a shift away from traditional manufacturing industries and a reduction in the levels of activity in construction as well as a move towards tourism and other services besides somes 'revival' in primary industries. The employment structure is:

	National	Meltwood
Primary	4%	5%
Secondary	24%	21%
Construction	8%	6%
Services	64%	68%

During the period 1971–81 the numbers in employment declined in the area around Meltwood. Manufacturing jobs dropped by 33%, construction by 19% and primary industries by 9%. These losses were partially compensated by a gain of over 18% in the service sector. Urban areas were hit hardest with some of the 'inner city' communities affected especially badly. The adverse effects of these changes in the overall economic structure had been mitigated by some slight increase in the overall population of the area and the college's ability to recruit from other regions especially in subjects in which it had a high reputation, notably Computing and Business. This strength is now being eroded by stronger competition and an ageing population. Regional age structure is:

	1971	1981	1986
Children (0–16)	24%	22%	20%
Work age	58%	58%	58.5%
Retired	18%	20%	21.5%

The influence of these changes on the divisions of the school has varied significantly. Some subjects have gained from their good national reputation as well as the growth in their subjects. This has been especially noticeable in the division of Business and Management. In other fields, the impact has been inconsistent. Innovations such as the Telecommunications Technology programme and a speciality in Rock Music have been successful. The progress made with these initiatives encouraged a large number of similar 'launches' during 1985–6. Relatively few of these were successful.

The problems of structural and economic change have hit the divisions of Construction and Environmental Studies, Mechanical and Production Engineering and Social Sciences especially hard. It is anticipated that the challenges facing these subjects will increase over the next few years. This is especially true given the constitutional changes of April 1989 and the shifts in funding occurring at the same time.

Until the present review, the College's central promotional expenditure was small. Meltwood City Council had insisted that most of the spend was part of its overall education budget. The college expenditure (£) on promotion is:

	1986	1987	1988
Media expenditure	9000	9350	8320
Prospectus	16000	18000	17500
Brochures, etc.	6500	7000	5750
Open day	4000	1500	5000

Divisions have been able to use their own budgets to supplement this. It is hard to be precise about the amounts spent but these appear to range between the £7500 spent by Business and Management and the £450 invested by Social Sciences.

The issue

The Director of the Polytechnic has called upon the heads of the three divisions to advise him on the development policies that should be adopted after Vesting Day. He is especially keen to hear their comments on:

- how the management effort should be organized, especially the split between central and divisional activities
- the ways in which the college and the divisions should direct their efforts
- levels of expenditure and forms of activity.

The task

Produce recommendations on these issues.

Chapter 9

Personal development

Enterprise is human quality. Those who wish to realize this potential are accepting a personal responsibility to develop or express this capacity. Formal education is only part of this process. Mark McCormack comments[1] about his own training in Law at Yale:

> A law school graduate, on the day he or she picks up the sheepskin, is like a learner driver who has studied everything about the science of driving but has never driven a car. In both cases, the heart of the matter lies not in abstract knowledge but in the sharpening of innate talents by experience
>
> Mark McCormack, *The Terrible Truth About Lawyers*, p.11

The raw material for developing personal enterprise is common to all people. Most have a similar mix of physical and mental attributes. The time available varies very little. Opportunities to learn are presented from many quarters. Despite this, ~~only~~ *nobody* ~~a minority~~ realizes their full potential.

Thinking

Neustadt and May[2] are among the leading writers on thinking, and the way individuals and groups approach the analysis and resolution of problems. They centre their analysis of thinking on political enterprise. They ask why some politicians avoid and others encounter difficulties. They build their analysis of their achievements on the way these leaders think about problems. Neustadt and May highlight the limited amount of time that is spent in the systematic, prior analysis of issues before decisions are taken and action implemented. Decisions are taken without sufficient, good quality 'thinking time'.

Their study concentrated on the failure of US leaders to learn from history. Failures often occurred because politicians did not think in a structured way before they acted. They suggest that action was generally based on either 'solutions looking for problems' or false analogies. In each case, more time invested in following a few simple rules at the start might have avoided long-term difficulties. This notion – 'act in haste, repent at leisure' is a valuable starting point for any person seeking to make the best of a situation.

'Get into the habit of writing things down'. This is the fundamental premise of most attempts to improve the quality of analysis. The basic technique can follow the Neustadt and May recommendation that 'things *known*, *unclear* and *presumed* be written down – if only on the back of an envelope'. The approach adopted might follow the *describe – what you know; what you don't know and what you need to know* – advice given to aspiring journalists. The essential disciplines lie in:

* taking time to think
* thinking about the issue(s) first
* arriving at solutions only after the issue is understood
* building up a word picture of the situation.

The relationship between analysis and conclusion is especially important. It takes very little skill to find a justification for virtually any choice or decision. To avoid this precipitous choice or action requires a prior analysis which incorporates as much relevant information as possible even if the material gathered is uncomfortable because it does not fit in with the preconceived ideas or assumptions. Mistakes are better made on a sheet of paper than in a workplace.

Special emphasis is placed on drawing analogies with relevant prior situations. This is not because history repeats itself. It is based on the proposition that the same coalition of circumstances may provoke a similar array of responses. This is especially true if those involved are conditioned by similar circumstances. This stresses the value of properly understanding those whose response will determine success or failure.

The systematic analysis of the behaviour and attitudes of others involved in a project or decision is an integral part of producing solutions that will work. A useful approach involves the construction of a simple chronology of their past work and achievements. It is hard to sell innovation, mobility and change to a colleague who has worked all her life in the same firm. Force field analysis based on this understanding might indicate the ways in which their responses can be influence and change effected.

Alongside these disciplines, the simple journalist's questions of 'where', 'who', 'how', 'why', 'when' and 'what' provide a useful framework on which to build thinking. Outside pressure is probably the greatest barrier to the serious consideration of issues. Effectiveness depends on being able to 'create time and space'. This is similar to the way great sportsmen seem to have that bit more time than their lesser rivals to do the right thing. It expresses a capacity to impose their timing on events rather than react to outside pressures. Confidence is part of this. The individual must feel in control. This shows itself in a determination to keep interruptions to a minimum and organize blocks of time for considering issues.

Time management

Creating time and space is not easy. The pressures to hurry from one crisis to another can be seen in most forms of enterprise. There is some evidence that an ability to 'cope under pressure' and 'handle crises' is more satisfying for the individual than avoiding the problem in the first place. The cost to the venture of this type of management is high. It is useful to employ some basic techniques to get the best use of the time available. This is the one commodity shared out in equal amounts to everyone.

Time is best viewed as a resource which can be allocated well and a good return earned or allocated badly and wasted. This suggests that the first step in getting the best value lies in understanding how it is used now. Auditing time can be done several ways. The most basic involves the creation of a time-use sheet. This is a simple daily calendar of how time is allocated. The time-use calendar is arranged as:

Date		Day	
Time	Activity	Control	Notes
08:00			
08:30			
09:00			
09:30			
10:00			
10:30			
11:00			

Each element in the time-use calendar has a role. The day and the date indicates the extent to which time use varies. It is worth doing the audit regularly and on different days. The activity taking places shows what is happening. There is some work which is unnecessary or can be delegated. Some undertakings merit more time than is spent. The calendar should highlight these features on the way time is spent. Control flags the extent to which the individual can determine the extent of involvement. A student may have no choice about attending a lecture or taking a test. The chairman of a company might be obliged to go to a board meeting. Some things can be avoided or delegated.

An appreciation of how time was used in the past can guide its use in the future. This assumes an understanding of the tasks to be completed. This may not be true. The second step in the better use of time is the creation of action lists of the type outlined below.

Priority	Item	By whom	By when

Each task to be completed should be itemized. This will soon give a picture of the scale and feasibility of the programme of work. Some tasks can be allocated to others. This should be done in time for them to produce good-quality results. This calls for time to be invested in proper briefing and guidance. This preparation should acknowledge their state of knowledge and capabilities. Realism in completion dates assumes some need to recycle actions or amend behaviour. This highlights the importance of priorities. Some tasks are essential. They need to be done. Others are less important. It would be nice if they were done. The former should take priority. The excellent Video Arts film *The Unorganised Manager* makes a valuable distinction between important and urgent tasks. It is easy to confuse urgency with importance. The latter always takes priority. Absolute preference is given to important *and* urgent work.

Faced with several tasks, scheduling events for the greatest effectiveness is essential. The first step involves the allocation of sufficient time for each piece of work. The sequence has a marked influence on performance. Often the hardest and most onerous work is put off until last. This is a mistake. It means that the most daunting pursuit is undertaken when reserves of energy are at their lowest. Fatigue will affect performance.

The persistence of this approach probably reflects the old examination adage – get an easy question under your belt. The difficulty with this tactic is that it fails to acknowledge the diminishing returns for effort which characterizes examination responses. The first two to three pages of an essay answer probably accounts for most of the marks. Extra space given to a very good response has only a marginal effect on grades. Normally it is better to invest effort in generating increased returns with a weaker answer than squeezing the last mark from a stronger response.

A disciplined approach to the work undertaken can be based on the mnemonic AID. Activities can be categorized as Action, Information, Dump. This is especially useful in dealing with correspondence.

Stress

Time pressures and the accompanying sense of lack of control are major sources of stress. This is not necessarily a bad thing. Stress is a natural part of life. The human body has evolved to cope with anxiety. Some of the physiological responses which occur at the level of the autonomic nervous system improve the body's ability to perform. Adrenaline and noradrenaline are

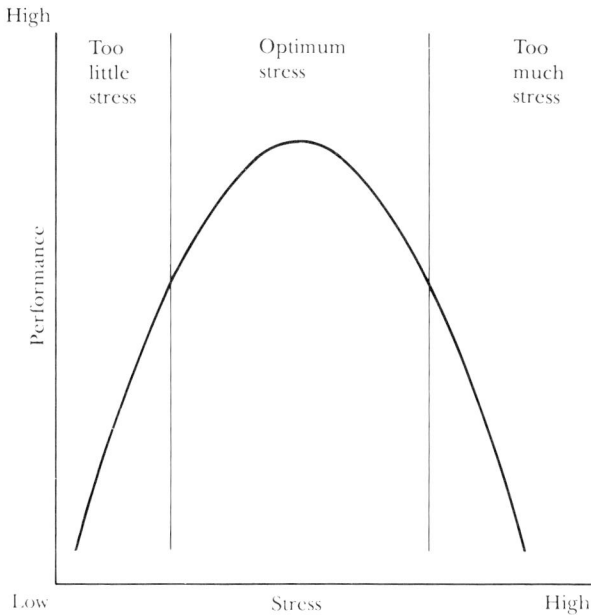

Figure 9.1   Relationship between anxiety and performance

powerful stimulants, speeding up reflexes, increasing heart rate and blood pressure, raising blood sugar levels, and raising bodily metabolism. The result is increased short term capacity and performance, as blood is carried to the muscles and to the lungs, energy supplies are boosted and responses sharpened.

Performance is improved but only for a time and up to a certain level. A reaction is inevitable as the body's ability to cope with this stimulus deteriorates and perform-ance declines. The bell-shaped curve described in research[3] describes the relationship between anxiety and performance (Figure 9.1).

Cooper and Marshall[4] place the causes of stress into seven classifications (Table 9.1).

The adverse effects of a failure to manage stress increase over time. These can include:

- Reduced attention span
- Memory failures
- Aversion to planning
- Irritability
- Sense of powerlessness
- Absenteeism
- Lack of energy
- Unpredictability
- Easily distracted
- Slower responses
- Hypochondria
- Emotionalism
- Speech problems
- Insomnia
- Cynicism

In extreme cases, drug abuse, violence and suicide threats can occur. Action to mini-mize these risks is the main challenge to stress management.

Recognition of the problem is the precondition for successful action. Several of

Table 9.1 Stress classification (after Cooper and Marshall[4])

Category	Stressor
1. Individual	Ambiguity Motivation Change
2. Job	Too much time Too little time Poor physical conditions Lack of training
3. Organization's interaction with outside	Company/family conflict Company/personal values
4. Operations	Poor consultation Restrictions on behaviour Office politics Industrial disputes
5. Relations within enterprise	Relations with boss Relations with colleagues Poor delegation
6. Career development	Overpromotion Underpromotion Lack of job security Frustration
7. Role	Role conflict Role ambiguity Responsibilities for others

the symptoms are outlined above. Some are easier to recognize in others than in ourselves. The more obvious early warnings are moodiness, lack of satisfaction or enjoyment in leisure pursuits and failure to concentrate on issues. Cooper and Marshall[4] highlighted many of the causes of stress in their research.

Tackling stress

The ways of tackling stress can be divided into three broad categories: pre-stress schooling, stress management and post-stress adjustment.

Pre-stress schooling

This involves remembering a number of approaches to stress avoidance. Learning to say 'no' is perhaps the most important. The feeling that there is too much to do and too little time to do it might be valid. It can only be avoided if new, excessive responsibilities or tasks are rejected. There are some aspects of life which induce more stress than others. These should be avoided where possible. Often these are linked with frustration. Fighting battles that cannot be won is a primary source of avoidable stress. Obessiveness causes stress in the individual and among colleagues. The fear of saying 'no' may reflect other concerns. In work, subordinates may take on work because they feel undervalued and seek positive feedback. The creation of strategies for getting feedback is important. Much responsibility for the problem lies with superiors. They can reduce stress among their staff by making demands realistic, giving feedback, listening and avoiding inconsistency.

Stress management

This takes many forms. Rest is probably the best immediate response as fatigue and stress are common partners. Rest may not be possible without distraction. But some forms of distraction can make the situation worse. Those which stimulate the same bodily reactions are especially dangerous. 'Comfort' eating, for example, produces no lasting comfort and increases many stress inducing concerns. Dehydration is a physical symptom of stress. Drinking large quantities of alcohol increases dehydration: this again worsens the situation. Diversion of attention helps by transferring attention to less stressful issues. It provides an opportunity to identify alternative solutions to the challenges being faced.

Meditation and relaxation exercises are effective at reducing tension and overcoming the physical consequences of stress. Meditation operates at several levels. Its simplest form involves concentrating energy and attention at a single idea, theme or object which emerges from a stream of consciousness. Some approaches to meditation emphasize the value of a *mantra*. This is a single word or phrase repeated over and over. All other ideas are driven from consciousness by this notion. Physical release of pent-up emotion or energy works for some. Running or energetic sport shifts attention from the problem while using up the energy released by stress. The optimal responses are often personal. Everyone subject to stress should find a stress management strategy.

Post-stress adjustment

The post-stress adjustment of behaviour and response is important to avoid the long-term dangers. Physical fitness is valuable. Many of the symptoms of stress are physical. The less able the body is to cope, the greater the risk. Other behaviour changes are equally important. Problems of role ambiguity and conflict can only be resolved through discussion and negotiation. This may mean identifying, with colleagues, the factors which provoke stress. Normally, it is better to change lifestyle and work pattern than accept the risks of long-term damage through stress. Toffler[5] underlines the value of 'stability zones' for those facing regular and considerable stress. These might be places or situations within which the individual feels secure. Recognizing and using these will help in coping with stress. Regular reviews of work and behaviour are parts of this process of adjustment.

Negotiating

Many of the causes of stress outlined above – role ambiguity, overwork, lack of security, etc. – reflect a failure to establish a satisfactory work situation. Often, this is not the outcome sought by those involved. Very few firms or managers define jobs to give their employees or colleagues the maximum stress. They do not want the poor performance that this involves. Customers seldom seek to undermine their suppliers by giving impossible deadlines and poor prices. In the vast majority of cases, the source of an unsatisfactory outcome is poor negotiating by either, or both, parties.

Few accomplishments are more important, or more often neglected, in developing individual enterprise than negotiating skills. They affect every aspect of the enterprise from its creation and the early discussions with supporters or bankers to its prosperity based on satisfied colleagues and clients. Negotiation occurs when two or more parties recognize that a specific result can only be achieved if those involved consent. They agree to seek this outcome through discussion and bargaining. It contrasts with the use of power or competition to achieve ends. Negotiation is meaningful only where the parties involved are free and genuinely desire agreement. Within these parameters a range of techniques can be applied to maximize the benefits for either party.

Alex Leighton's comment 'To the blind, all things are sudden', vividly illustrates the value of preparation in negotiation. This should include a serious attempt to understand each party's *minimax* position. This outcome is the *mini*mum possible and the *max*imum sought by each. The ability to see the situation from the other person's perspective is especially useful in the three key phases of negotiations – opening discussion, conflict resolution and concluding an agreement.

Opening discussion

The quality and contribution of the opening discussions depend on the extent to which the preparation allows one party to seize the initiative and shape the agenda. The broad objectives and framework for discussion should be established at this stage. Fisher and Ury[6] supply some basic rules for making progress at this stage:

• Avoid arguments about positions: they distract. Nothing is added to the substantive discussion if the main issue is shrouded by justifications of a specific posture.

- Keep the real issues to the fore: they matter. This means keeping personalities, histories and precedents in the background.

Some approaches to success at this stage bear fruit throughout negotiations. The traditional hard/soft tactic means deciding early on to take one of these stances. The hard approach sees negotiations as a conflict to be won. The soft emphasizes agreement. The prisoner's friend ploy brings the two together but requires two negotiators on one side. One adopts a hard, the other a soft approach.

Fisher and Ury[6] suggest that a more sound approach recognizes the negotiator's interests in both the substantive issue and the relationship. These should be separated and every attempt made to minimize any negative impact from the relationship by not 'deducing their intentions from your fears', 'blaming them for your problems' and by 'giving them a stake in the outcome'.[6] Success in the initial phase depends on appreciating the opponent's position and breaking down any negative impressions.

Conflict resolution

The bulk of negotiations consists of incremental progress based on conflict resolution. Here the dominant requirements are:

- *Reconcile interests not positions* – that is the purpose of this phase. When both parties are seeking an outcome, the result matters, not the positions held before the discussions.
- *Build in options* – these allow for progress. Unless there are several ways of getting to a solution; a hold-up on one, can create an impasse.

The simple act of asking *why* and *why not* can keep discussions moving forward. Another useful mechanism involves checking whether it matters more to you or your opponent. It is worth conceding something that matters more to your rival than to you to sustain progress and establish 'credit'. The cascade strategy can be effective in breaking down log-jams. This is based on the identification of all areas of agreement, even the very small. These loosen the log-jam and provoke a breakthrough. The 'virtuous circle' strategy of finding routes to mutual gain performs a similar function.

Concluding an agreement

Concluding an agreement turns on the ability to recognize opportunities for maximum, enforceable gain. The bargain will need to be acceptable and provide substantive benefits. This means:

- *Making it saleable* – everyone will need to deliver or the process will start again.
- *Making it specific* – this requires a specific and objective statement of outcomes and ways of enforcement.

People undertake negotiations. This human dimension is especially important in the closing phases. It creates opportunities and constraints. Mutual trust might mean that fears are minimized. Battles of will produce waste. The option of saying 'no' and walking away always exists. The speed with which satisfactory negotiations can be concluded depends largely on:

- the quality of prior preparation
- the system of review and appraisal used in negotiations

Negotiators depend on their skills as communicators to progress discussions and win support for their conclusions. Without the ability to win backing, the deal will soon fail.

Communication

David Bernstein[7] opens his discussion of 'Communication in Business' by quoting from Jacques Maisonrouge of IBM

> Most management failures result from, or are accentuated by, a failure to communicate somewhere along the line. Recognition of this need to communicate ought to be written into the job specification of every chief executive and senior manager.

This comment does not go far enough. The same principles apply in very small businesses and in every business situation. Difficulties and failures persistently occur because owners fail to communicate their needs, ambitions or offers to bankers, workers and clients. In the public sector, poor communication can be linked with low teacher moral, dissatisfaction among nurses and disillusion among students. Individual conflicts and disagreements are often linked with a failure to apply some fundamental principles of communication. This is equally true for work inside and outside the enterprise. It is as valid for the reception as the transmission of messages. Put another way, listening skills can be as important as prowess as a speaker. Business failures can be attributed to the failure of managers to listen as often as their failure to express themselves.

Recognition of the two-way nature of communication is *More honour'd in the breach than in the observance*. The ways in which messages are interpreted is shaped by a host of factors. Many of these are outside the direct control of those taking part. Neither the lecturer nor the student will be able to affect the hot, muggy atmosphere in the lecture theatre. Negotiators for a merger between two rival companies will not be able to re-write a tradition of hostility and distrust. Participants take into a situation a history of views, experiences and prejudices. These are affected by the ways they interact, the physical conditions and the people themselves. Students soon recognize the poorly prepared lecturer. A teacher gets to know those who stay up late and don't prepare work. It is against this background that communicators 'send or receive messages in an effort to create meaning in their own minds ... or in the minds of others.[8]'

The task of those wishing to manage communication more effectively lies in structuring and organising these *signals* to achieve their desired ends. These are just four communication channels: visual (sight), auditory (sound), olfactory (smell) and tactile (touch). Each can be used to create an impression. The salesman passes material around his audience to reassure them of its quality. The restaurateur has smells coming from the kitchen as the menu is read. In the vast majority of institutional contexts visual and auditory channels dominate. Managing these is the primary task of the communicator.

Creating the right environment is an important first step. This should minimize negative bias and gain the greatest benefit for the message. Negative bias can come from several sources. The appearance of the individual transmitting the message has a marked effect. This should reassure the audience and add credibility to the message. Eye contact establishes a bridge between those taking part. The physiology matters. There are limits on the amount of information that can be absorbed. This is reduced by lack of trust, emotion and distance.

The presentation

The underlying rule that communication is centred on the receivers focuses attention on *their* objectives. The presentation which does not address the issues which concern clients, in terms they understand will not succeed. The manager who talks to workers about a change in work practice and leaves them with the wrong impression has failed. The way the audience receives and interprets the message is more important than the manner in which it is sent. The rules which guide the formal presentation illustrate many of the principles which underlie all effective communication. These are:

1. Specify the message to be sent.
2. Define the audience.
3. Adjust the message to the capabilities of the audience.
4. Review the medium employed.
5. Fit the message to the medium.
6. Design presentation for clarity.
7. Reinforce verbal with visual signals.
8. Provide opportunities for feedback.

The intent and the message fit best when proper preparation has taken place. In formal presentations this means writing the presentation in full before editing down.

In written communication it involves allowing time for editing and proofreading. Interpersonal communication works best when the initiator has thought through the issues in advance. The parliamentary adage 'never ask a question, unless you know the answer' is equally valid in managerial situations. Final preparation should be undertaken from the audience's perspective. This goes beyond an examination of their characteristics to an attempt to appreciate what they seek from participation. A research report will have one lesson for a fellow researcher, another for a policymaker. The former might want information on methodology and technique, the latter seeks guidelines and recommendations for action.

Most communication involves summaries of the knowledge held by the sender. The lecturer will not be saying everything she knows about a topic. Managers do not describe every facet of a topic. The form of the summary reflects the medium and the audience. The script prepared for the presentation will be pared down to a series of cue cards or headings. The executive summary opens the substantive research report. There are severe limitations on the amount of material that can be retained from any form of communication. These are affected by time and relationship. Jones[9] found that retention of content at the end of a lecture was only 50%, dropping to 25% after a fortnight. Attention span declines rapidly after a fairly short time. This can be extended by the use of stimuli such as visual aids. It can be reduced by the form of the presentation and the environment. Normally, points should be introduced, illustrated, related to the audience and repeated.

The venue should be chosen to support the message. The fashion of 'managing by walking about' recognizes that there are times when it is best to communicate on another's territory. The manager's office helps reinforce authority but may not put subordinates at their ease. Formal presentations require a venue that is large enough for the audience to see and hear. Non-verbal signals through visual aids and body language ought to reinforce the message. Choice and preparation of aids calls for considerable skill. Blackboards and flip-charts are flexible. They can be used to break down barriers and establish rapport with the audience. This can be destroyed by poor writing. Slides and overheads can create a powerful structure, emphasize and explain key points. They are inflexible. The amount of material contained is limited. Words less than 24 points in size will be hard to read at a distance.

Today Today
24 point   10 point

Figure 9.2 Different type sizes

Feedback is a help not a hindrance when it is well managed. Feedback is employed to reinforce, clarify and redirect messages. Reinforcement occurs when the feedback enables the sender to develop a point or issue. A manager might use questions to illustrate the benefits of a wage deal to specific groups. Clarification happens where confusion or distortion is tackled. This is often linked with a redirection of the message to meet the needs of specific participants.

The use of presentations as a model for communication has two central weaknesses. First, it presumes a high degree of source control. Second, it employs a single source model of transmission. Most enterprises have a variety of formal and informal communication networks. Briefing meetings, newsletters, meetings and noticeboards are among the tools used to organize the flow of communication. The grapevine is a powerful feature of the informal process. It can perform positive and negative roles. Skilled leaders use the grapevine to sound out responses to novel ideas and developments. The impact of bad news can be softened by leaking information. The type of bargaining position to be adopted in union negotiations can be flagged. The grapevine can reduce risks and define what is acceptable without confrontation. There are risks in reinforcing the contribution of the grapevine. Rumours can spread misleading information. Morale can be undermined if opposition groups win control of the network.

Networking

There is growing evidence that successful enterprise relies on the effective use of networks of relationships.[10] These are: communication systems, patterns of relationships and ways of looking at authority.

Communication networks take many forms. These include hub, Y, chain, circle and all channel systems. The typical entrepreneurial firm is hub-based with the proprietor acting as the centre around which the network operates. Client/customer relationships are often Y-shaped. The account manager will take information from two sources, organize and structure the material and pass it to clients. Bureaucracies are chain-based. Material follows a simple and formalized 'chain of command'. Circle-based networks are usually based on equal contributions by the parties. A seminar group will tend to operate on this basis. The all-channel structure offers the maximum satisfaction for all members. This is especially effective for research and development work.

Each structure has strengths and weaknesses. The hub is highly centralized. This gives the leadership or entrepreneurial group a great deal of control but at the cost of group satisfaction. The links with the entrepreneur are very gratifying for individual group members but weaken other managers. The Y-shaped network is less centralized and predictable. It widens access to information and gives greater authority to line managers. The chain structure reduces ownership and involvement by members. This is important where routine and system are more important than individual initiative. Circular networks have minimum central direction and distribute ownership widely. Learning situations gain from this type of 'group ownership'. The 'all-channel' structure is low in central direction and control. This links it with creative or research situations in which flows occur on a *need to* not a *required to* basis.

The networks of relationship that an enterprise creates provide a framework for business development and a support system for growth or adversity. The effort that is invested in managing these alliances can generate substantial returns in most aspects of the venture. Personal relationships can provide advice, leads and reassurance. The approach of Gerald Eadie, a successful Scottish entrepreneur, illustrates this. When faced with a problem, he turns to contacts or firms who face the same challenge. He asks them how they tackle the issue. He tries to understand how their experience can help him deal with the same issue. Building up contact lists is a continuous process. Business cards are collected. 'Contact books' are maintained. Databases created. They link the venture to a wider field of expertise.

The growing importance of knowledge or expertise-based enterprise has raised questions about traditional authority systems. New technology-based firms have found that hierarchies based on power and authority pose problems in creativity and consensus-based situations.

> Tandem is founded on a well ordered set of management beliefs and practices. The philosophy of the company emphasises the importance of people: 'that's Tandem's greatest resource – its people, creative action, its fun' ... Top management spends about half of its time in training and in communicating ... Tandem has no formal organisational chart and few formal rules ... Tandem seems to maintain a balance between autonomy and control without relying heavily on centralised or formalised procedures, or rigid status hierarchies
>
> Terence Deal and Allan Kennedy, *Corporate Cultures*,[11] pp. 9-10

Workplace-based hierarchies reflected the needs of mechanical and electromechanical technologies. These depended on large numbers of workers coming together to perform centrally directed, relatively uniform tasks. The mill, the car factory, even the large branch of a bank operated this way. The technology worked best when the efforts of large numbers were mobilized under central direction. Many new industries do not benefit from this amount of control. Software engineering, computing, design and new technology-based firms are underpinned by technologies which operate equally well through distributed networks. The workers do not need to be in the same place. Co-operation and creativity is as important as discipline and standardization. This scenario shifts the emphasis in enterprise management from control of subordinates to stimulating the best from collaborators.

Self development

Enterprise development is characterized by rapid shifts in the needs of the participants. Cuts in government help for the Arts might require an increased effort to raise sponsorship. A tax change can create opportunities for a charity to raise new finance. Cuts in interest rates may encourage new investments. Those involved in the venture will need to adapt and respond to these flows. The importance of certain skills will alter. The ability to fill out an application form for a government grant, to lobby politicians, will become more/less important than skills in designing a promotional campaign. Finance from Brussels might become more important than finance from Edinburgh or London. Developing the right portfolio of skills and knowledge is a constant challenge for those involved in enterprise.

Formal programmes of education, training and information gathering abound. Large organizations constantly review the offerings available. Some firms allocate a fixed percentage of their wage bill to education and training. It is sometimes suggested that 2–3% is a minimum. Others operate on a less-structured basis. They send people on programmes when a need can be clearly identified. The opportunities range from formal certificated courses such as MBAs, to open entry seminars and workshops.

Pilkington's, for example, send many of their managers on MBAs. They have a highly structured approach to the type of MBA and the manager's needs. In the public sector, the NHS has invested in the development of a Diploma in Health Service Management. Beside this, it sends senior staff to leading management centres where they will work alongside executives from the public sector. The Committee of Vice-Chancellors and Principals has organized a specialist centre at Sheffield University for University management. It arranges short courses for Heads of Departments. The Training Agency has taken a lead in developing short courses for managers in small- and medium-sized firms. Many private firms are active in this area. Bankers and accountants arrange special seminars for their clients. Others operate on a wholly commercial basis. They arrange courses with a view to making a profit from the event.

Traditionally, development programmes were initiated by employers. Their interests dominated. This is changing. Ownership and control is centred on the employee.

> We need to place more onus on individuals to manage their own careers. This is healthier for the individual, should help to reduce problems arising from career blockages in later life, and should reduce cases of serious mismatch.[12]

Self-directed learning places several demands on individuals and enterprises. It encourages both to seek and create opportunities to realize their full potential. It highlights the importance of continually adapting and upgrading skills and knowledge. It brings out the value of support groups within ventures. It links personal development and human resource strategy and places both at the heart of the venture.

Appraisal is constant. It takes place every time a task is attempted or interaction occurs. It is a judgement about the extent to which the competencies exist to complete a job. Performance appraisal is carried out formally in most large organizations. Self appraisal provides a framework for personal adjustment to circumstances. It has many advantages over institutional appraisal. It minimizes conflicts of loyalty,[13] reduces the preoccupation with technique[14] while encouraging stronger links between appraisal and action. There are a variety of approaches to systematic self appraisal. They have in common:

- Establishment of a regular routine of annual or biannual assessment.
- Creation of a set of criteria which make sense to the individual and are relevant to the venture.
- Distinguishing some form of performance measures.
- Identification of the means to meet personal development needs.

It is advisable to involve someone else as a mentor or adviser in this undertaking. This can be done formally or informally. It may involve a trusted outsider. Non-executive directors can perform this role. It helps individuals step outside their normal roles and explore their development needs. Successful enterprise calls for the progressive improvement of knowledge and skill through personal development.

Leadership

There is probably no aspect of enterprise more highly valued, more hotly debated or more fraught with risk than leadership. It poses a challenge to individuals and societies which it is hard to meet and even harder to ignore. It is not a function of technical skill.

> Undeniably, De Lorean began his career equipped with engineering skills that bordered on genius, plus an inexhaustible supply of energy and ambition. One can only guess with sadness at what an enormous contribution he might have made. Ironically, it is the engineer's definition of success – 'does it work' – that points up the barrenness of his subsequent career.
>
> Ivan Fallon and James Strodes, *De Lorean*, p. 431[15]

It does not reflect lofty ambitions:

> Most of Carter's initiatives came to nought. He himself repudiated the tax rebate scheme. Congressional campaign financing died in committee. Most of the pork barrel projects were restored. Reorganisation and zero-based budgeting produced disappointing results. Hospital cost containment met unconquerable resistance. Social security reform would be rewritten on the Hill; tax and welfare reform would die *aborning*.
>
> Richard Neustadt and Ernest May, *Thinking in Time*, p. 67[16]

Leadership is 'the process whereby an individual exerts a positive influence over the behaviour of others without the use of coercion'.[17] This modest definition omits the four issues which have dominated thinking about leadership:

- Is leadership an intrinsic characteristic of certain people?
- How much does the behaviour of the led affect leadership behaviour?
- Do certain situations produce particular leaders?
- Can leadership be developed?

There is evidence that certain characteristics are closely associated with leadership. These include fluent speech, relevant knowledge, personal control, interpersonal dominance, creativity, self confidence, desire to achieve, acceptance of responsibility, interest in achievement, interpersonal skills and willingness to participate.[18] All these features are not shown by all leaders. Some will be more highly esteemed and more important in certain situations. This highlights the importance of the behaviour of the led and the situation in shaping leadership.

People affect the contribution of a leader's role. It is accepted more easily during periods of external threat; when established authority systems are not working; where internal conflict exists and where it is bolstered by tradition or success. The developing enterprise is likely to experience most of these situations. Need is, however, no guarantee that successful leadership will emerge. Northern Ireland was desperate for industrial leadership before De Lorean. The erosion of presidential authority before Carter made most Americans want him to succeed. The same pattern of need and leadership failure recurs throughout history:

> Jean II, who succeeded his father, Philip VI, could have served Machiavelli as model

for Anti-Prince. Impolitic and impetuous, he never made a wise choice between alternatives and seemed incapable of considering the consequences of an action in advance. Though brave in battle, he was anything but a great captain. Without evil intent, he was to foster disaffection to the point of revolt and lose half his kingdom and his person to the enemy, thereby leaving his country leaderless to meet its darkest hour.

> Barbara Tuckman, *A Distant Mirror*, p. 126

Attempts to shape and develop leadership skills can be seen throughout history. The advice given by her nobels to Queen Amalasuntha of the Ostrogoths on the education of her son illustrates their views of the right leadership training for a king.

> O lady, you are not dealing justly by us, nor doing that which is expedient for the nation, in your way of educating your son. Letters and book learning are very different from manly courage and fortitude, and to hand over a lad to the teaching of greybeards is generally the way to make him a coward and caitiff. He who is to do daring deeds must be emancipated from fear of the pedagogue and be practising martial exercise.
>
> Procopius, *The Persian, Vandal and Gothic Wars*,
> quoted in R.C. Davis, *A History of Medieval Europe*[19]

Most approaches to leadership education attempt to improve both the quality of the decisions or choices made by leaders and their acceptance by others.

Vroom[20] has concluded that; 'managers can learn to become more effective leaders'. John Adair[21] in his book on developing leadership skills highlights three related tasks which the leader must perform to perform his role (Figure 9.3). He presents awareness, control and progress as the building blocks of leadership.

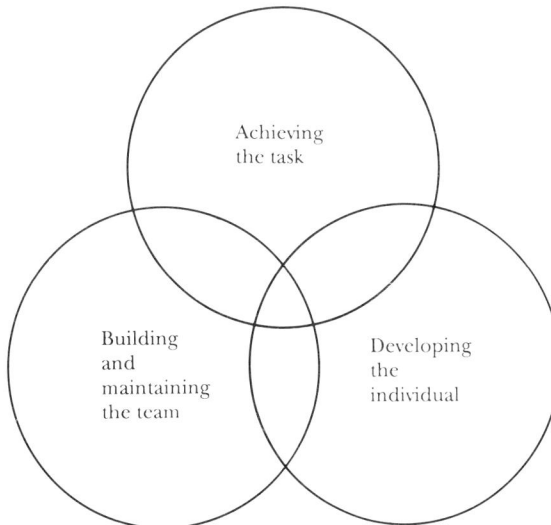

Figure 9.3   What a leader has to do

The first task in leadership development involves creating awareness in oneself and among others of the job to be done and roles to be performed. The leader thinks through the situation and is in a position to properly guide others. Behavioural, psychological and contextual factors will affect performance. Effective leaders are sensitive to the situation faced. These are taken into account in the way the briefing is delivered and structured. Any confusion over expectations or responsibilities will reduce the effectiveness of individuals and the group. Boosting these planning, briefing and situational skills underpins leadership development.

This is underscored by the promotion of control skills. These combine self and group control. There is nothing effective or attractive in loss of self control. It shows weakness, provokes reactions that cannot be predicted and distorts judgement. Some personal trick for retaining self discipline especially when provoked is invaluable. Breathing exercises are useful. Exhale through your mouth more than you inhale for a few moments. A deliberate smile can help. The time to 'blow your top' is in private when the consequences can be predicted and contained. Group control depends on knowing what is expected of a situation and managing the situation to achieve these goals. In dealing with others, the principle of public praise and private criticism has won many leaders, allies and supporters.

Chairing meetings

A skilful chairperson illustrates many of these group control skills. The purpose of the meeting will be defined and reviewed in advance. Some attempt to predict the key issues will be made with close colleagues. Prior discussions might avoid time-wasting debate. Compromises are easier in private than in public. Agendas and papers should be distributed in advance. The Chair or Secretary ought to be fully aware of any procedural rules or standing orders. At the meeting, the Chair should be more concerned with process than content. A Chairperson with strong views on a topic should vacate the Chair for this issue or delegate the argument.

Gauging the views and sense of the meeting is a primary responsibility. A specific speaker is less important than the reactions of the audience. The power to choose speakers is useful. It can draw out important but reticent views. The Chair should not be afraid to employ these to counterbalance the more vigorous speakers. It is vital that the Chair reduces any tension and appears in control. A sense of humour and an ability to appear reasonable are invaluable. Judging the moment to summarize and close the debate is crucial. Some pre-test for consensus is advisable especially when the mood of the meeting is emerging. The pre-test is an attempt to summarize the views of those involved. It is the responsibility of the Chair to agree deadlines for progress, set review dates and allocate action.

Making progress as a leader or with the task needs a willingness to learn or adapt. Successful leaders learn from watching others. They relate these lessons to their own experiences and situations. The adage – when you stop learning, you're dead – has a special relevance to leadership. Advancing the task calls for two distinctive features of leadership. These are: the ability to identify solutions, not problems; and the skill to transfer ownership of the solution to those with responsibility for implementation. In both of these, the core talent lies in keeping close to those being led. Bonar Law summarized this well when he said 'I must follow them. I am their leader'.

Barbara Tuckman[22] illustrated the danger of losing this link;

> Three outstanding attitudes – obliviousness to the growing disaffection of constituents, primacy of self-aggrandisement . . . [the] illusion of invulnerable status – are persistent aspects of folly.

This dual view of leadership, the individual and the group is well summarized by Tom Peters.[23] He describes his leadership tools: develop an inspiring vision; manage by example; and be visible. These are linked to a system of empowering others by listening to them, deferring to those at the sharp end of the enterprise, delegating good things, not just bad things, and championing the interests of achievers over constrainers.

Conclusion

Successful enterprise depends on the ability to fully realize human potential. People provide the 'edge' which allows voluntary agencies to meet complex needs in challenging situations. Their talents enable small firms to convert raw materials to products and services. Their abilities allow drama groups to perform, civil servants to interpret needs and scientists to gain new insights. The challenge of enterprise lies in converting this potential to achievement. Each member of a venture has a responsibility to develop this potential in himself or herself and their colleagues.

There are a series of steps in this process. A strategy for harvesting this latent capacity is essential. It is based on an appraisal of needs and capabilities. Pressure of events puts a premium on time management. Change calls for skills in negotiations. Once the knowledge needs are identified, their value and level can be established. Public agencies are generally managed through a system of consensus. Chairmanship is an important technique. Members of the group look for leadership especially in defining the goals of the venture, defining the core skills and managing the capabilities of members. The energy of each participant and the venture will need to be directed to maximum effect. Sustaining this effort of self development will involve dedication and commitment.

> The Hill, though high, I covet to ascend
> The difficulty will not me offend,
> For I perceive the way of life lies here;
> Come, pluck up, heart; lets neither faint nor fear;
> Better, though difficult, the right way go,
> Than wrong, though easy, where the end is woe
> > Bunyan, *Pilgrim's Progress*, 1678

The creation of a role model through a commitment to self development will help the venture besides the individual.

Case Study

Personal Development

A careful appraisal of the way time, energy and effort is invested lies at the centre of improved personal performance. Over the next week, keep a detailed diary of the way your time is spent. Map this in terms of productivity and pleasure.

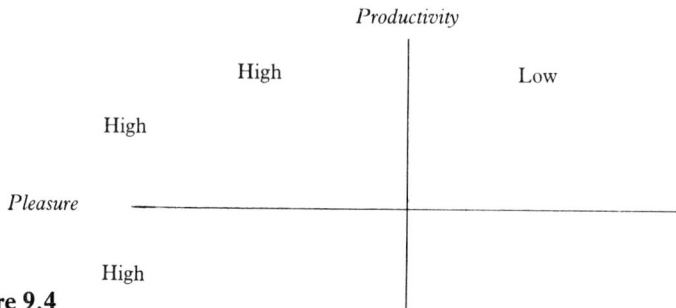

Productivity

High   Low

High

Pleasure

High

Figure 9.4

Task

Relate this analysis to the reasons why your time is spent either unproductively or without enjoyment. Develop two strategies to avoid investing time in activities that are unproductive and disagreeable. Look for ways of making this time more productive and/or agreeable.

References

1. McCormack, M.H. (1988) *The Terrible Truth About Lawyers*, London, Collins.
2. Neustadt, R.E. and May, E.R. (1988) *Thinking in Time*, New York, The Free Press.
3. Yerkes, R.M. and Dobson, J.D. (1908) Relationship of strength of signal to rapidity of habit formation, *Journal of Comparative Neurology*, vol. 15, pp. 459–82.
4. Cooper, C.L. and Marshall, L. (1977) *The Management of Stress*, Personnel Review, **4**, no. 4.
5. Toffler, A. (1970) *Future Shock*, London, Bodley Head.
6. Fisher, R. and Ury, W. (1981) *Getting to Yes*, London, Hutchinson.
7. Bernstein, D. (1984) *Company Image and Reality*, Eastbourne, Holt, Reinhart and Winston.
8. Baird, R.A. (1977) *The Dynamics of Organizational Communication*, New York, Harper and Row.
9. Referred to in Handy, C. (1985) *Understanding Organizations*, London, Penguin, p. 357.
10. Foy, N. (1980) *The Yin and Yang of Organisations*, London, Grant McIntyre.

11. Deal T. and Kennedy A. (1982) *Corporate Cultures*, London, Penguin.
12. Hodge, R. (1987) Commitment to management education and development. *Management Education and Development*, 18, part 3, Autumn, pp. 194–203.
13. Gouldner, A.W. (1985) Cosmopolitans and locals: towards an analysis of latent social roles. *Administrative Science Quarterly*, 2, pp. 444–80.
14. Hogan A. (1986) A Question of Appraisal? *Management Education and Development*, **17**, part 4, Winter, pp. 315–23.
15. Fallon, J. and Strodes, J. (1983) *De Lorean*, London, Coronet.
16. Neustadt, R.E. and May, E.R. (1988) *Thinking in Time*, New York, The Free Press.
17. Kempner, T. (1971) *A Handbook of Management*, London, Penguin.
18. Stogdill, R. (1974) *Handbook of Leadership*, London, Macmillan.
19. Davis, R.C. (1963) *A History of Medieval Europe*, London, Longmans.
20. Vroom, V.H. (1982) Can leaders learn to lead? In Hampton, D., Summer, C. and Webber, R. *Organizational Behavior and the Practice of Management*, Glenview, Illinois, Scott, Foresman and Co.
21. Adair, J. (1983) *Effective Leadership*, London, Pan.
22. Tuckman, B. (1984) *The Pursuit of Folly*, London, Penguin.
23. Peters, T. (1987) *Thriving on Chaos*, London, Pan.

Chapter 10

Group work

The relationship between the individual and the group lies at the core of enterprise development. The group provides both a challenge and an opportunity to those individuals seeking to realize themselves through enterprise. The challenge lies in the constraints which the group imposes on the person. Groups have rules, values and norms of behaviour which members are expected to recognize and generally obey. There are penalties which can be imposed. Even an arch-individualist like Mark McCormack[1] can say:

> Don't go one-by-one with the boss. If you win the battle you're probably going to lose the war. And the more right you are, the more damage it will do in the long term.

Working within these limitations, to tap the potential of the group, is the recurrent challenge of enterprise. Andrew Grove[2] highlights this, when he comments that 'a manager's most important responsibility is to elicit top performance from his subordinates.' He is describing the opportunities which can be tapped when an individual works through others. They can channel their energy, resources and expertise. These assets can extend and complement those provided by the individual. The entrepreneur's primary contribution often lies in acting as a catalyst to release this group potential and help the team achieve far more than earlier seemed possible.

The creation of synergy or making $2 + 2 = 5$ is sometimes seen as the primary contribution of enterprise. This calls for a sensitivity to group situations. It may mean subordinating part of self to the needs of others. John Adair[3] illustrates this with rhyme: *A Short Course On Leadership*:

> The six most important words . . .
> 'I admit I made a mistake'
> The five most important words . . .
> 'I am proud of you'
> The four most important words . . .
> 'What is your opinion?'
> The three most important words . . .
> 'If you please'
> The two most important words . . .

'Thank you'
The one most important word . . .
'We'
And the least most important word . . .
'I'.

An understanding of groups and the ways they affect ventures can be the difference between realizing an opportunity and missing a chance.

Pervasiveness

Most people spend the bulk of their lives in groups. These can be informal or formal. Informal groups are those which are *not* deliberately formed to achieve specific objectives. Friends meeting regularly for dinner, a family or casual acquaintances meeting at a sports event are examples of informal groups. They have power and influence but this is not applied in a systematic way to achieve specified goals. Their influence changes over time. They shape attitudes and values but seldom in a structured and organized way. At times their influence is considerable. Family pressures might make a manager reluctant to work long hours, relocate or accept new responsibilities. The group of colleagues meeting over lunch in the college refectory can carry and shape rumours about proposed changes. A clique within an amateur dramatic group can make the work of the director easy or hard. These informal groups are built around the people involved. They change or evolve with the membership.

Formal groups exist to serve specific purposes. There is usually some element of thought and design invested in the structure. The goal or purpose will often be open to review. Political parties, charities, public institutions or commercial concerns are the more obvious forms of formal group. Within these, there will be other formal groups established to perform tasks and achieve objectives. The Young Conservatives provide a means of addressing the specific interests of young people within the Conservative party. The sponsorship committee of a charity will be expected to seek corporate support for certain activities and events. The finance department of a museum is charged with managing its funds. The R&D department of a firm undertakes research which it expects to convert into new products.

The division between the formal and informal is useful for analysis and definition but can imply a false separation. People move between one and the other. They can co-exist. They influence each other. The informal group determines values and attitudes and the formal group shapes behaviour. Specific actions are, however, affected by attitudes. The enthusiasm and commitment of individuals to a venture is swayed by the attitudes of friends, family and members of social groups. Some ventures successfully tap this support. Work in the media is highly esteemed by many social groups. This makes it easier for those involved to recruit talented people. Other work, for example, in heavy manufacturing industry does not have this status. This influences recruitment, retention and payment systems. It can create a national problem. The low status given to engineers in the UK is linked with the decline in the UK's industrial and economic base.

Roles

Within an enterprise, groups can perform a variety of roles. These include:
- allocation of tasks
- people development
- liaison
- negotiation
- individual support
- identification of expertise
- creating a sense of identity
- control of operations
- information processing
- communication
- review and evaluation
- pleasure
- idea development.

Each of these has a value for the enterprise and its members. Very large organizations can overwhelm their members while losing control of their operations. The formation of smaller sub-groups or teams makes it easier for members to relate to each other and the task(s). Control and evaluation is easier when work is broken down into smaller projects which the team can handle. The KISS maxim, *Keep It Simple, Stupid*, highlights and gains from organizing work into simpler and more manageable tasks.

Group dynamics

Although all groups are capable of performing the above roles, some are more effective and others operate differently. The reasons for these variations lie in the way they are set up, their remit, the structure and the way the members work together. Groups are created for a variety of purposes. They can be temporary. A Vice-Chancellor will bring together a group of senior academics to prepare the university's bid for funding under the Training Agency's Enterprise and Higher Education Initiative. It is assumed that the group will break up once the task is completed. A polytechnic Director might establish a Directorate for Academic Services. This might be a permanent restructuring of these operations. The way the group is created will influence the group.

Staff drawn together 'temporarily' will usually be able to pool a wider range of skills. Much of this will not be directly relevant to the task. The ability of the chairperson or co-ordinator to mobilize this wider portfolio of skills quickly determines the effectiveness of the group. This type of team can be created quickly and may be able to identify more radical solutions. It is usually strong on policy and weak on implementation. The strengths and weaknesses of permanent groups mirror those of transient bodies. They take longer to set up but will see a task to completion. They can draw upon more relevant, specialist skills. They can be 'held responsible' for their work in a more clearly identifiable way. More effort will be invested in design to ensure the right skills base, optimum size (large enough to do the work but not much larger), that relationships can be established and that there exists a balance between homogeneity for implementation and heterogeneity for creativity.

The structure of the group will influence its effectiveness. Size is very important (see Table 10.1).[4,5]

Table 10.1 Size band structure of groups

Size band	Feature
2–5	Greater member satisfaction, greater anxiety, more likely to achieve consensus
5–11	More accurate decisions, greater creativity
11+	Wider external networks, more conservative

The internal organization and its relation with the external environment affects the way work is carried out and overall performance. Groups with formal and closely defined roles are better at carrying out repetitive tasks. More open structures encourage creativity. Smaller groups with shared experiences and values are resilient and capable of heavy workloads.

Group-think

The willingness of more cohesive groups to work together and share aspirations can adversely affect judgement. This is especially true when the group feels challenged by outsiders. Janis[6] described this phenomenon as 'group-think'. It occurs when the search for identity with the group and agreement undermines judgement and reduces the willingness to reassess policies. Janis identified eight symptoms of Group-think.

1. *Invulnerability* – Members are over-optimistic. This leads them to take excessive risks with little serious consideration of alternatives.
2. *Collective rationalization* – Contrary evidence is dismissed through explanations which avoid serious reappraisal of assumptions.
3. *Inherent morality* – The group is so confident of the rightness of its actions that doubts are rejected.

4. *Stereotyping* – Critics and opponents are allocated a stereotype which eliminates the need to seriously consider their position or response.
5. *Pressure* – Demands for loyalty are used to repress doubts and keep members in line.
6. *Self-censorship* – Members suppress their questions to retain group esteem.
7. *Illusion of unanimity* – This is maintained vigorously. Silence is treated as agreement.
8. *Mindguards* – Specific individuals take on the task of controlling information flows and restricting those ideas which might challenge the consensus.

Examples of group-think can be identified in a host of situations. Firms become locked into a new product launch despite overwhelming evidence of its likely failure. Political leaders convince themselves that a policy must be seen through. Leadership groups in public bodies persuade themselves that 'there is no alternative'. The higher the self belief, the tighter the security, the more ego and judgement become confused and the greater the risk of group-think. Avoiding this risk calls for:

- *Leaders* who encourage debate and resist the temptation to lock themselves into solutions
- *Resistance* to unnecessary security
- *Endorsement* of review and evaluation

The creation of an effective team of co-workers and collaborators reduces the risks of 'group-think' beside mobilizing the talents of its members to group goals.

Team building

The notion of a team adds a further dimension to the idea of people working together. It implies a harmony, a cohesion and a sense of additionality. These may not be present when individuals work together. The harmony grows from the support members give to each other. When a team member has problems, the others cover and help. This happens spontaneously. The leader's role becomes guidance and help not direction. The cohesion comes from the different but complementary skills each member brings to the joint task. Teams can handle several tasks but they deal with them together.[7] The additionality is based on the team's ability to achieve more together than as a collection of individuals. In sport, the failure of collections of stars contrasts with the successes of less glamorous but more cohesive teams. Keller[8] found that cohesiveness was the best predictor of the success of R&D groups.

Teams do not emerge spontaneously or naturally. Their creation depends on an awareness of their value in a situation and a team building and maintenance effort. Teamwork is not necessary in all situations. Many of the Arts are individualistic. Writers and painters work on their own for most of the time. Athletes often need back-up but their achievements are usually private. Some teams are very short lived. A national sports team will be drawn together for a very short period and broken up as players return to their clubs. Emergencies can spontaneously produce the type of bonding and team work that can takes years to build in normal circumstances.

Team building usually follows a cycle of problem recognition, team design, adjustment and recruitment, bonding, performance and review. Sharing is a crucial element in team building. This starts with a collective grasp of the same task or goal. Members will sublimate some element of themselves to the challenge faced by the group. A soccer player passes to a colleague in a better position to score. The nurse ignores the impatience of the surgeon in the operating theatre. The star accepts a lesser part in a play. The soccer team wins but the individual gets less glory. The surgical team pioneers a new technique but the nurse is unfairly criticized. The play is a success but the star shares the limelight.

Team design is based on three related activities:

1. Work diagnosis
2. Individual work
3. Collaboration.

The analysis of the task indicates the resources required for success. The ways assets will be deployed need to be understood and communicated by all members of the team. Clarity of objectives and assignments helps participants to focus their efforts. Some flexibility is advisable especially where good-quality communication is available. An appreciation of the contribution of the members to each aspect of the work will help them to weld their skills together. Performance indicators are useful.

Feedback sustains progress and a direction. Information, advice and positive and negative comments bolster teamwork. In the initial stages, this pattern should be established. The 'team' should pool ideas, describe resources and skills available and acknowledge any limitations or shortages. Some attempt ought to be made to outline the ways gaps will be filled. Cover for colleagues is a crucial part of this.

Although the leader has a disproportionate effect on teamwork each member has an active part to play. Listening and responding skills are important. Effective listening means:

- *Getting ready to listen:* This is shown by sitting upright, not slouching, watching the speaker and avoiding distractions.
- *Listening actively:* Feedback is at the centre of this. Points made by the speakers will be questioned mentally by the listeners. Note-taking helps. A verbatim record is impossible but key points help the listener to master the ideas.
- *Withholding evaluation:* An open mind reduces the risk that premature judgements will reduce interest and attention.

Co-operation is an integral element of team work. This involves encouraging others to play their part, tolerance of failure and consistent efforts at bonding the group. Progress reviews are an integral feature of reinforcing teamwork. An understanding of the factors that motivate members will help the leader direct its endeavours profitably. Money can play a part in motivation but sense of achievement, recognition, interest, prospects of advancement and intrinsic interest are equally valuable.

Delegation

Teamwork calls for trust and respect for all those involved in the enterprise. This creates opportunities for delegation. Most entrepreneurs find this difficult. The notion that it is sometimes necessary to invest an hour to save five minutes sits badly with them. Impatience with others is often linked with a strong achievement orientation. Reluctance to delegate is increased when poor delegation produces poor results. The mixture of a sense of being indispensable and poor performance by a subordinate is a great ego booster. It reinforces a feeling of being indispensable but as the saying goes: *The graveyards are full of indispensable men.*

Successful delegation can increase the productivity of most members of the enterprise. It works when the delegator trusts those to whom tasks are transferred. Ideally, it involves some choice by both parties. It works when time and effort is invested in providing the knowledge and skills to do the job. Initially, this will take longer than merely doing the work. It is an investment for longer term returns. The activities delegated ought to be a mutually acceptable mix of work. Merely 'dumping' unpleasant chores is neither fair nor effective.

Feedback and guidance precede increased discretion. Blanchard and Johnson[9] highlight the value of early and frequent feedback. They talk about 'one minute praising' and 'one minute reprimands'. The former emphasizes the gains from immediate feedback based on specific successes. The approach to reprimand combines immediacy and detail with a strong sense that the issue has been dealt with. Too often resentment and bitterness build up after a criticism because people feel that they, not their actions, are unsatisfactory.

> The second half of the reprimand: Shake hands, or touch them in a way that lets them know you are honestly on their side.
>
> Blanchard K. and Johnson S. *The One Minute Manager*,
> London, Collins, 1983

Some pattern to activities and ownership of results will increase the job satisfaction and initiative of subordinates. These will be linked to accepted performance criteria and periodic review. Delegation poses an additional challenge to the enterprising. It imposes a separation between responsibility and activity that is alien to their world view. The central dilemma of delegation is that the work can be delegated but accountability remains.

International comparisons

Much of the recent literature on the way enterprise and organization can be linked has been influenced by the success of Japan and other high growth economies.[10] Ventures in these societies seem more effective at sustaining enterprise without provoking conflicts between the individual and the group or between groups. Consensus-based management has demonstrated its ability to innovate and change without much of the conflict seen in the UK. This can be seen in new businesses, new product development, private, voluntary and social group behaviour. There is a suggestion that a restructuring of some areas of traditional conflict especially worker – employer relations is occurring. Sir Pat Lowry, the Chairman of ACAS (the Advisory and Conciliation Service) commented:[11]

> For years I accepted that in an uncertain industrial relations world the one certainty was that because management objectives and employee relations do not always coincide, conflict in the employment relationship was inevitable. Now, I am not so sure ... [if] we accept that even the possibility of conflict would be an industrial relations defeat, we are far more likely to avoid it.

Other aspects of international links are influencing the ways groups work.

Many projects are moulded around international groups. This occurs in most forms of enterprise including private industry, the Arts, sport and voluntary work. The development by Electrolux of a new fridge-freezer illustrates how this works in commerce:[12]

> Under the leadership of Heikki Takanen, a Finn based in Stockholm, the product was designed and developed for 'global' markets by a multidisciplinary task force from Europe and the United States, meeting sometimes on one side of the Atlantic, sometimes on the other. Much of the design work was done in Italy, but the product was engineered in Finland with Swedish assistance and with particular marketing input from Britain.
>
> Lorenze, C., Birth of a Transnational, p. 83

International collaboration is longer established in the Arts and sport. This probably reflects the universal nature of these activities. In turn, it is possible to link the openness and tolerance to other approaches seen in these fields with a cosmopolitan perspective. The increasingly international orientation of voluntary activity reflects communication systems which highlight issues, the global nature of some topics and the greater power of international agencies. Action by Live Aid to tackle starvation in Ethiopia was provoked by TV pictures of the suffering. Greenpeace draws together volunteers from across the world to attack the worldwide issue of environmental damage. Success may not be possible without the backing of international agencies like the European Commission or the United Nations. None of these organizations can achieve their goals unless ethnocentric approaches to the combination of enterprise and organization are replace by internationalism.

Conclusion

Most of those who see themselves as enterprising have some suspicion of groups, organizations or institutions. Often, this reflects a fear that the group will develop a life of its own. Parkinson[13] vividly illustrated the ways in which the establishment can grow regardless of the task to be performed.

> Here are some typical figures. The strength of the navy in 1914 could be shown as 146 000 officers and men, 3249 dockyard officials and clerks, and 57 000 dockyard workmen. By 1928 there were only 100 000 officers and men and only 62 439 workmen, but

the dockyard officials and clerks by then numbered 4558. As for warships, the strength in 1928 was a mere fraction of what it had been in 1914 – fewer than 20 capital ships in commission as compared with 62. Over the same period the Admiralty officials had increased in number from 2000 to 3569.

Parkinson C., *Parkinson's Law*, p. 20

There is little evidence that this tendency to grow and overwhelm has lessened over the years. Those seeking to drive a venture forward are right to be wary.

The challenge lies in keeping control of the group, using its resources well and encouraging enterprise within it. Control is not a matter of using power and authority. Skilled leaders seldom exercise brute force especially against their colleagues. The best way to win commitment and motivation is by ensuring shared ownership of policies and their implementation. This requires an effective dialogue between all members of the group. Skills in planning, team building, chairing and communication are important. These can minimize waste and confusion while making sure that objectives are achieved.

Some pitfalls are easier to identify than avoid. Parkinson's[14] 'Law of Triviality' which states that *the time spent on any item of the agenda will be in inverse proportion to the sum involved* is recognized by committee Chairs everywhere. The difficulty lies to avoiding this problem. Some responses seem easy – fixing in advance the time to be spent on an item and avoiding repetition simply keeping control of events. But, groups have their own dynamics shaped by rules, values and norms of behaviour. The long debate on a 'trivial' item can flag wider concerns. A team starved of access to the leader and trying to manage with poor communication will use every opportunity to extend and widen discussion. Recognition of these symptoms, a willingness to learn, allied to sustained control, marks out the effective team member regardless of the specifics of his or her role.

Groups facing complex and managerial situations need to develop those skills which help members to act independently. This reflects the nature of managerial work. Burgoyne[15] has described the distinguishing features of this type of activity as:

- complex and varied
- hard to programme or easily predict
- dependent on working through others
- cross cultural and interfunctional.

The value of stimulating commitment, building teamwork and recognizing personal and group needs is well documented.

Currie[16] describes the way the needs of the individual and the group are integrated in management development for police inspectors. Bowden[17] spotlights similar issues in quality management in the NHS. Main[18] describes the attempt to replace 'old style boss – employee relationships' with 'participative management' in Westinghouse as a 'cultural revolution'. Similar issues can be seen across the public, private and voluntary sector. They symbolize the importance of uniting the person and the organization to create enterprise success. Each needs to adapt to the other. 'We' might replace 'I' as the focus of attention. Creating opportunities replaces controlling behaviour as the purpose of organization. This creates an environment in which enterprise acts as the primary catalyst for synergy.

Case study

The project brief

Draw up a brief for a small team to work on. Start by setting up a brainstorming session to identify likely projects. After this draw up a shortlist and select one. Allocate roles within the group. Organize a programme of meetings based on the schedule of events to complete the project.

Each member of the group should act as the chairperson in turn. Each person's skills in this and other roles should be appraised by colleagues. Create a system for feedback and performance apppraisal. At the end of the project, highlight the learning outcomes alongside the task outcomes.

References

1. McCormack, M. (1984) *What They Don't Teach You at Harvard Business School*, London.
2. Grove, A. (1983) *High Output Management*, London, Pan.
3. Adair, J. (1983) Effective Leadership, London, Pan.
4. Manners, G.E. Jr. Another look at group size, group problem solving and member consensus. *Academy of Management Journal*, **18**, no. 4, December (1975) pp. 715–24.
5. Hackman, R. and Vidmar, N. (1970) Effects on size and task type on group performance and member reactions. *Sociometry*, **33**, p. 51.
6. Janis, I.L. (1972) *Victims of Group-Think: A Psychological Study of Foreign Policy Decisions and Fiascos*, Boston, Houghton-Mifflin.
7. Payne, R. and Cooper, C. (1981) *Groups at Work*, Chichester, Wiley.
8. Keller, R.T. (1986) Predictors of the performance of project groups in R&D organisations. *Academy of Management Journal*, **29**, pp. 715–26.
9. Blanchard, K. and Johnson S. (1983) *The One Minute Manager*. London, Collins.
10. Pascle, R.T and Athos, A. (1982) *The Art of Japanese Management*, London, Penguin.
11. Sir Pat Lowry The industrial relations outlook: confrontation or co-operation? *Journal of the Royal Society of Arts*, June (1988) pp. 500-6.
12. Lorenze, C. (1989) Birth of a transitional. *The McKinsey Quarterly*, Autumn, pp. 72–93.
13. Parkinson, C.N. (1986) *Parkinson's Law*, London, Penguin.
14. *ibid.* p. 69.
15. Burgoyne, J., Boydell, T. and Pedler, M. (1978) *Self Development: Theory and Applications for Practitioners*, Aldershot, Gower.

16. Currie, B. (1989) Designing a management development course for police inspectors. *Management Education and Development*, **20**, part 4, pp. 273–89.
17. Bowden, D and Gumpert, R. (1988) Quality versus quantity in medicine. *Journal of the Royal Society of Arts*, April, pp. 333–42.
18. Main, J. (1989) Westinghouse's cultural revolution in Rukeyser, W. *Working Smarter*. London, Penguin, pp. 70–80.

Chapter 11

Networks and information

Stephen Jobs, one of the founders of Apple Computers, visited the research laboratories of Xerox Computers in the early 1980s. He saw computer researchers use a hand-held device to perform many of the functions done by keyboards on conventional machines. His interest increased when he found that Xerox saw no future for this device. Soon, the new range of Apple computers were using a similar gadget to control key aspects of its operation. The 'mouse' was born. Other 'point and shoot' devices soon followed. The *G*raphical *U*ser *I*nterface (GUI) is now as common as the keyboard. Xerox, the originators had missed their opportunity.

For Xerox, it was an intriguing case of history repeating itself. Three decades earlier, the Haloid Company of Rochester N.J. had tried to persuade their giant neighbours; Eastman Kodak, to become their partners in developing a new electronic copying technology. After Kodak rejected their approach, Haloid turned to IBM. The computer giant's rebuff meant that less conventional sources of backing, notably the University of Rochester, were used. By this time the firm had changed its name first to Haloid Xerox then Xerox. IBM's failure to recognise the potential of the people behind Xerox and their inventiveness had echoes in its own history. It was NCR's failure to appreciate Tom Watson Jnr. and the computer technology he espoused that provoked him to join and shape the success of IBM.

Innovation, change and development generates more interest and discussion in a modern industrial society than virtually any other subject. In a sense this is inevitable, as it is in the process of technical change or a society's willingness to harness technology which distinguishes industrial society from earlier eras. Deane[1] puts the associated *increase in the flow of inventions or of ideas for change suitable for incorporation into the productive process* at the centre of the industrialisation process. The successful management of change has been associated ever since with corporate and national economic success. The factors which underpin effectiveness in the management of change are central to many explanations of varying competitive performance over the last century.

A hundred years ago, following the Great Recession, Tom Vickers had explained how:

In the doldrums of the 1870s and 1880s, Vickers' reaction to the Great Recession was

> to innovate a way through it, exploiting rather than mislaying their technical strengths
> ... in the Depression of Trade ... [and] turned about to face the ill wind, and, to
> beat through them, created a new business
>
> Trebilcock[2]

The same sentiments would find many echoes in modern academic and popularist
literature:

> Top companies ... see innovation not as another overhead that the company needs
> to stay in business but as a flexible tool in the competitive game
>
> Goldsmith and Clutterbuck[3]

> The market share of British companies in many international markets (for example engi-
> neering products) has declined because of a failure to introduce new and better quality
> products to meet competition from overseas sources
>
> Baker[4]

Recognition of the importance of this issue has been matched by a growing awareness
of the difficulties associated with managing development. The complexity of the underlying processes of invention, innovation, development and adaptation, is becoming
more clear. The interaction between internal management practices and wider adjustments to the environment poses additional dilemmas for the researcher or policymaker
interested in the area.

There are, however, some areas of broad consensus. Rothwell[5] points out that
*all modern studies of the technological innovation process emphasize the importance of
demand specification to innovatory success*. The attempt to understand the interaction
between demand and the supply of new products and services is a major preoccupation
of modern business. It reflects a wider concern with change and its positive and
negative effects on enterprise. Research draws on many sources notably business
history, economics and organizational theory. Some studies seek to build a picture
of the ways individuals, firms, industries and communities are affected by change.
Others explore the ways in which the opportunities which emerge are effectively
exploited.

Many assumptions have been confounded. This has been a feature of the subject
since Charles C. Duell, Director of the US Patent Office in 1899, commented 'everything that can be invented has been invented'. Around the same time Lord Kelvin,
President of the Royal Society, was confident enough to assert that 'heavier-than-air
flying machines are impossible'. Enough has been learned to give important cues
to the ways people, firms, institutions and societies can manage progress more effectively.

The importance of information

Information, knowledge and data are the sources from which the enterprise gleans
the insights to renew itself and adapt to evolving conditions through innovation.
The importance of adaptation and response is seen at the corporate level in terms

Table 11.1 Proportion of sales from recent introductions

Industry	Products less than 5 years old
Buildings and construction	45
Chemicals	29
Clothing	67
Electrical machinery	38
General machinery	41
Fabric metal	21
Food, drink and tobacco	11
Furniture	57
Iron and steel	21
Leather	54
Paper	24
Plastics	50
Print	38
Textiles	50
Miscellaneous	64
Stone, glass and clay	24
All	38

Source: Baker, M. J., *Market Development'*, Harmondsworth, Penguin Books, 1983.

of the proportion of sales accounted for by-products launched in the relatively recent past[6] (see Table 11.1). This process of renewal is commonly described in terms of the useful heuristic of the *product life cycle* (PLC). This suggests that individual products pass through a series of stages of development. These are commonly described in terms of introduction, growth, maturity and decline. This framework has been used as a basis for several related propositions about the process of technical change. Among the most popular are the notions that:

- life cycles are getting shorter
- ranging from core products is the key to growth
- strategies for extending the life cycle are dangerous or profitable (depending on perspective).

Figure 11.1 shows that stages of the product life cycle are linked to the most popular approaches to extending through new products or new markets. Underlying each of these concepts are potentially valuable insights. The proposition that life cycles are getting shorter highlights the rate of change and the extent to which discontinuous change is occurring. The emphasis on ranging is a useful antidote to the preoccupation

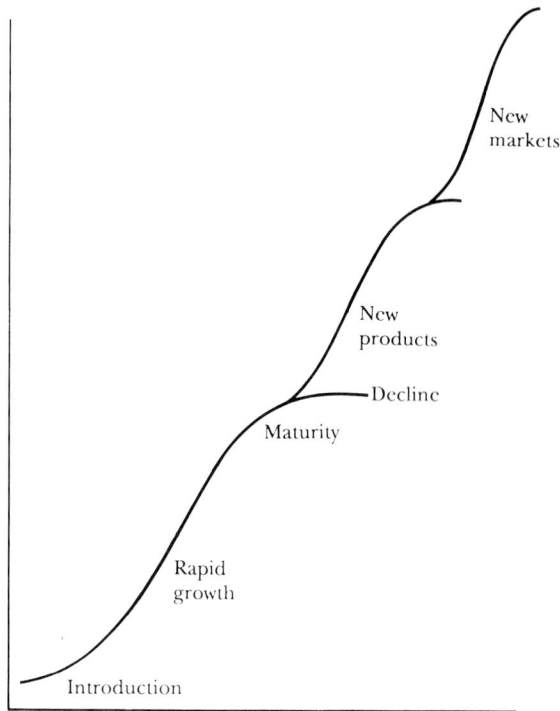

Figure 11.1   Extending the product life cycle

with single product/single-market models prevalent in some disciplines. These indicate both the usefulness of the PLC as a rule of thumb and its limited value as a research tool. It forces investigators to define the facets of innovation they are studying. It is, however, hard to define either the length of each stage or the lifespan of a product. Some for example, bread, can last indefinitely while others, such as a popular record disappear quickly. The complexity of these phenomena vividly illustrates the value gained from good quality and constantly updated and relevant information.

> Ideas without information are pretty worthless. Information without ideas can still be useful. The best of all is abundant information supplemented by ideas. The mistake, which so many people make, is to assume that collecting more information will do away with the need for ideas.[7]
>
> Edward de Bono, *Opportunities*, p. 17

The link between information and enterprise is constructed from function and worth. Material is gathered to serve a purpose and employed because it has a value. This is illustrated in the ways information is employed in undertaking a project and preparing a report. The underlying ideas are usable in a variety of situations.

Managing an information based project

The research-based thesis, project report or dissertation provides a most complex, information 'hungry' environment. Those involved in enterprise will find the underlying disciplines invaluable in virtually all investigative project work. The entrepreneur starting a new commercial enterprise requires a business plan based on a coherent structure. A research paper without a clear framework will ramble and confuse readers. The initiators of a charitable venture need a clear understanding of the role and purpose of their work. A project report needs to be clear and relevant to the brief. A theatre group blends a sense of direction with personal insights. A dissertation gets its direction from knowledge of the literature and insights from the evidence gathered. Underlying each of these aspects of enterprise is a use of networks and information.

Defining the task

At the core of any project is a definition of the task or work to be done. The researcher and the entrepreneur share several common problems. Both have a body of knowledge to draw on but it is inadequate. Established wisdom provides the hypothesis, the questions, an insight into the opportunity, even a view of the most promising way forward. Enterprising investigators will generally make the initial mistake of trying to do too much in the time available. Fascination with the issue blinds enthusiasts to the limitations of resources. The final-year student seeking to understand the implications for technology of high-temperature superconductivity has much in common with the entrepreneur striving to launch a new business based on teleshopping. Unless they are uniquely skilled or backed by the equivalent of Huber Corporation's superconductivity experts or Tesco's retail specialists they will fail. Successful enterprise depends on an appreciation of the challenge faced and the resources needs. In research, this means a summary statement of the issue and the hypothesis to be tested. In a commercial enterprise, the equivalent is a description of the business and an answer to the question: *why will I succeed?*

Project search and initial development

In the research situation, the investigator often faces the same need to seek out ideas and projects as the potential entrepreneur. A similar range of opportunities exists as those outlined in Chapter 2 (Figure 2.4). The primary, initial assignment lies in defining an achievable project and programme of work that can be undertaken. It is useful to ask:

- why is the project interesting?
- what is known about the issue?
- is success dependent on forces outside my control?

- how much help is needed?
- is the help easily and readily available?

The preparation of a time-based plan of action, with contingencies built in, often provides useful insights. The time plan (below) from the fictitious University of Inverness Enterprise Project indicates just some of the constraints based on a 'final-term' project:

4 June	Hand in project
30 May	Give proofread version to typist
25 May	Receive proofs from typist
11 May	Provide final draft for typist
7 May	Revise and edit final draft (r1)
23 April	Start final write-up
17 April	Collate information (r1)
6 April	Send out reminders to respondents
23 March	Mail survey
19 March	Type up final questionnaires
12 March	Review pilot survey
7 March	Start pilot survey
1 March	Draft questionnaires (r2)
26 February	Complete initial literature review.

Some of the basic planning ground rules are outlined above. The most basic is 'plan from the end-date'. It is easy to look forward and believe time stretches out indefinitely. This is dangerous in itself and can be fatal when absolute and practical restrictions exist. A typist might not drop existing plans to squeeze this report in. The print room will not be able to reschedule other work. The last minute rush can destroy the value of earlier painstaking work. The reviewers' irritation at poor English, recurrent spelling mistakes and bad presentation will soon blind them to intrinsic merit.

At most stages of a project some scope for recycling work is necessary. The (r) identifies the more common areas. The draft is unlikely to be 'right first time'. The initial sort through responses will not bring out all the main issues. Questionnaires take several efforts to get things right. In this illustration a project based on a mail survey is proposed. The scope for delays and difficulties is as great in personal questionnaires and experiments. Some problems are shared. Equipment failure with an experiment is akin to the respondent refusing to answer. Sitting in front of a person who clearly has no knowledge of the issue is as wasteful as finding that the computer is 'down' or the equipment is broken.

In research projects Murphey's Third, Fourth and Fifth laws are a sure guide to planning:

- Murphy's Third Law
  In any field of scientific endeavour, anything that can go wrong, will go wrong.

- Murphy's Fourth Law
  If there is a possibility of several things going wrong, the one that will cause the most damage will be the one to go wrong.
- Murphy's Fifth Law
  If anything just cannot go wrong, it will anyway.

It is, however, unlikely that the researcher will be able to use Maier's Laws to win past the astute client or supervisor. These are:

- If facts do not conform to the theory, they must be disposed of.
- Knowledge advances more by what it has learned to ignore than what it takes into account.

Information gathering

There are two discrete but related elements which make up the information gathering process. The first is the systematic search through available sources of data. The second is the use of networks of contacts to increase access to existing and new sources beside adding insight into the material. It is useful to review the sources of material that will be relevant to a project in terms of ease of access and availability. Information that exists within the enterprise and has already been collected for another purpose is normally easier to obtain and use than external and new material. This internal, secondary information comes in many forms. It might be letters of complaint or compliment. It can be figures on failure rates and rejects. Organizations store vast amounts of data but then proceed to ignore it.

One British university recently found that it had relatively small numbers of non-European students. The decision was made to increase attendance at recruitment fairs, spend more on promotion and send more staff abroad on recruitment visits. These had no significant effect. Later a group of students working on a project discovered that the problem did not lie with the number of applications. The university had always received relatively large numbers! The difficulty lay in converting applications to entrants. The processes employed were slow. Rejection rates were high. Departments were not enthusiastic as the prevailing view was that the resources allocated by the university for these students were poor. One professor pointed out that the staff:student ratio for home students was 1:12 but for non-EC students it was based on 35% of the fee. This meant that the effective student ratio was 1:18. The details about numbers, processing time and rejection rates were easily available from the admissions office. The information about faculty attitudes required some primary investigation. Primary research is designed chiefly to answer specific questions. The students found that talking to staff inside the institution gave them valuable insights into the topic. Many firms have discovered that tapping the market, technical or other knowledge of their employees can save time and money on external studies.

Some subjects require external information. The work by the university mentioned above was prompted by data gleaned from the *Universities Statistical Record*. This source is typical of the vast archive of material that is gathered by government, international agencies, voluntary bodies and private firms. It would be impossible to itemize the sources of this data. The broad categories are international, domestic, public and private.

International

Public

International organizations have emerged to link countries and groups. They provide an extensive reservoir of data on a host of topics. Among the most prominent are the UN and EC. Some of the accessible sources of information are outlined below.

- United Nations Reports and Directories, e.g. *Directory of International Statistics, Demographic Yearbook, Statistical Yearbook*. Also specialist agencies such as UNESCO, UNCDAD, The World Bank and the International Monetary Fund and OECD produce period reports on a host of issues.
- European Economic Community, e.g. *Bulletin of the European Communities, Economic Survey of Europe, General Statistical Bulletin*. The commission is an important source on data especially in those areas which reflects its main interests: Agriculture, Economic Development, Social Policy (notably education and training but including culture and women's issues), Technology and Regional Development.

In most parts of the world, inter-regional collaboration is increasingly important. Customs unions and economic groupings play an increasingly important role in gathering and sorting statistical data. These include:

- in Eastern Europe – CMEAD (The Council for Mutual Economic Assistance or ComeCon*),
- in Latin America – LAFTA (The Latin American Free Trade Area),
- in South East Asia – ASEAN (The Association of South East Asian Nations).

The best local sources of this material are the specialist libraries that exist in universities, polytechnics, central institutions and research units. Units like Leeds University's Institute for Commonwealth Studies and Warwick University's Centre for Social History can be invaluable to the specialist investigator.

Domestic

The state gathers, collates and provides information on virtually every aspect of life in the UK. A visit to any HMSO bookshop gives some indication of the extent and depth of this activity. Research reports on Roman Settlements in Britain vie for space with guides to the beaches of southern England. The *Guide to Official Statistics* pub-

---

* It remains to be seen how the role of ComeCon will evolve in the light of the changes in Eastern Europe.

lished by HMSO is the best overview. Each year the *Annual Abstract of Statistics* summarizes the key data gathered by the Central Statistical Office. The material available directly through central government gives only part of the picture. Specialist arms of government, notably the Research Councils, Training Agency, Universities Funding Council and Arts Council publish reports on issues touching on their interests.

The UK government is not unique. Most national governments provide a range of public information. The extent and quality of the material reflects the resources available to the research community and state policy towards disclosure. US material is especially extensive and maintains high standards. Sources range from the Government Printing Office, the equivalent of HMSO, through to specialist institutions such as the National Science Foundation. Access is possible through agencies of overseas governments operating in the UK. JETRO, the Japanese trade organization, is typical of those operating in the UK. It provides information on Japanese trade. Specialist libraries exist in some universities and colleges. Some embassies have libraries with current material.

Private

International

The commercial provision of information is an international industry. The *International Directory of Published Marketing Information* is probably the most comprehensive UK listing of private, commercial and published research. Firms like the Economist Intelligence Unit complement their domestic activities with overseas studies. These range from detailed, industry specific studies like their *Motor Industry Review* to regional reviews of several sectors, for example *Marketing in Europe*.

The best sources of this material are the specialist libraries. Typically, these are in major business schools such as London Business School and Manchester Business School or large chambers of commerce such as the City Business Library at the London Chamber. Admission to these facilities is generally restricted to members. Casual use might be allowed with advance notice. Economic and business information is more widely available than virtually all other categories. Trusts, foundations and international agencies will commission studies of other areas of activity. They might allow access to this information to some researchers. The British Academy has a crucial role in the Humanities.

Domestic

Countries with mature economies or established research industries are usually well endowed with private sector, information companies. Most will concentrate on commerce. In the UK the *Directory of the Market Research Society* is the best source of information on these firms. Many of these companies and some specialist enterprises have turned their attention to the Arts, science, public policy, etc. For example Segal Quince is a leader in research on technology policy. As a rule, access to their work is possible only through their clients or sponsors. The Design Council or Scottish Design Council are typical of the organizations which might supply material from studies commissioned by them. Their annual reports are useful sources of information on this type of investigations. Some larger research companies donate reports to specialist libraries. Frost and Sullivan have adopted an especially positive attitude to disseminating information which their clients are willing to release

External, secondary sources of information are especially valuable in establishing what is know already and the likely sources of further material. Good examples of the ways this material helps researchers can be found in related studies carried out by previous investigators. University, polytechnic and central institution libraries will usually hold large stocks of research studies by students. A cursory examination of one library found projects on:

- Smart cards in France
- Management of soccer clubs
- Banking for overseas students
- Computers in Arts departments
- Recycling computer paper
- Liaison between local emergency services
- Marketing universities
- Shakespeare's Globe Theatre
- Tree planting projects
- Fostering
- Biotechnology.

The cost and time involved in data collection increase as investigators move beyond local and available data. The illustration in Figure 11.2 gives some indication of the shape of this curve.

Presenting information

The use of secondary information imposes a number of disciplines on the researcher. The basic ground rule is that all material should be acknowledged and fully referenced. This serves three basic purposes:

1. It ensures that the reader can check facts.
2. It acknowledges the contribution of others.
3. It helps future researchers.

The practice in referencing varies. Often, those commissioning the work will spell it out in advance. A publisher like Heinemann, a periodical or a government department will provide its writers with guidelines. Some procedures have achieved wide

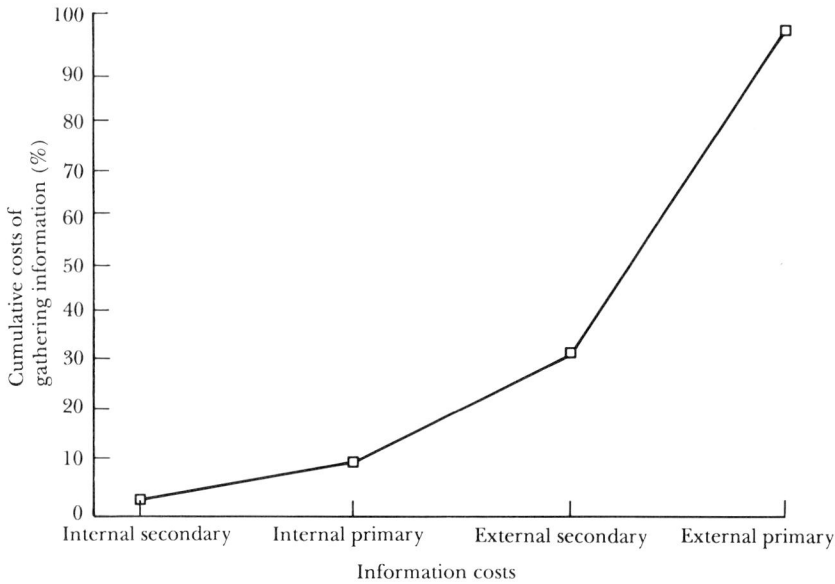

Figure 11.2

acceptance. The following ground rules are drawn from Turabian's invaluable *Manual for Writers*.[8]

- The names of authors are given in the normal order as per the publication, e.g. Charles B. Handy. Generally, the first name is given in full with second name, initial only. The full name is followed by a comma. This is normally varied where the author is very well known, for example T.S. Eliot.
- Journal article references will usually include details of author(s), full title, name of periodical (underlined), volume number, date, issue and page numbers.
- Book references contain author(s), full title (underlined), edition, location and name of publisher, date, volume and page numbers of any citation.
- Other periodicals are more easily identifiable by date. This should be included with the title and location, for example; 'investment clubs make a come-back', *Manchester Evening News*, 23 February 1989, p.35. Where the location or source is not easily identifiable by the reader it should be given in parentheses. It might be a small town, *The Chronicle* (Durham), or a foreign periodical, *La Stampa* (Milan).
- Official reports and documents will usually include the originating or authorizing body e.g. Department of Employment, the full reference number, for example Cmnd. No 1254, date, volume, publication and page numbers.
- Commercial documents will be referenced in a fashion similar to a government report with the firm, other specific referencing, date, publisher and pages included.

The procedures for tables and figures are framed with the same eye to making it easy for the reader to examine, interpret and check data.

Most institutions supply guidelines for presenting material but some general rules are worth bearing in mind. Ehrenberg[9] has highlighted the value of keeping data simple and avoiding redundancy. It is tempting to take figures to the second or third decimal place. At the very least, it shows how much work has gone into their production. But it is seldom needed and can mislead. In Table 11.2 the figures in column (a) are harder to use and suggest a level of turbulence that does not exist.

Table 11.2 Example of a misleading table
27 Students at Art Centre Productions

Performance	(a) Students (%)	(b) Students (%)
The Commissar	17.36	17
Chopin Recital	16.53	17
Mortal	17.11	17
Mazeppa Cossacks	16.85	17
Swing Band	19.75	20
Shirley Valentine	20.35	20
Battlefield Band	17.45	17
Average	17.91	18
Standard deviation	1.39	1.4

Source: Annual Report of Inverness University, 1988.

Other useful disciplines in presenting tables or illustrations are:

- every table should be numbered
- each needs a title
- place next to the first reference to the data
- give clear captions
- clearly state measures (units, percentages etc.)
- provide useful summaries (e.g. averages)
- show sources
- with illustrations, show scales
- for graphs, indicate legends and keys.

Tables or figures are not self-explanatory. A brief discussion, outlining the key issues or features ought to be placed alongside the table or illustration.

Gathering external primary information

In many projects, the point is reached when investigators go outside their own organization to collect data which is specific to the venture. Existing data may be dated.
It might cover the specific issues raised. There can be important gaps. This phase
in the inquiry allows the researcher to choose the issues to be tackled, the population
and the method of gathering data. Decisions about the hypotheses to be tested are
among the most important faced in the study.

A valid hypothesis satisfies several criteria. It will relate to a wider body of knowledge. Normally, this means that it is grounded in previous research or established
wisdom. A hypothesis should be framed in a form which allows conclusions to be
drawn using the data gathered. This link between the material gathered and the
topic ought to be transparent. The concept of falsification is valuable at this stage.
This means that the data can lead to the rejection of the proposition or its acceptance.[10]
A clear link between the material gathered and the hypotheses under investigation
is the best means of ensuring control over the volume of information gathered. The
old football adage *if in doubt kick it out*, is invaluable in choosing the areas to cover.
The besetting sin of inexperienced investigators is the effort to cover too much material
and lose track of the key issues.

Choice of the population to study is made in terms of who to study and how many.
The former emerges from the initial brief or prior study. The target group might
seem natural. An investigation of 'smart card' use among young people in France
indicates the relevant population. It is harder to decide who to survey on the issue
of marketing universities. There is likely to be a public relations officer in the registry.
He or she will probably say that departments are more important to many aspects
of marketing than any central office function. Job titles can mislead. A buyer will
only advise others on many key choices.

Some form of pilot survey is an essential step in eradicating these confusions. It
will seldom be possible to include every member of a population in a study. Cost,
access and other barriers will intervene. A sample can be drawn which represents
the total population. These can be drawn up using some form of random technique
or a purposive approach can be employed. Random samples 'represent' the population
by providing each member with an equal opportunity to be chosen. Randomness
avoids the risk of bias being built into the sample. Purposive samples involve an
element of direction by the investigators. They choose the 'quota' of representatives
for insertion or 'judge' who is included for the purpose.[11] There is a close link between
the choice of who or what to study and the technique employed. The basic research
options are; experiment, observation and interrogation. The great value of experiments
lies in the extent to which variables can be controlled. A stately home can cut its
prices to see if more people will visit. A gardener might employ a sonic gun to drive
away pests. A college can offer a new course to attract unemployed graduates. In
many situations it is hard to control all the forces which can affect the outcome.
A change in the weather, coinciding with the price cut, will drive up the number
of visitors anyway. New neighbours might fail to keep pests down in their garden,

increasing their numbers in the neighbourhood. The Government can introduce a new policy requiring all unemployed graduates to take further study or lose their unemployment benefits.

Some questions are hard to fit into an experiment. A firm will be reluctant to expose its new product to public gaze. Questions about future inventions are equally difficult to reach this way. Experiments can be very costly. The issues might be very wide ranging or hard to fit into a valid experimental design.

Observation is a useful alternative. Simply watching operations and behaviour can provide insight and understanding. Librarians watch and learn how readers use their facilities. It helps optimize the location of products and services. Observing operators use computers gives useful insights on keyboard design. New products have been derived from monitoring the way workers or consumers use equipment or appliances. The apparent simplicity of observation does not eliminate the need for careful application of formal techniques. Design of the experiment takes time and discipline. The area, location or group is chosen with the same attention to methodology and representativeness as other approaches. The strength of the classic studies in participant observation; 'Streetcorner Society'[12] and 'Wildcat Strike'[13] comes from the marriage of core discipline and vivid detail.

Interrogation-based techniques include mail-out, telephone and personal interviews. These are employed to gather quantitative and qualitative information. Respondents are asked questions which range from the qualitative to the clearly numerical – how often was an item purchased and what quantities? Surveys are undertaken which encompass thousands of people. In depth interviews, group discussions and projective methods allow researchers to explore more complex issues. Attitudes, values and expectations are open to investigation in this way. The choice of methodology depends on a mixture of the topics under examination and the importance of individual response.

The mail-out or postal survey allows the investigator to reach large numbers of people at a relatively low unit cost. Respondents complete the questionnaires at their leisure. They can dig out any information required. Interviewer bias is minimized as the questionnaire is the only point of contact. Virtually everyone can be reached by post. Language barriers are minimized. The technique has several notable weaknesses. Response rates are quite low. It is common to see less than 30% of questionnaires returned. Spoiled returns are frequent. This reflects the lack of help available when the questionnaire is being completed. Long or very detailed questionnaires are very susceptable to this. Respondents get bored or lose interest. This can distort the sample. Those concerned about a topic are more likely to reply. The study, however, might seek to describe the total population. This is less of a problem when attention is centred on special interest groups. Postal surveys can be slow. It is usual to allow several days for the questionnaires to reach respondents. Several weeks are needed to provide for sending reminders and getting returns.

Telephone surveys overcome several of the difficulties with postal studies. Direct access to the respondent increases returns. The interviewer can clarify problems and reassure the interviewee. The telephone ensures a fast reply. Some traditional difficulties with this approach are disappearing. A large majority of the population and virtually all business can be reached. Gaps exist with some groups notably the old, poor and young. The immediacy of the method places a premium on brevity and reduces the willingness to search out information.

Personal interviews provide the best opportunity to explore some issues. The interviewer can establish a rapport with the respondent. This enables more time to be spent and greater detail examined. Interviewer bias is minimized by adequate prior thought and training. Adjustments are made in response to circumstances but *only* in line with previous plans. The 'face-to-face' situation enables a skilled interviewer to weigh answers and add an element of observation to the formal response. This technique is very flexible. Large amounts of quantitative information can be gathered beside attitudes and other qualitative material.

The 'in-depth' personal interview is the most popular method of gathering qualitative information. In some circumstances, group discussions and projective techniques add valuable insights. The 'group discussion' usually involves a small number of people with a specific interest or shared characteristic. They are interviewed together to bring out issues in which a distinctively 'group' dimension exists. A group of young people will, for example, give a different response to questions about fashion, trends, etc. than each on their own. The dynamics of the group situation, the interaction between members, shape the response in the group.

Some situations are fundamentally group based. Industrial purchasing is sometimes described as coalition buying because a number of different people take part in the choice. The 'group' situation provides an opportunity to explore the way they work together. Managing a group discussion to maintain direction and structure takes skill and experience. These abilities match those of the good chair but add the capacity to probe key issues and obtain a usable response.

Sometimes, the researcher attempts to uncover views, beliefs and attitudes that are not fully recognized by the interviewee. The reasons behind some choices and decisions are not easy to establish through direct approaches. A range of projective techniques has been developed to explore these issues. These include sentence completion, word association, story boards and cartoon tests. Each is used to create a situation in which respondents employ their own words to develop a point or describe a situation. The apparent lack of structure allows the interviewee to go beyond the obvious or formal response. The skilled researcher can derive insights into the influences behind conscious words or thoughts.

Sentence completion requires the respondent to finish a series of sentences on a topic without pausing to think through answers. A mix of specific answers and the overall pattern forms a picture of the views held about issues. Word association serves a similar role but usually on more specific questions. A series of words are put to interviewees who are expected to state the first word that comes into their head. Flying might be linked to danger, planes to crashes. This will add further insights to the reasons why a group are low users of air travel. Story boards are usually simplified representations of a situation. The respondent is asked to describe or tell a story about the situation depicted. The way the situation is interpreted gives a useful insight into views. Cartoon tests are a variation on this. The interviewee is asked to put words in the mouths of the characters depicted. These approaches can be very stimulating but they are very dependent on the researcher's interpretation. Some critics comment that they say more about the researcher than the respondents.

The value of the results generated from each approach is largely dependent on the design of the tool used (often, the interview based questionnaires) and the skill of the interviewer. The *KISS* rule – *Keep It Simple Stupid*, is crucial. Respondents never have the time and seldom share the level of interest of the researcher. The time expected should be kept to a minimum. The early elimination of redundant or doubtful questions saves the researcher's time and increases response rates. Ambiguity in a question can be fatal. Anything that can be misinterpreted *will be* misinterpreted. Only one issue can be dealt with in each question. Questions about sensitive or personal information are the most common reasons for rejection. Generally these are best avoided or left to the end.

The use of specialists or links with professional bodies offer the best ways to maintain standards. Where this is not possible, the literature provided by recognized institutions can help. This can range from practical guides such as The Market Research Society's guide to *Standardised Questions*,[14] to manuals like the British Overseas Trade Boards *Checklist on Undertaking Export Market Research*.

Confidentiality

The maintenance of confidentiality and respect for privacy is an integral feature of good research. Respondents look for some reassurance on this before giving information. Sometimes this is not clearly stated. It should, however, be respected unless the interviewee specifically releases the material. A similar form of self-discipline extends to privacy. There is no 'right of access' to people or their knowledge. Pressure to get an answer is counterproductive. It devalues the response and undermines the research.

Contacts

The search for the right people to interview and meet is very demanding and time consuming. More specialized and detailed endeavour pose greater problems. The larger, more public sources – electoral register, telephone directory, etc. – are easy to obtain, but many of those included will not be relevant. Commercial lists are more specific but can be expensive. Some projects are linked with particular trades, industries or professions. Contacts are available through these groups. The *Directory of British Associations*[15] is one of a series of similar guides covering prosperous countries. In more distinctive fields of enquiry a version of the snowball approach is necessary. It depends on the use of one contact to lead to another. This way the total steadily grows by accumulation.

Report writing

The final report on the project, endeavour or study is the culmination of the programme of work. It serves to draw the prior work together. Typically, it is passed on to others for action. It can have an archival role but this is normally limited. The structure and content ought to contribute to these four broad goals:

- summarize results
- validate work
- outline conclusions and recommend action
- store material for further reference.

The primary role of a report is to: guide the reader(s); draw conclusions and take action. This determines the structure.

The structure for reports is:

- Acknowledgements
- Abstract or Summary
- Conclusions and Recommendations
- Brief or Project outline
- Methodology
- Substantive Argument or Main Text
- Findings
- Research team
- Bibliography and References
- Acknowledgements ⎫
- Appendices   ⎬ as necessary.
- Glossary   ⎭

Conclusions and Recommendations are normally presented at the start. This is a marked contrast to the essay or narrative style of writing. Often, the report opens with an abstract or summary. This is sometimes called the Executive Summary. The Conclusions and Recommendations draw together the findings and make clear recommendations for action to be taken or lessons to learn. Wheatley[16] makes the comment often ignored by writers that *conclusions should conclude*.

A similar directive can be applied to recommendations. These should be implementable and within the competence of those receiving the report. It might be useful to make wider proposals but the recipients are normally looking for guidance on their future actions. It helps to restate the original brief or remit for the project at that point. It has probably changed over the course of the project. Flagging these modifications and the reasons for change assist readers to relate the report to their expectations. The primary responsibility of those preparing the report lies in ensuring that it tackles the issues it was asked to address.

A report will stand or fall on the quality and rigour of its methodology. The procedures adopted – especially the population studied, the means of gathering data and disciplines applied – determine the value placed on the work by readers. They look for relevance to the issues and scientific validity in technique. Validity is founded on a commitment to objectivity, consistency in approach and an assumption of replicability. The latter is especially important as recipients will assume that someone else conducting the same study would find the same things.

The form and content of the substantive argument or main text is dictated by the issues identified in the remit. The sections and subdivisions are built around the hypotheses or topics stipulated in the proposal. The task is to provide the reader with a logical structure which brings out salient issues and justifies conclusions and recommendations. There is a dangerous temptation to use this to show how much effort was invested by the researcher. This wastes space and alienates readers. There is no need to summarize all the evidence collected, e.g. through tabulating the results of each question. The value of the main text lies in summarizing key issues and directing the reader's attention. The best place for detail or background information is the Appendix. A summary of the findings ought to follow the substantive argument.

Recipients of a research report generally expect some indication of the composition of the team preparing the report. The References and Bibliography provide a comprehensive listing of the sources of support material. This recognizes the contributions of others while creating an opportunity for readers to delve further into source material. References point out works that are used in the report. The Bibliography is made up of relevant, related work.

It is sometimes necessary to acknowledge the contributions of others. Normally, this means that they have had a major contribution to shaping the report. Appendices contain detailed background material. Specific information on the research tools used and the main body of material gathered can be presented. Ideally, the content is determined by the need to provide scope for readers to delve further into the information on which the findings are built. A Glossary provides an opportunity to define or explain technical or unfamiliar terms used in the report.

Copyright

Report writers are affected by Copyright Law in two ways. First, the law determines the ways in which previously copyrighted material can be used. Extensive use of material gathered by others without permission is illegal. Second, writers are protected by the same laws. Some statement of the copyright ownership ought to be included at the start of the report.

Conclusion

The information and knowledge industries have emerged as powerful forces in the modern advanced economy. This largely reflects the importance placed on science, technology and commercial intelligence in modern societies. Increased familiarity with the sources of knowledge has increased people's confidence in their ability to gather and deploy information. Entrepreneurs seek information on potential purchasers from a Frost and Sullivan report. Arts graduates dig through the *Directory of Grant Awarding Bodies* to find trusts interested in Commonwealth literature. Scientists use international databases to identify relevant prior work. Each is part of a complex network of information providers and users. All have the opportunity to use superior intelligence to their advantage.

Recognizing the opportunity is only the tentative first step in gaining the benefit. Stephen Jobs was not the first person to be shown round the Xerox laboratories where their revolutionary prototype products were on show. McLaren showed his Baby Buggy to many potential producers of 'baby buggies' before he decided to go into production himself. The clues are available to everyone, but most fail to draw them together in a form which creates an opportunity. Search processes are central to this. Kokubo suggests that Japanese firms are building their technology search strategies around three broad strands – exploitation of mature technologies, blurring borders and technological breakthroughs. These approaches make research and development and hence information strategies central to the operations of the enterprise. This pivotal role allied to the rate of change places a premium on the skills associated with information gathering, analysis and dissemination.

The information can come from a variety of sources. Art Fry of 3M links his development of 3M *Post-It*™ note pads with a chance conversation on a golf course and an irritating problem with the bookmarks he used in his hymnal. The better use of information creates opportunities for enterprise in virtually every context. Hospitals, public utilities, charities and voluntary groups are as likely to benefit as corporations, entrepreneurs, writers or performers. Their ability to gain relies on their willingness to apply some basic skills. The value gained depends more on the application of system and discipline than the investment of large resources. An open and inquisitive approach to information allied to confidence and insight has probably generated more successful enterprises than any other combination of forces.

Case study

The research report

In the months before Vesting Day, the Council of York Polytechnic invited MDE Services to conduct a research study of the market(s) which the Polytechnic would have to satisfy in order to prosper. They were interested in attitudes of different client groups to their offerings. These included local employers, current and potential students, policymakers and intermediaries. The following tables give some indication of the findings.

Tasks
1. *Identify the key findings from this study.*
2. *What does the research tell you about the challenges facing the college?*
3. *What additional information does the college need in order to enhance its position?*
4. *What additional data is needed to make marketing recommendations?*

Table 11.3 Provinces of company training

In-house activity (entirely)	40%
In-house (partly)	35%
Public sector providers	15%
Private sector providers	10%

Table 11.4 Locus of Training Decision

Local	55%
External	45%

Table 11.5 Knowledge and views of Locally Provided Courses (number of respondents)

Course	Yes	No
Appropriate for new staff	18	43
Appropriate for existing staff	16	45

Table 11.6 Form of Contact with College

Form	Number
One-off (by chance)	3
One-off (problem driven)	2
Occasional (chance)	2
Occasional (planned)	7
Frequent (planned)	8

Table 11.7 Number of Main Points of
Contact

Careers service	4
College staff	5
Individuals (third party)	8
YTS staff	12

Table 11.8 Organizational Approaches to College

	Yes	No
Organization *has* approached	15	46
Organization *would* approach	21	40

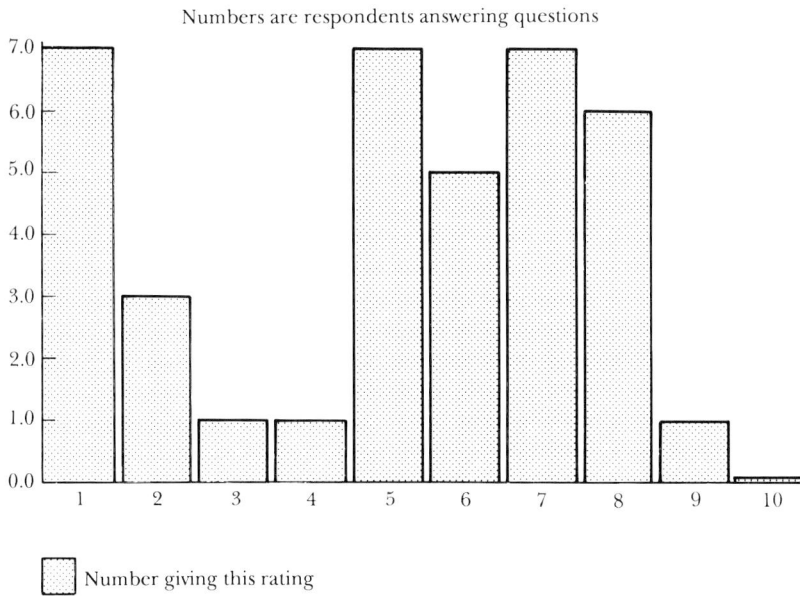

Numbers are respondents answering questions

Number giving this rating

Figure 11.3   Overall rating of college. 1 is very low; 10 is very high

Numbers of those rating

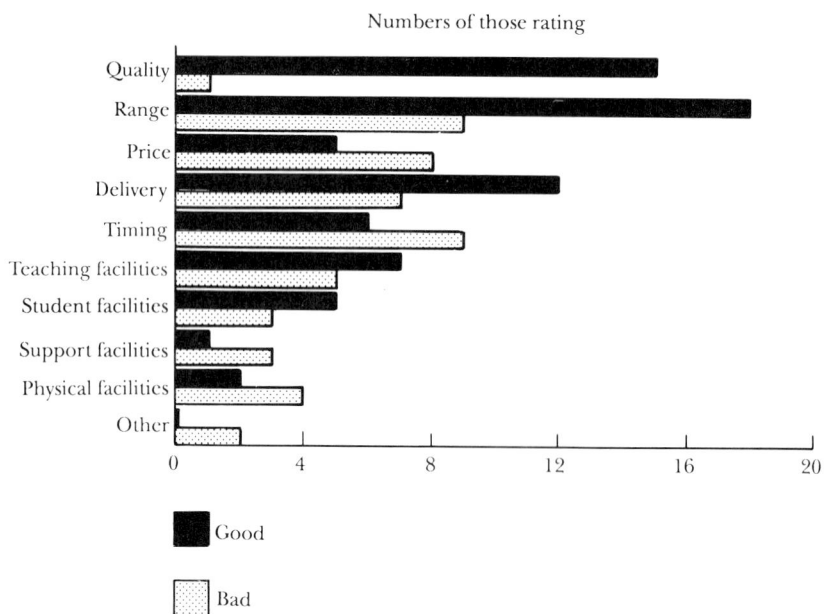

Figure 11.4   Rating of features of college

Table 11.9 Potential end users: sample structure

Group	Male	Female
Employed – mature school leaver (pre-1980)	24%	21%
Employed – recent school leaver (post-1980)	5%	12%
Unemployed – mature school leaver (pre-1980)	9%	11%
Unemployed – recent school leaver (post-1980)	16%	8%

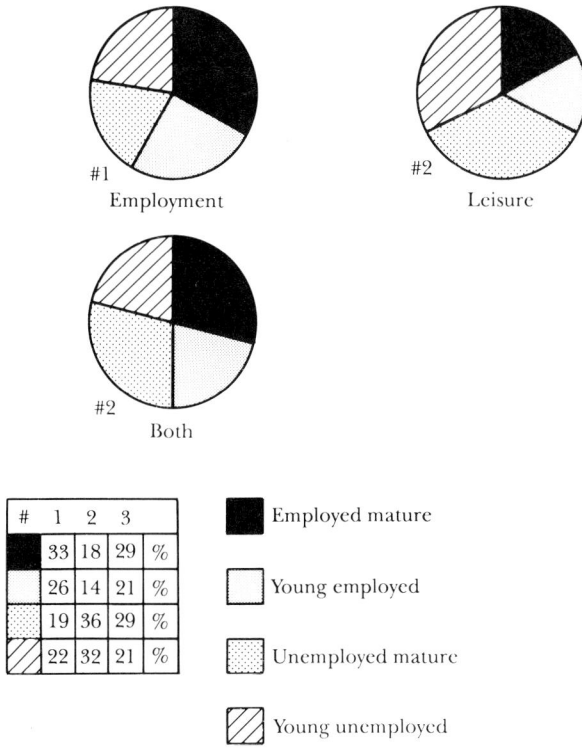

Figure 11.5 Take-up and interest in Polytechnic courses

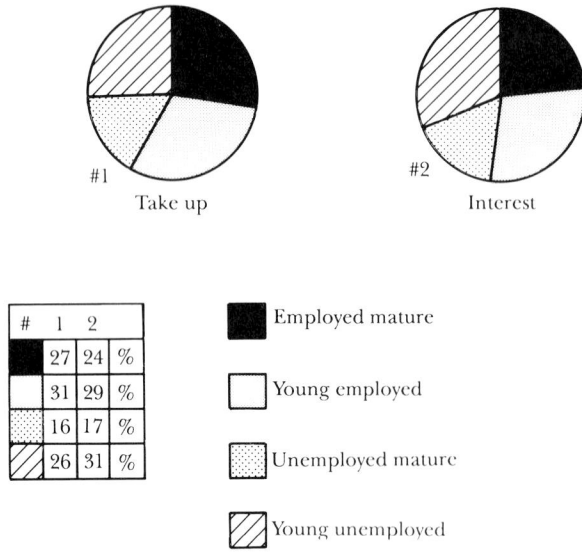

Figure 11.6   Take-up and interest in college programmes by potential clients

Table 11.6 Percentage awareness of Employment and Leisure Courses, from total sample

Group	Employment	Leisure	Neither
A	11%	17%	11%
B	4%	10%	7%
C	2%	8%	5%
D	7%	7%	11%

In all tables:

A are employed, mature school leavers (left school; pre-1980).
B are employed, recent school leavers (left school; post-1980).
C are unemployed, mature school leavers (left school; pre-1980).
D are unemployed, recent school leavers (left school; post-1980).

Table 11.7 Action Taken to Progress Career Related Courses

Action	Group			
	A	B	C	D
Nothing	33	35	28	31
Enquiry	10	15	22	21
Enrolled	16	15	19	26
Completed	30	29	8	11
Unknown	1	4	13	11

Table 11.8 Action Taken to Progress Non-Vocational Courses

Action	Group			
	A	B	C	D
Nothing	30	55	35	42
Enquiry	20	20	34	29
Enrolled	21	10	11	21
Completed	23	14	8	4
Unknown	6	1	12	4

Table 11.9 Sources of Information

Source	Percentage
Advertising	30%
Word of mouth	20%
Enquiry	15%
Advisory	10%
Job centre	10%
Don't know	26%

References

1. Deane, P. (1969) *The First Industrial Revolution*, Cambridge, Cambridge University Press.
2. Trebilcock, C. (1977) *The Vickers Brothers*, London, Europa Publications.
3. Goldsmith, W. and Clutterbuck, D. (1984) *The Winning Streak*, London, Penguin.
4. Baker, M. (1983) *Marketing: Theory and Practice*, London, Macmillan.
5. Rothwell, R. (1986) Innovation and re-innovation: a role for the user. *Journal of Marketing Management*, 2, no. 2, pp. 109–23.
6. Baker, M.J. (1983) *Market Development*, Harmondsworth, Penguin Books.
7. De Bono, E. (1978) *Opportunities*, London, Associated Business Programmes.
8. Turbian, K.L. (1982) *A Manual For Writers of Research Papers, Theses, and Dissertations*, London, Heinemann, pp. 82–193.
9. Enhrenberg, A.S. (1976) *Data Reduction*, Amsterdam, North Holland.
10. Popper, Sir Karl. *The Logic of Scientific Discovery*, London, Hutchinson.
11. Crimp, M. (1981) *The Marketing Research Process*, London, Prentice-Hall, p. 29.
12. White (1981) *Streetcorner Society*, University of Chicago Press.
13. Gouldner (1965) *Wildcat Strike*, Harper & Row, New York.
14. A. R. Wolfe (ed.) (1973) *Standardised Questions; A Review for Market Research Executives*, London, The Market Research Society.
15. CDP Publications, *The Directory of British Associations*, London, CDP Publications Annual.
16. Wheatley D. (1988) *Report Writing*. London, Penguin.

Chapter 12

Individuality, enterprise and the future

The thesaurus entry for 'vision' lists 'outlook', 'aberration', 'illusion' and 'prophecy' among the alternative terms. Each depicts some aspect of the way enterprise is viewed. The outlook is largely based on a view of the world which concentrates on challenges not problems and emphasizes individual responsibility. This stress on the individual has a powerful appeal to those who share John Stuart Mill's view[1] that:

> He who lets the world, or his own portion of it, choose his plan of life for him has no need of any other faculty than the ape-like one of imitation.

The esteem in which this outlook is held has varied over time and between communities. Mill's favourable view was overtaken for much of this century by a suspicion that devotion to the individual was inseparable from exploitation of the group.

The dark side of individualism and enterprise is expressed by D.H. Lawrence:[2]

> He saw the stream of miners flowing along the causeways from the mines at the end of the afternoon, thousands of blackened, slightly distorted human beings with red mouths, all moving subject to his will. He pushed slowly in his motor car through the little market town Friday nights in Beldover, through a solid mass of human beings that were making their purchases and doing their weekly spending. They were all subordinate to him. They were ugly and uncouth, but they were his instruments. He was the god of the machine.

This outlook poses a challenge to advocates of enterprise. It marks the need to bring out the continuing contribution of enterprise to achievement while linking it to social justice.

Much of the recent argument for individual and group enterprise has centred on its benefit in creating jobs, stimulating innovation, establishing new markets and stimulating competition. The bulk of recent evidence indicates that small enterprises generate most new jobs. These ventures are more effective at innovation especially during their early years. This is linked with some success on opening new markets domestically and overseas. The direct gains are linked with the positive effect these ventures have on larger organizations. They are capable of challenging a comfortable consensus and established organizations.

Enterprise and organization

The challenge posed to accepted thinking by Rossetti, Millais and Hunt through the Pre-Raphaelite Brotherhood provoked change and development in the visual arts. 'Big Science' is regularly confounded by the achievements of smaller groups and its dependence of individual insights. Philip Marcus arrived at his explanation of the nature of the Great Red Spot of Venus by looking at the issue in a new and different way. New businesses challenge established firms in the same way. Anita Roddick built the Body Shop by looking at the market and the relations between cosmetics and their users in a new way.

They are not always successful. It is, however, the possibility of challenge that matters. It forces large organizations to monitor the environment closely if they wish to survive. The same awareness of opportunity gives potential entrepreneurs hope that they can 'buck the system' *and win*. These are important features of the development process in Britain and North America.

The relationship between enterprise and institution ought to be symbiotic. The small firm's innovations emerge from the R&D investment that the corporation cannot exploit. Small theatrical groups can experiment and explore ideas in ways that are impossible for large national companies. The large surgical team, using the latest technology depends on the small care group to nurse the patient back to health. The balance between the parties varies between situations and over time.

In Japan, there exists a culture which:[3]

> finds it difficult to accept strong individuals and Japan has a group-orientated society that prefers working through equality based consensus.
>
> Shoichi Saba, 1989

This cultural dimension to social and economic behaviour cannot be ignored. There are, however, circumstances which highlight the merit of enterprise and lessons to be learned about its effective and constructive role. The value is greatest where there is an identifiable personal contribution to success, gain from knowledge, insight or creativity and a low cost of entry. The cost of entry is not absolute. Change, turbulence or lack of clear direction makes it easier for enterprise to make its mark. Mill's reply to the view that this emphasis on the role of the enterprising individual will lead to abuse of the group still carries weight:

> There is no natural connection between strong impulses and weak conscience.[1]

Some activities are individual by nature. Many art forms are characterized by dominance of the private over the public. Writers, painters and many in the performing arts build their work on the ability to impose themselves and their view on a work. Their approach to enterprise is shared with those scientists who confound accepted belief. They hold onto their conclusions despite the reservations of their peers. Much sporting endeavour is private. The loneliness of the long distance runner strikes a chord with all those involved in creating and shaping an enterprise.

In the UK this debate has a special relevance. Economic decline has reached an alarming level. Sidney Pollard observes that 'there has been no failure like it in world history'.[4] Weiner develops this by commenting that 'the leading problem of modern British history is the explanation of economic decline'. The management of enterprise lies at the heart of this debate. The scope for achievement through endeavour is well documented. The levels of innovation and rate of change seen today create an especially fertile environment for creativity and initiative. Opportunities exist but in a competitive environment. Exploiting these openings calls for a combination of will and skill.

Some observers see the occurrence of this combination as largely a matter of chance. Stephenson, Watt, Telford, Brunel, Cadbury and Pilkington were shaped by different experiences but went on to innovate and create. Their enterprise was an aberration. Background, education and training had a minimal effect.

The counterview spotlights the profound differences in culture and development which seem to distinguish the more successful economies from Britain. This approach is based on two propositions. First, the more people who aspire to realize themselves through enterprise the greater the chance that some will try. Second, the greater their skills in venture management, the less likely it is that those who try will fail. Put differently, the larger the pool, the less the leakage, the greater the reservoir of talent for society to rely on. The dramatic growth in business formation by women in the UK and elsewhere gives some insight into this process.

The United States Small Business Administration reported in 1985 that over the previous decade the number of female business owners grew by 74%. They now account for 37% of all enterprises. Business receipts from women-owned businesses increased from $44 billion to $53 billion in 1983 alone. Similar trends in the growth of female entrepreneurship have been reported in other countries. In Sweden and Finland over a quarter of all owner managers are female. In India new business formation by women is growing rapidly.

In the UK, recent estimates by James Curran of the number of self-employed men and women display a 'sharply upward trend which has accelerated in the 1980s'.[5] Between 1981 and 1983 male self-employment increased by 2%. Female self employment increased by 24% over the same period.[6] This growth mirrors wider shifts in the pattern of female employment. There has been an increase in the number of women in the workforce and the continuity of their working lives. According to Catherine Hakim the traditional bimodal employment life cycle[7] – the first phase prior to the birth of the first child, the second after the youngest reaches school age – is being eroded. Women are spending more of their potential working life in paid employment.[8] So far, this has not led to a major shift in their career opportunities in large organizations. In 1965 only 5% of all working women were managers or employers. This was the same in 1980.[8] Sara Carter *et al*. notes that self-employment, building a new business, has emerged over the last decade as an important means of addressing the glass ceiling effect – the phenomenon by which women can see the top but cannot reach it.[9]

The use of enterprise to overcome barriers is long established. Nonconformists, migrants and other 'out-groups' used enterprise as the primary means to overcome the social and economic barriers facing them in the last century. In some senses the Industrial Revolution was an incidental by-product.

> They were self made men, or at least men of modest origins who owed little to birth, family or formal education ... protestant dissent of the hard Independent, Unitarian, Baptist and Quaker rather than the emotional Methodist type gave them a spiritual certainty and a contempt for useless aristocrats.
>
> Hobsbawm, p. 222[10]

The same pattern can be seen in the achievements of new migrant groups in the UK, North American and Europe during the late nineteenth and mid-twentieth centuries. Their desire for development allied to new opportunities is a potent combination.

Enterprise and education

Today's opportunities are closely linked with shaping, using and applying knowledge. Science, wisdom and intelligence create openings for enterprise. There are some basic preconditions for success. Access to knowledge and recognition of its value is essential. Attitudes of educators and students play their part. Butler's[11] venerable Professor of Unworldly Wisdom asserts that:

> It is not our business to help students to think for themselves. Surely this is the last thing anyone who wishes them well should encourage them to do? Our duty is to teach them to think as we do or, at any rate, as we hold it expedient to say we do.

This fits comfortably with the *ex cathedra* lecture, the transmission of established knowledge, the view of the student as a passive vessel for received knowledge. The notion of the active learner, partnership and mutual development challenges this perspective.

The strength of project based or Action Learning lies in the assertion of the usefulness of knowledge. It has value, can be used and can be turned to, throughout life, to resolve issues and tackle problems. This does not mean that only knowledge which is currently and obviously functional has value. Insight, understanding and value turns on the way intelligence is used. Project work has a wider value in a society which has suffered from poor management and internal conflict. It brings people together to tackle issues in a collaborative and supportive way. Action Learning highlights the value of planning and integration. At the same time, it builds up that range of talents from leadership to teamwork which lie at the heart of successful enterprise.

Corelli Barnett[12] has demonstrated the extent to which British society lacked these skills even during times of apparent success. He quotes[13] a 1944 War Office memorandum which states that:

Probably the most outstanding single cause of failing to reach maximum production efficiency in wartime is scarcity of skilled management.

The pattern has been repeated throughout the ensuing half century as the UK's trading position and resource base deteriorated.

The distinctively UK (or more accurately English) isolation of education and industry has been remarked on by observers of the last 200 years. Hobsbawm[10] notes that:

> The Germans possessed institutions of technical training like the Prussian *Bergakademie* which had no parallel in Britain. The French Revolution created that unique and impressive body the *École Polytechnique*. English education was a joke in poor taste, though its deficiencies were somewhat offset by the dour village schools and austere, turbulent, democratic universities of Calvinist Scotland which sent a stream of brilliant, hard working, career seeking, and rationalist young men into the south country.
>
> Hobsbawm, p. 47

The theme of separation and ignorance recurs in analysis of the aftermath of the First World War.[14]

> Science itself was a remote world of specialists; industry, outside of the few firms traditionally associated with the provision of war stores was almost equally unknown
>
> Max Beloff, p. 179

George Tolley[15] returns to this notion of separation and mutual suspicion in his description of the UK in the mid-1980s:

> I am persuaded that lack of recognition of the achievement and the necessity of industry, of the process of wealth creation as a whole, is not our major cultural problem. Our major problem is the distrust of education, not the distrust of industry.

In part, this is a function of the separation of acquisition of knowledge from its use. This is seen in English graduates who never go to the theatre and avoid buying books; engineers whose main career aim is to work in a bank; business graduates who assume that communication is studied rather than implemented. The continued dominance of the essay, the lecture and individual rather than group work can be seen across education. This will sap the confidence in education of those who never write an essay, listen to a lecture and spend their working life in groups after leaving school or college.

> The old joke about the Professor who – went into the lecture theatre in Chicago and said, 'good morning' and the class said 'good morning' back; went into the lecture theatre in Paris and said 'good morning' and the class ignored him; went into the lecture theatre in Leeds and said 'good morning' and the class wrote it down – still has an edge to it.

The shift towards using knowledge and lifetime learning reinforces the perceived worth of education. This is a localized phenomenon. It will continue in this way while access to education is restricted and the system operates in a piecemeal and poorly integrated fashion.

The age participation rates in the UK post-16 (i.e. numbers continuing their education) are low for a society which strives to compete in modern technologies. This is especially evident in the number following and completing qualifications in the sciences and technology. The UK has low take-up rates which are made worse by the tendency of UK scientists and engineers to move out of their discipline on completing studies. The links between the schools, colleges, polytechnics and universities are poor. Some progress has been made in constructing bridges and eroding suspicion. Access programmes have improved institutional links. The barriers between education, training and development are crumbling. Increased experience of education, greater diversity, better links and mutual appreciation provide the best hopes of adapting successfully to new challenges.

New opportunities and new responsibilities

The 1990s offers a host of new opportunities and responsibilities. The creation of the Single European Market will establish a European 'home' market of 300 million. The collapse of the barriers to trade and movement between Eastern and Western Europe can double this 'market'. The effects go far beyond commerce. Education is moving towards a pan-European identity. In higher education, initiatives like the Erasmus, Commett and Eesprite are initiating openings for greater collaboration and integration. The opening up of Eastern Europe is posing a new set of challenges. Know-how funds are creating new opportunities. Collaboration in science, education and commerce will form the foundation for deeper and healthier long-term relationships. In Asia, the events in Tiannamen Square are likely to delay but not stop progress towards a society in which individual enterprise can flower. Greater freedom for the peoples of Sub-Saharan Africa, Latin America, the Middle East and Asia is hard to separate from new opportunities.

Sustainable development imposes new responsibilities. Enterprise is not exploitation. Consumers, producers, intermediaries – all members of a society – have a wide range of obligations to others. These extend beyond economically and socially disadvantaged people to other species and future generations. The technological, commercial and behavioural opportunities for misuse are now so great and so widespread that everyone has a duty to address them. Population pressures in developing countries have an immediate impact on the environment. Growing numbers of landless peasants can only turn to virgin territory to meet their needs unless realistic alternatives are presented to them (Table 12.1).

A mixture of individual enterprise and social responsibility offers the best hope of delivering solutions that work. Individual accountability is central to enterprise. It means that all those involved in endeavours are part of the solution as well as part of the problem.

The Single European Act vividly illustrates the opportunities which will be open to enterprise. It strives to build a more unified European economy. The primary purpose of forging this Single Market is to reduce those barriers to trade which add

Table 12.1 India: Landless Rural
Households (Brown *et al.*, 1986)

Year	Landless households (millions)
1961	15
1981	26
2000	44 (projected)

to costs and inhibit growth. The fragmented nature of the European market makes goods and services more expensive. Barriers exist which make it hard to sell products which are cheap in an EC country, into another. A car selling for under £4000 in Belgium can cost over £5000 in the UK. Industrial products, services and supplies can show the same variations in price. Institutional constraints, regulations inhibit competition and add to costs. The Single Market is designed to help those ventures which adopt a European perspective to grow and develop in new and exciting ways. The European Trade Union Confederation has underlined the need to wed these commercial opportunities with social responsibilities. The Social Charter tackles issues of trade union rights, job protection and health and safety at work. It seeks to frame a 'level playing field' for fair competition.

Eastern Europe poses a different type of challenge. The size of the market – 100 million excluding the Soviet Union, 350 million including the USSR – plus the extent of shortages is tempting many new entrants. Most acknowledge the risk but find it easier to play down their wider obligations. The exploitation of Eastern Europe as a reservoir of cheap labour or dumping ground for production processes which are unacceptable domestically is wrong. Beside this, it will quickly produce a backlash that will be hard to control or contain. The challenge is to wed the short-term needs of locals and entrants with long-term, self-sustaining development. This calls for innovation and flexibility by those initiating ventures and enterprise by locals.

The value of enterprise is widely acknowledged in developing countries. Successful economies in South East Asia have established systems of support for new endeavours. These include specialist development banks like Bank Bumiputra in Malaysia. This targets its efforts on the indigenous Bumiputra population. Education for enterprise is playing its part through organizations like the Centre for Entrepreneurial Development in India.

Global events, notably the climatic changes provoked by alteration in the ozone layer and carbon emissions have brought home the interdependence of the different parts of the world. Between 1982 and 1986 subsidies to farmers in North America and Europe increased by between 300 and 1000%. This stimulated greater food production. Food surpluses in North America and Europe forced world prices down. Peasant farmers were either forced off the land to crowded cities or pressed to bring new land into production. Both process had a negative effect on the environment.

Enterprise development over the next decade will take place against a background of increased expectations of environmental and social awareness.

Conclusion

Many of the challenges facing communities today will not be resolved by greater resources or traditional responses. They will call for novel solutions and an acceptance of risk. Biological abundance and cultural diversity have been crucial elements in the ability of individuals and groups to survive. It may be inconvenient to recognize to rights of a distant community or an alien species. The same group might supply a vital component for future success, even survival. Recognition of these challenges and duties is an integral element in shaping enterprise today.

The development process is a mixture of providing opportunities throughout education. These might be inside the curriculum through formal courses like the Stirling University MSc in Entrepreneurial Studies. They will extend across the curriculum through initiatives like the Enterprise and Higher Education Initiative. Each stage in education creates opportunities. Young Enterprise reaches primary as well as secondary schools and give an active role to managers. Mini-companies capitalize on the skill and enthusiasm of teachers. The successful programmes are integrative. They break down the barriers between industry and education. Their separation weakens the ability of a community to respond to the new knowledge-based industrial revolution. The best schemes build bridges between disciplines. Opportunities for enterprise exist within the Arts, Science and Humanities but new facets emerge from cross-disciplinary and interdisciplinary work. The combination of diverse elements into a new reality lies at the heart of enterprise.[16]

All this will mean facing up to challenges. The willingness to storm established positions is a feature of all forms of enterprise. The learning process and support system will reflect this. Learning Through Doing is part of this. Educators will change. They become part of a support system, not its masters, and enhance their role. The value gained from working with them reinforces a desire to maintain and sustain collaboration through a lifetime of learning. This feeds on the energy, drive and creativity of enterprising people, groups and communities. The resulting innovations and adaptations shape the communities in which they live.

References

1. Mill, S.J. (1984) *On Liberty*, London, Penguin.
2. Lawrence, D.H. (1966) *Women in Love*, London, Penguin, p. 250.
3. Saba, S. (1989) The Japanese style of doing business, *Journal of the Royal Society of Arts*, October, pp. 715–20.
4. Sidney, P. (1976) *The British Economic Miracle*, London, Edward Arnold.

5. Curran, J. (1986) *Bolton Fifteen Years On: A Review and Analysis of Small Business Research in Britain 1971–1986*, London, Small Business Research Trust.
6. Department of Employment, *Employment Gazette*, October 1986.
7. Hakim, C. (1979) *Occupational Segregation*, Department of Employment Research Paper no. 9, London.
8. Martin, J. and Roberts, C. (1984) *Women and Employment: A Lifetime Perspective*, London, HMSO.
9. Carter, S. *et al.* (1988) *Female Entrepreneurship*, Department of Employment, Research Report.
10. Hobsbawm, E.J. (1962) *The Age of Revolution*, London, New English Library.
11. Butler, S. (1872) *Erewhon*.
12. Barnett, C. (1986) *The Audit of War*, London, Macmillan.
13. PRO; CAB 101/406 Paper before the Munitions Management and Labour Efficiency Committee of The Production Efficiency Board, 17th November, 1944.
14. Beloff, M. (1960) *Imperial Sunset Volume 1 1887–1921*, London, Methuen.
15. Tolley, G. (1990) Satanic mills and secret gardens. *Journal of the Royal Society of Arts*, February pp. 204–10.
16. CEDEFOP (1989) *Management Education for Small and Medium Sized Enterprises in the European Communities*, Berlin, European Centre for the Development of Vocational Training.

Index